The Cosmic Christ

The Cosmic Christ

FROM PAUL TO TEILHARD

GEORGE A. MALONEY, S.J.

SHEED AND WARD: NEW YORK

Library of Congress Catalog Card Number 68–13852

Imprimi Potest:
Robert A. Mitchell, S.J.
Provincial, New York Province
Society of Jesus
September 1, 1967

Nihil Obstat:
Leo J. Steady, Ph.D., S.T.D.
Censor Librorum

Imprimatur:
†Robert F. Joyce
Bishop of Burlington
May 15, 1968

The Nihil Obstat and Imprimatur are official declarations that a book or pamphlet is considered to be free of doctrinal or moral error. No implication is contained therein that those who have granted the Nihil Obstat and Imprimatur agree with the contents, opinions or statements expressed.

Manufactured in the United States of America

To My Mother and Father

CONTENTS

INTRODUCTION

To say that modern man is confused and without a center or a ground for his being is to repeat clichés already overworked in the literature of existentialism. Still, modern man sees his world exploding and expanding with a frightening degree of complexity and multiplicity. A helpless atom, he is bombarded by myriads of material creations, all threatening to destroy his oneness-in-being.

Mircea Eliade, in *The Sacred and the Profane,* has shown that primitive man instinctively sought to center, and thus unify, the indeterminate, amorphous mass of his daily experience. He found this center within himself toward which his total person could be ordered as toward the ground of his real self. He drove a stake into the earth, thus symbolizing the pinning of a snake's head—a sign of chaos and irreality—to the ground. This spot on the earth gave him a second center, and upon it he built his home. Next, he joined his clansmen in a hunt, and where the prey was killed he built his temple, the center of his social community. He chose a mountain top as the center of his cosmos, and there he encountered the Supreme Reality of his world.

Christian man does not need to search for the center of his being, the center of his home, the center of his social community and of his cosmos. That center became a reality when the sacred intersected the profane in the person of Jesus Christ. God, the supreme reality, became centered in a human body. "The Word became man and lived among us" (Jn. 1:14). Man now had a center toward which he could direct his whole life. "All things came into *being* through him and without him there came to be not one thing that has come to be" (Jn. 1:3; emphasis added). All things have their true reality when grounded in Christ. He is the Alpha and the Omega (Apoc. 1:8) of all created beings and "in him we live and move and have our being" (Acts 17:28).

This is the vision of Christians of all times. The sacred in the person of Jesus Christ is the center now of the profane, giving it its order, its unity, its fullest reality. Through the profane element of his human body, Jesus Christ has inserted himself into our lives and into our cosmos. Because that human body died and was raised to a new and glorious life in the resurrection, that sacred center is still inserted into the profane of our lives and of our cosmos. He will never cease being the center.

Still, Christians not only believe that all reality comes under his dominion, but also hold by deepest faith that Jesus Christ, through and in his resurrected body, is working to accomplish the fulfillment of all creatures. By an interior force of attraction called love, he draws to himself human beings, capable of recognizing and acknowledging him as their center of true being. Christian faith brings with it the awesome possibility and obligation of building within ourselves a sacred temple, of relating ourselves to a center who is the risen Christ, living within us. "Do you not know that you are God's temple and that God's spirit dwells in you?" (I Cor. 3:16).

From within man, Christ permeates and leavens the profane world of "the flesh and the devil" in order to make "all things in Christ," as St. Paul so forcefully puts it (Col. 3:11; Eph. 4:6; 1 Cor. 15:28). It is Christ who fills all things and in whom everything is held together (*cf.* Col. 1:17).

Young people today search hungrily for beauty that will not perish or diminish, yet they become ever more frustrated in their search as they are torn in multiple directions by senses and passions that become quiescent only through exhaustion or boredom. They openly reject instructors and religious leaders who "have the answers" for all questions even before they are posed. No rational demonstrations convince them of ultimate realities; only the open encounter with life in all its freshness and rawness and unpredictability has meaning for them. They hunger for direct, full experiences now, not tomorrow.

This "Now Generation" has a passionate yearning, a hunger, for life, and more life. In sports car or on the dance floor, the quest is for life, and *now*. Pop art with its clashing colors and aggressive design is another indication of the modern generation's burning thirst for life. But its music, with its frenzied beat and abrupt rhythms, reveals the pent-up suffocation of an inner *élan vital*. Jack Kerouac, in his book *On the Road,* expresses this craving for vitality:

> Uproars of music and the tenorman had it, and everybody knew he had it. Dean was clutching his head in the crowd, and it was a mad crowd. They were all urging that tenorman to hold it and keep it with cries and wild eyes, and he was raising himself from

a crouch and going down again with his horn, looping it up in a clear cry above the furor. . . . Everybody was rocking and roaring. Galatea and Marie with beer in their hands were standing on their chairs, shaking and jumping. . . . "Stay with it, man!" roared a man with a foghorn voice . . . Boom, kick, that drummer was kicking his drums down the cellar and rolling the beat upstairs with his murderous sticks, rattlety-boom![1]

Modern man with a nervous, often frantic physical vitality —at times bordering on the brutal—nevertheless betrays his ancestral hunger for a life that no finite creature can finally satisfy. He stalks about a universe teeming with possibilities of greater life-experience, with promises and prospects of fuller life and happiness. He is ever reaching out for new thrills, yet ever drops his hands empty at his sides, gazing into seemingly infinite expanses of future possibilities, basically homeless, wandering through a void that yields nothing of its secret to him.

In our modern age, scientific discoveries have opened to us a world of almost infinite complexity. As man faces an ever-expanding universe, he fears that which he cannot dominate. He feels that he is swimming desperately in an ocean of opposing forces which he cannot order. He feels his own inability to make out of the amorphous mass of created beings around him an integral part of his own reality.

For those who believe in a God who transcends this sense world, or for the confused and frustrated who would like to believe in something or someone bigger or more enduring than this fleeting pleasure or that past joy, there is a desire or an unexpressed hope to approach such a Transcendent Being *immediately*. Rituals and rites, symbols and priests, have apparently lost most of their usefulness for this generation.

The modern Christian experiences a greater conflict, perhaps, than the non-Christian in his conscience. The nihilistic void of modern existence contradicts the basic beliefs of his Christian faith. He is not necessarily aided by his creed in solving everyday problems. In a religion unfortunately presented to him as a flight into another world, he vainly tries to reconcile his strong attraction to the world with a basic distrust of it.

Our age presents modern Christians with a religious crisis that ultimately centers on the person of Jesus Christ. Does the Christ traditionally presented to them in religion classes and Sunday sermons have relevance for them, absorbed as they are in fashioning a new and exciting world? How can they find him, the source of all life, in this complex, ever-changing world of today?

For they reject openly any appeal to an "other-worldly" spirituality. Dietrich Bonhoeffer, the German Protestant minister put to death by the Nazis at the age of thirty-nine in 1945, captured the modern attitude toward a religion of flight:

> We are other-worldly ever since we hit upon the devious trick of being religious, yes, even "Christian," at the expense of the earth. Other-worldliness affords a splendid environment in which to live. Whenever life begins to become oppressive and troublesome, a person just leaps into the air with a bold kick and soars relieved and unencumbered into so-called eternal fields. He leaps over the present. He disdains the earth; he is better than it. After all, besides the temporal defeats he still has his eternal victories, and they are so easily achieved. Other-worldliness also makes it easy to preach and to speak words of comfort. An other-worldly Church can be certain that it will in no time win over all the weaklings, all who are only too glad to be deceived and deluded, all utopian-

ists. . . . Man is weak, that's just the way he is; and this weakling man is open to the religion of other-worldliness. Should it be denied him? Should the weakling remain without help? . . . No, the weak man should receive help. He does in fact receive help from Christ. However, Christ does not will or intend this weakness; instead, he makes man strong. He does not lead man in a religious flight from this world to other worlds beyond; rather, he gives him back to the earth as its loyal son.[2]

But the other-worldly Christian flees from the creatures of this world as things evil or tending toward evil. By rejecting God's created world such a Christian acts as if he believed that God could not be found in the world he created, that his kingdom is not to consist in the transfiguration of his world into a "new creation," a "heavenly Jerusalem," but that he is to be found outside of and in spite of this world. Everything in this world is viewed pessimistically, as a hindrance or obstacle or, at best, as no help to sanctification. Teilhard de Chardin characterized this type of Christian as one who will repress his taste for the concrete and material, to focus his interest on purely religious objects. He will live narrowly within the limits of a sacralized world which will seek to rule out of his life as many "worldly" objects as possible.

The opposite reaction, equally arising from a distrust that God's kingdom could be really relevant to this world, is a complete immersion in this world as the total milieu of man's existence. Such a belief includes an extreme optimism that trusts solely in man's resourcefulness to create by his own efforts a "lasting city" on this earth. The premise of such utopian "secularism" is that all religions, including Christianity, are irrelevant for the only "world" there is.

Recent Christian thought reveals a reaction both to other-worldly spirituality and to complete secularism. Led by Maurice Blondel, such writers as Henri de Lubac, Hans von Balthasar, and Karl Rahner stressed the unity between God and his world, between the supernatural and the natural, between grace and nature. Starting with an optimistic vision of God's dominion over his created world and a trust that he could and would attain the end which he intended in creating this world, these thinkers insisted that God was to be encountered precisely in and through the world, the very world cursed by God. "Cursed be the ground," God said to Adam, ". . . thorns and thistles shall it bring forth to you" (Gen. 3:17–18). Yet God so loved the world as to give his only-begotten Son who came to establish his kingdom on this earth. This kingdom, wherein Christ becomes present to his creatures, is hidden within the material world, like a leaven in a mass of dough. Faith shows us Christ immanently working to transform and complete God's creation. Instead of fleeing the material world, we are to encounter Christ there. All created beings exist through Christ and are sustained in their being by Christ's activity. He is the Logos, the image according to which not only man but all creation is fashioned. Through him each creature will attain its completion. "All things came into being through him, and without him there came to be not one thing that has come to be" (Jn. 1:3). ". . . in him were created all creatures in the heavens and on the earth. . . . All have been created through him and for him" (Col. 1:16–17).

St. Paul more than any other early sacred writer beheld Christ immersed in and energizing the created, material world. In Paul's captivity letters (cf. Chapter I), Christ is shown as the center of unity for all that has been created. Paul would wish to lead us high up on the mountain of faith to gaze over the whole universe below. If we share his faith, we shall see Christ as the center and focal point toward whom and from whom all beings flow, verifying Heidegger's insight that truth is ultimately full reality. All beings have their ontological intelligibility and are "true" to the degree that their relationship "in being" to Ultimate Reality is comprehended.

Christ is not to be separated from material reality. All reality is already christologically structured by the incarnation whereby God inserted himself into his creation.

The "immanence" thinkers, although they recognize a clear distinction between the natural and the supernatural orders, the secular and the sacred, the world and the Church, do not seek to separate them in their concrete reality but to unite them through the finality of God's continuous creative act that is vitally related to God's redemptive and sanctifying activity.

In his unpublished work, *Comment je vois* (1948), Teilhard de Chardin speaks the mind of these thinkers in complaining of the various distinct acts in the drama of human salvation conceived as independent of each other. He rather binds them together by his vision of the creative union. For Teilhard there is no creation without an incarnation and no incarnation without redemption. These fundamental mysteries of Christianity are but three "faces" of the one great mystery, the divine process of pleromization, the fulfillment or perfecting through the unifying reduction of the multiple.

Christian Secularity

To avoid a mistaken "incarnational" optimism that would depict Christ as undergoing a series of "incarnations" in our world completely independent of the activities of human beings, a more recent current of thought has evolved, largely from the premises laid down by Jacques Maritain in his *True Humanism.* This school of thought is best described as *Christian secularity.* It is not to be confused with secularism; rather, it is just the opposite, and stands as the main modern answer to it. Some of the leading Catholic proponents of this new thought, besides Maritain, are Karl Rahner, Johannes Metz, Gustave Thils, J. Mouroux, W. Ong, John Courtney Murray, and the three Dominicans, M. D. Chenu, E. Schillebeeckx, and Yves Congar. Like-minded leading Protestant theologians include Dietrich Bonhoeffer, Bishop John Robinson (author of *Honest to God*), and Harvey Cox.

These thinkers point out that for the pagan Greeks, the world was inhabited by numinous beings. Because God was not conceived by the Greeks as transcendent, he became the immanent director of the entire cosmos. The world of gods and the world of men became one. God became many gods with a small *g,* while man became Man with a capital *M.* Judaeo-Christianity, aware of its true mission, exalted the other-ness of God, his absolute transcendence. Creatures are absolutely worldly because in no sense are they God. For this reason the early Christians were considered by the pagan Greeks as atheists (*atheoi*) because they denied the existence of immanent gods fashioned according to man's own liking. The God of the Old and New Testaments had spoken and revealed himself as he "who is." Completely beyond all imperfection, independent absolutely from all material creatures, God was utterly distinct from creatures as Being is distinct from Becoming, as Allness is distinct from Nothingness.

Still, early Christian thinkers did not despise the world but recognized it ontologically for what it truly is. It is not God. It possesses by its nature nothing of God's inner life; it is not "holy"; it is not sacral. Thus a severe yet, in itself, truthful objectivity was strongly established in their minds and attitudes toward the material things of the world.

But more importantly, Christians were thus able to see how fully gratuitous was God's giving of himself to the world that was so "other" than himself. Into a "secular," not-godly world, God sent his own Son to communicate through his material world with mankind. In the historical person of Jesus Christ, God and human beings communicate in a relationship hitherto unknown. It is precisely in Christ's humanity, which is not the infinite, sacred God, the fullness of being, but is worldly, distinct from God, finite, dependent on God for its existence, that God can reveal his great goodness and love. Through Christ, he communicates his being to something other than himself.

In the Incarnation humanity reaches its fullness and perfection because through Christ's humanity "worldly," non-godly humanity is united, through God's infinite act of love, with God himself. In the hypostatic union, human nature receives the existence of God in the person of Jesus Christ. His humanity remains ever humanity; it is never swallowed up or sacralized. Yet the humanity of Christ, especially in his human consciousness, reaches the maximum of self-transcendence. The human nature of Christ in the intimate divine communication within itself reaches its fullness of being. All its capacities, potentialities, as created by God, are completed in sharing God's life.

But the historical Christ is more than the apogee of humanity. This truth, if pressed too far, could circle back to the Arian heresy, which so exalted the humanity of Christ that it denied his divinity. Christ is, as Karl Rahner expresses it, even more than the peak of cosmic realities. He becomes the goal toward which the whole cosmos is moving and in whom the cosmos will find its completion. In Christ we have God's gift of himself to us, irreversibly given. God can never withdraw his self-giving because he is now incarnated in the living person, Jesus Christ. God has given himself to us through other finite creatures by giving extrinsically of his perfections in a finite, imperfect, participated mode of existence. But the incarnation reveals God's *intrinsic* giving of himself, the gift of his very inner Life to mankind in a visible, human form, an autonomous, human consciousness, that can never be reversed or extinguished.

Briefly and simply stated, therefore, through the hypostatic union, in an historical event that unfolded in space and time, that is, in the incarnation of the Second Person of the Trinity, God has given himself totally to mankind. If God has given himself irreversibly to us through Christ, then Christ must be not only God's instrument but God himself. The promise of God to give himself to us absolutely is realized completely and irreversibly in the hypostatic union.

Schillebeeckx writes:

In Christ, and through him, human existence has become the objective expression of God's absolute communication of himself to man, and by the same token, the objective expression of the human response to that total divine gift. . . . The human existence of Christ, taken with all its determinism and all its human implications, is the personal life of God, the Son. This means that the entire temporal dimension and the unabridged reality we call profane can be assumed into a God-related life, given that in the Son the eternal has presented itself personally within temporal and terrestrial realities. The very definition of the hypostatic union is exactly that. This also reveals the fact that thanks to Christ all of human history is swathed in God's love; it is assumed into the absolute and gratuitous presence of the mystery of God. The worldly and the temporal remain worldly and temporal; they are not sacralized but sanctified by that presence, that is, by the God-centered life of Christ and of his faithful.[3]

Thus, we see that man and the whole concrete world are dependent on Christ for their fullness of actuated being. The world has been given to us as a manifestation of the love that God has for each of us. This does not mean that we are to regard the material things of the world only as "instruments" for the spread of the kindom of God. We see already that each material creature has its own intrinsic value and proper relationship to Christ, its own finality. But its full completion cannot be attained unless man, made to God's image and likeness inasmuch as he possesses an intellect to know God's love and a will to respond to that love, recognizes the inner relationship of his given creaturehood to Christ and develops it accordingly.

Genesis tells us that God made man dominant over the whole material universe. He enjoined man, before the Fall, to "be fruitful and multiply; fill the earth and subdue it. Have dominion over the fish of the sea, the birds of the air, the cattle and all the animals that crawl on the earth" (Gen. 1:28). Man has the power through his free will to use, rule, dominate, and direct the entire universe; but this power has been given so that through the proper exercise of it he can subordinate his will to that of the Supreme Ruler. This is what many of the Eastern Fathers, such as St. Cyril of Alexandria and St. John Damascene, affirmed: it is in the fact that God has bestowed on man power and dominion over the non-human cosmos that we see in man the "image and likeness" of God. As co-creator with the immanent divine Logos present in the cosmos, man is to achieve the fullness of his being.

Christ is still living and cooperating with us in the restoration of dominion, first over ourselves and then over the nonhuman cosmos—a truth forgotten by many theologians and spiritual writers today. But this was the most evident and viable truth grasped by the early Christians, and it led to the Chalcedonian definition which provided the basic teaching for an integral christology.[4]

It is necessary to establish an intimate relationship between ourselves and Christ, first, in order to bring about within us the "new creation," "sons of God," coheirs with Christ of Heaven; and secondly, to effect the transformation of the total cosmos under Christ's actual dominion. To effect these two goals we must become convinced of the intrinsic value of all material beings and of our relationships with them.

We Christians must ask ourselves today, "Would we not be distrusting God and constructing a caricature of him if we thought he were not interested in our teeming cities? Are the millions of urban citizens not equally destined by his creation to share his life, as were those of a more bucolic society of humans who served him in a different social and cultural environment?" This modern, urban existence cannot be something manufactured only by man. If he is faithful to his promises, God must be concerned with every phase of it. Through such an environment, God will communicate himself to man. Many of us live our whole earthly life in such urban circumstances. In these circumstances we must receive God's communication of himself to us. Amos Wilder sums up:

> If we are to have any transcendence today, even Christian, it must be in and through the secular. . . . If we are to find Grace it is to be found in the world and not overhead. The sublime firmament

of overhead reality that provided a spiritual home for the souls of men until the eighteenth century has collapsed.[5]

To believe that one can find God only in retreat from modern society is to disbelieve that God is all-loving and all-powerful. He does want to reveal himself to us through his living Word, Jesus Christ, precisely as Christ is to be found in our present world.

Cosmic Christology

But how does one find Jesus Christ shining "diaphanously," as Teilhard de Chardin expressed it, through our material world? How does a housewife harassed by the problems of a growing family, a student coping with the apparently conflicting views of science and religion, and an unskilled laborer in his working hours find Christ? Is there any reliable method that will help men bridge the chasm from the profane to the sacred? In short, how can we, so absorbed in the material, encounter Christ *today* and make a meaningful, total response to him?

The following chapters do not embody such a method. Their purpose is to present a vision of Christ in his relation to the world, shared across the ages by many Christian theologians for whom Jesus Christ was encountered in and through the material cosmos. This book treats, as architects of this tradition, Paul, John, Irenaeus, Clement of Alexandria, Origen, Athanasius, Basil, Gregory Nazianzen, Gregory of Nyssa, Cyril of Alexandria, and Maximus the Confessor. The concluding chapters treat Teilhard de Chardin's christological contribution and the development of contemporary Christian secularity. Inclusion of Teilhard means, of course, that the early vision of Christ's cosmic presence has far from faded in our modern age. Through his scientific research, his philosophical and theological studies as a priest, and, above all, through his own striking integration of these diverse roles in an extraordinary personality, he has succeeded in recapturing the same vision of the cosmic Christ so dear to earlier Christians. De Chardin recaptured and assimilated this vision into his whole being and succeeded in expressing it in terms that men, groping in the new complexities of the twentieth century, could understand and make a part of their living experience.

Their Christian faith presented to all of these men a Christ-in-the-cosmos. By assuming a material body, God inserted himself into the heart of his created cosmos. By his death and resurrection, Christ, in his gloriously spiritualized humanity, became present, and is even now present, to the cosmos in a new manner. Not only is he the exemplar, the Divine Logos according to whom, as St. John tells us in his Prologue, God created all things and in whom all things have their being, but also he is this Body-Person who has become the working agent to effect the fulfillment of God's plan of creation. The Fathers' vision reveals the structure of cosmic Christology: Christ, the God-man, is the redeeming and fulfilling center of the total created universe. This theme, traced through their writings, is the subject of this book.

As articulated by the leading theologians of the ancient Church, it was a vision shared by the early Christian communities and provided the framework and background for their "life in Christ." After St. Maximus the Confessor (seventh century), for reasons too many and too complex to be developed here, Christ's dynamic presence and activity in the world was not sufficiently stressed. There was an eclipse of the cosmic dimension in the study of christology, as theological reflection about Christ became largely a science of excessively rigorous rational concepts. The view of Christ as the life of the world, in the world, bringing life to the world, was increasingly obscured, only to be brilliantly recaptured by Teilhard. This vision cannot be learned as one learns from a teacher a fact of history or a solution to a mathematical problem. We can only hope that, having been exposed to their intense response to Christ encountered *in* their universe, we too will be led to glimpse that which "eye has not seen nor ear heard" but which will be revealed to those who believe in him.

I

ST. PAUL'S COSMIC DIMENSIONS OF SALVATION

"Saul, Saul, why do you persecute me?" From the first encounter with Jesus Christ, Paul met the Savior of the world as the cosmic Christ. He had set out to persecute the followers of the man named Jesus, who had been put to death in Jerusalem for blasphemously claiming, in substance, that he was God. But along the road to Damascus, Saul became Paul, and Jesus became for him the living Son of God, "the image of the invisible God, the first-born of every creature, because in him were created all creatures in the heavens and on the earth" (Col. 1:15).

That haunting voice seared Paul's being: it was never to be forgotten. The implications of Christ's words gradually became clearer to Paul through years of prayerful encounter with his Lord. A steady progression in Paul's thought can be discerned in his epistles, as his christology takes more specific and more extensive form. Many modern New Testament exegetes have pointed out the gradual development of Paul's christology as he composed his pastoral letters to answer exigencies that arose in the early churches he administered. In the initial stage of development, we find the Pauline emphasis placed on a basic creed that was formulated undoubtedly by the first church in Palestine. The death and resurrection of Jesus Christ were professed in faith by the church as a pledge of future resurrection and entrance into the heavenly kingdom. Paul stresses our own future resurrection which will be realized when Christ returns triumphantly in his parousia (I and II Thess. and I Cor. 15).

Paul next develops the concept of the power of Christ's death and resurrection, not as looking forward to the parousia but here and now exerting its influence in the living Christian. Through his glorious resurrectional life Jesus Christ lives in a new way in the souls of men. His death and resurrection are being accomplished in Christians even in this life (Rom. and I Cor.). Man is raised to a new life, the very life of Christ, by which he is changed from the "old man" to the "new man," "in Christ."

The final period of development gives us the best expression of the dimensions of Paul's cosmic christology. Here he strives to define more precisely Christ's relationship not only to individual human beings but also to the whole cosmos. Christ appears as the center of unity, drawing all things back to their origins. Since the world was created for Christ (Col. 1:6), it must be recapitulated or reestablished in and through him under whose power all creatures must one day be united (Col. and Eph.).

The final period of Paul's development is evidenced most clearly in his letters of captivity, especially Colossians and Ephesians. In these letters we must look for the cosmic dimensions of his christology. The other two periods, of course, give us details which offer a fuller understanding of this christology.

Paul's Attitude toward the World

Paul deals with the created world, the cosmos, in antithetical comparison with the "new creation" that Christ came to bring to the world. St. John in his First Epistle tells us that we have been born of God, but the whole world is under the influence of the Evil One (I Jn. 5:19). All creation, as coming from the hand of God, was good. In the presentation of this truth Paul shows great optimism, but his optimism stems from Christ who is the model according to which all things have been fashioned. The created world, at least as destined by God, is meant to be a reflection of the "invisible things" (Rom. 1:20). It is a reflection of the Logos, the perfect image of the Father.

He is the image of the invisible God, the first-born of every creature, because in him were created all creatures in the heavens and on the earth, both visible and invisible, whether Thrones, or Dominations, or Principalities, or Powers. All have been created through him and for him (Col. 1:15–16).

But this creation, which was to be perfected according to the cooperation of man with the Divine Logos, fell into a universal slavery to an extrinsic force. It was plunged into darkness, chaos, and death. To better explain this estrangement from God and from basic orientation toward God, Paul employs the apocalyptic symbols common not only to the Gnostic sects of his day but also to his own Jewish tradition.

The Jews had come into contact with the astrological symbols of the Babylonians during the Exile and readily used this imagery to work out their own religious cosmology.

Cosmic spiritual forces, external to God's intrinsically good creation, held the universe in bondage. The Prince of the World (Jn. 12:31), Satan or Belial, led the attack along with his intermediate powers, the Principalities, Powers, Thrones, Dominions. The Evil One, the god of this world (II Cor. 4:4), has prevented men from seeing the splendor of Christ, who is God's image (II Cor. 4:5). Paul describes the effects of sin quite graphically in his letter to the Ephesians where his use of the cosmology of his day is seen most clearly.

> Once, you were dead by reason of your transgressions and sins, in which you lived in keeping with the ways of this world, in obedience to the prince who exercises his power in the air, the spirit which is now active in the rebels. In fact we too, all of us, were in the company of such people, when we led lives enslaved to fleshy cravings, yielding to the desires of our flesh and its aims, and were by nature objects of wrath, just like the rest. But God, who is rich in mercy, was moved by the intense love with which he loved us, and when we were dead by reason of our transgressions, he made us live with the life of Christ. . . . Together with Christ Jesus and in him, he raised us up and enthroned us in the heavenly realm, that in Christ Jesus he might show throughout the ages to come the overflowing riches of his grace springing from his goodness to us. . . . We are his handiwork, created in Christ Jesus in view of good deeds which God prepared beforehand for us to practice (Eph. 2:1–4; 6, 7, 10).

Paul uses the popular picture of angelic powers that hover above our universe in the air, the cause of all chaotic elements found in our world. These powers were the cause of evil, both moral and physical, in an otherwise good but undeveloped universe. They were essentially destructive. Syncretistic Judaism assimilated from Greek and Egyptian religious philosophy the concept of semipersonal powers ruling the destinies of cosmic, social, and even personal history and joined this idea to the elaborate systems of angelology derived from Persian and Babylonian sources.

The Flesh and the Spirit

Like his successors Clement of Alexandria, Origen, and Christian theologians of all times, Paul strove to use the popular concepts of the times as an already existing vehicle by means of which he could teach his new converts from paganism or Judaism about man's "bondage to sin." Man without Christ, without hope of salvation, was exposed to the temptations of Satan and his cohorts. Through the "flesh" (*sarx*) Paul seeks to describe the total man, the flesh-substance, the whole man considered from the point of view of his eternal existence as opposed to any interiority. *Sarx* represents man in all his creaturehood in contrast to God—man, not only in his distance and difference from God, in his mortality and weakness, but also in his utter estrangement from God through sin. "All have sinned and lack the approval of God" (Rom. 3:23).

All of humanity, both the Jew of the Law and the pagan guided by conscience, has been tainted by sin, not only because "through one man sin entered into the world and through sin, death, and thus death has spread to all men because all have sinned" (Rom. 5:12), but also because sin has entered as a power subjugating man from without by using man's own physical flesh as the instrument for his estrangement from God. Paul personifies sin that invaded the world, "produced death for me" (Rom. 7:13), and held him in its bondage (Rom. 7:15), for sin rules as king in the realm of death (Rom. 5:21). We must not think that he regarded sin as a personalized spirit. But always and foremost, in his pastoral epistles, the persuasive teacher and preacher, he utilizes the popular conceptions of "principalities and powers" as intermediaries between God and man, personifying sin in order to inculcate in the hearts of his readers his own intense hatred for sin. By imaging in personalized terms the power of sin over man, Paul could arouse in his new converts an emotional hatred for evil much stronger and more effective than had he launched into an impersonal, philosophical discussion of why God permitted evil.

Sin wields an almost irresistible power over man, leading him away from God. One of its prime ways of enthralling man is through the flesh. Paul speaks of "sinful flesh" (Rom. 8:3) and the flesh as the "body of sin" (Rom. 6:6). Because he is carnal (*sarkinos*), man is "sold into the power of sin" (Rom. 7:14). Sin and flesh are not identified (Rom. 6:12–19; 8:3; 12:1; II Cor. 4:11). But in his realism Paul shows the flesh as the seat of all passionate desires, set awry as long as man does not ascend and put on the "spirit of Christ." The "flesh" element is not sinful by its nature, but *in fact* it opens the door to sin through inordinate self-love.

In the light of the flesh-spirit antithesis Paul highlights the redemptive work of Christ. Through the incarnation the Son of God broke through the barrier separating the realm of divinity and life from that of humanity and death, both physical and moral. Although personally sinless, Christ came "in the likeness of sinful flesh" (Rom. 8:3); for our sakes

"God made sin of him who knew no sin, so that in him we might become God's holiness" (II Cor. 5:21). Humanity was estranged from God through Adam's sin and the accumulated mass of subsequent sins. Christ took upon himself this same estrangement. Although united intimately with the Father, Christ in his earthly existence was in some sense not fully one with his Father. By taking upon himself our flesh he entered a humanity in a state of "unsalvation" which bore the sign of sin, namely, death (Rom. 5:12).

Not only is man infected with sin and death, but the whole of creation has been touched by the power of sin. Man was meant to be the master of the created cosmos; now the non-human cosmos suffers the fate of man. Because under the yoke of sin together, so also man and the non-human cosmos will be redeemed and fulfilled together. No part of the universe will be unredeemed when the Redeemer comes, for he is capable of uniting the universe with the Creator. This is the sense of Romans 8:19–22:

All creation awaits with eager longing the manifestation of the sons of God. For creation was made subject to vanity not by its own choice but by the will of him who made it subject, yet with the hope that creation itself would be delivered from its slavery to corruption, to enjoy the freedom that comes with the glory of the children of God. For we know that all creation groans and travails in pain until now.

Against this universal subjection to sin in which "All have sinned and lack the approval of God" (Rom. 3:23), Paul paints the goodness and mercy of God by showing how God made good that which man in the darkness of his sinful misery could not accomplish (Rom. 15:8–9; 11:32; 5:8).

"By sending his Son in the likeness of sinful flesh as a sin-offering, he has condemned sin in the flesh" (Rom. 8:3). Christ condemned sin in the flesh through his death and resurrection whereby he passed gloriously from the state of flesh (*sarx*) to that of spirit (*pneuma*). Confined to his human flesh, Christ was not able to share his divine life with other men. After his glorious resurrection he, "the last Adam, became a spirit imparting life" (I Cor. 15:45). The first representative man failed to resist sin; the second Adam would be man in the fullest sense by triumphing over sin, destroying death and its sting, and bringing all men at least the possibility of leaving their "carnal" condition of estrangement from God in order to put on the Spirit of life in God.

Resurrection Leads to the Spirit

Christ would effect the redemption of the universe by overcoming the flesh and leading it to spirit. All through biblical tradition we find death connected with Adam's sin. If Christ were to break sin's power, he would have to conquer death by the transforming glory of his resurrection in which his carnal condition, that is, the state of estrangement from God, would be transformed into the fullness of Spirit or life of God. As through his human body Christ as an integral part of humanity touched all men, so by the resurrection of his human body the bodies of all men and the whole universe would be given the possibility to be reoriented to God. This reorientation would lead eventually to a full resurrection in the spirit.

Paul stresses death-resurrection as a kind of thesis-antithesis in his letter to the Romans. ". . . Jesus Our Lord, raised from the dead, was delivered up for our sins and rose again for our sanctification" (Rom. 4:24–25). He affirms in Romans

5 that it is faith in his resurrection that sanctifies us, giving us peace with God through Our Lord Jesus Christ, "through whom also we have found entrance into this state of grace in which we now abide and exult in the hope of participating in God's glory" (Rom. 5:2). Our whole Christian faith hinges on the resurrection of the body of the Lord. "But if Christ has not been raised, your faith is groundless; you are still in your sins" (I Cor. 15:17). Our faith would be vain in the sense of empty, for Christ would not ontologically have reversed the sentence of death; thus, he would not have rescued men from their estrangement from God. He would not have restored to us the "spirit," that is, God's own life. To live in God through his full humanity, to live the divine life of the Spirit—this is why Christ had to rise and die no more. It is true that before his resurrection, he personally enjoyed the fullness of God's divine life. After his resurrection, however, he possessed it in his role as our living and life-giving Head. He passed from a "carnal" existence to one completely spiritual, "pneumatic." In this new modality or manner of existence Jesus Christ could transcend all space and time and apply the merits of his sacrifice, the sprinkling of his blood, whereby we could draw near again to God.

In summary, the raising of Christ's body is God's acceptance of the sacrifice whereby Christ, the perfect man, passes over from the condition of flesh (*sarx*), which was subject to death, into the new condition of spirit (*pneuma*), and thus becomes the life-giving Spirit, the Head of the new humanity, established by him as the new people of God. In Christ's death, God condemned sin in the flesh (Rom. 8:3). The power of sin was broken. The resurrection of Christ is uniquely important because his new and glorious life makes him the new Adam and the Lord of the universe, capable under this new modality of bestowing upon us the same life of the Spirit by making us sons of his heavenly Father.

St. John the Evangelist implies this same doctrine in explaining why Christ could not pour out his Spirit during his earthly existence. "As yet there was no outpouring of the Spirit, because Jesus was not yet glorified" (Jn. 7:39). Christ himself insisted with his apostles that "It is to your advantage that I depart. Unless I depart, the Advocate will not come to you; whereas if I depart [am glorified], I will send him to you" (Jn. 16:7). When his human body became glorified, it became for humanity the source of the Spirit, of eternal life.

Redemption of the Whole Universe

The indwelling Spirit that Jesus Christ sends us not only imparts to our souls the ontological life of God through grace but he exerts his influence on our bodies as well. "And if the Spirit of him who raised Jesus from the dead dwells in you, then he who raised Christ Jesus from the dead will also bring to life your mortal bodies because of his Spirit who dwells in you" (Rom. 8:11). But tied intrinsically to our material bodies that are destined to a future redemption through a spiritual resurrection is the whole universe. Genesis 3:17 speaks of a universal curse of God upon the earth and upon all material creatures through man's turning away from God. Man loses his dominion over the non-human cosmos; chaos, the result of sin, holds the universe in bondage until that bondage is undone through the Spirit of Jesus Christ.

Thus Paul ties up the destiny of brute creation with man's sanctification. He imagines the created universe empty of man, waiting for the manifestation of the sons of God. The material world was made subject to "vanity," that is, was misused by the pride of man, not by any choice of its own, but by that of man who cast the universe into the "slavery of corruption" (Rom. 8:21) by his sin. The whole of creation is, like a mother in agony before giving birth, groaning and laboring in pain "until now" (Rom. 8:22).

Christ's dominion over the whole universe is pictured most clearly in Paul's later epistles, those written in captivity, especially Colossians and Ephesians.

Shipped from Caesarea to Rome as a prisoner, Paul learned from his co-worker, Epaphras, of a rising heresy among the communities of Colossae, Laodicea, and Hierapolis. These Asiatic Christians, under the influence of a false cosmology, were filled with a morbid craze for speculation about the heavenly spirits and powers. False teachers maintained that the angelic powers, intermediate beings between God and men, and in whom the fullness of the Godhead, the *pleroma,* dwells, were also causes of creation (Col. 1:19; 2:9; 1:15–17). They could exert great power over the birth and destiny of men and were to be worshiped.

The gravity of the heresy consisted in the implicit denial of Christ's unique position as the sole mediator and redeemer of mankind. For this reason Paul stresses in two clear passages the uniqueness of Christ in his dual role as mediator and redeemer.

In Colossians 1:15–20 Christ's existence "prior to all creatures" means that all things are created and are preserved in their being through and for him. Earlier, in his Epistle to the Philippians, he had hinted at Christ's universal dominion over all creation: "It is he who by an exercise of the power which enables him even to subject the universe to himself will refashion our lowly bodies, conforming them to his glorious body" (Phil. 3:21). In the text from Colossians,

Paul points out certain created beings who exemplify the highest of all creatures in heaven and on earth, "both visible and invisible, whether Thrones, or Dominations, or Principalities, or Powers." All creatures, therefore, have been created through Christ and for him. But how Christ affects them after their creation is not stated until Verse 20. Christ's redemption of them consists in their reconciliation with the Father through his sacrifice on the Cross. "For it pleased God the Father that in him all fullness should dwell, and that through him God should reconcile to himself every being, and make peace both on earth and in heaven through the blood shed on the cross" (Col. 1:19–20).

Here we see a clear example of Paul's use of a cosmic setting, based on the cosmology of his times, to relate in a more dramatic way the full extent of Christ's dominion over all creation, visible and invisible. All creatures were created to be under the dominion of Christ. They had lost their proper orientation and had to be reconciled by the same Christ who is both their exclusive beginning and end. Their rebellion was put down but not completely destroyed. His work of reconciliation goes on in the universe still. C. K. Barrett summarizes this passage as follows:

> The ordered universe is now disordered, and has reached such pitch of rebellion that he who is the image of the Invisible God—Wisdom, Word, Torah, Urmensch, Microcosmos, call him what you will—can only retrieve the situation by shedding his blood and overcoming the power of death by experiencing it. This means that the work of the heavenly Man can be apprehended not in creation as it now exists, but only in the process of redemption.[1]

After Paul has maintained, against the Gnostic heresy that excluded part of the created world from the dominion of

Christ, the absolute power and dominion of Christ over all creatures, he insists in Colossians 1:22 that Christ "has reconciled you by his death in his human body, to present you holy and without blemish or blame in God's presence." This reconciliation is made actual by our adherence in faith to the message of Christ's gospel. This gospel must be preached to every creature under heaven (Col. 1:23). But only in Second Corinthians does Paul develop in greater detail the relationship between God and Christians in the reconciliation of man to the Father effected through Christ. Man's role is enunciated in the ministry of reconciliation by preaching the gospel to all creatures. This is a greater responsibility than merely preaching to other men. His ministry of co-reconciliation with Christ must touch even the non-human cosmos:

If, then, any man is in Christ, he is a new creation; the old state of things has gone; wonderful to tell, it has been made over, absolutely new! All this comes from the action of God, who has reconciled us to himself through Christ, and has entrusted us with this ministry of reconciliation. We know that God was truly reconciling the world to himself in Christ, not reckoning against men their sins, and entrusting to us the message of reconciliation. We are, therefore, Christ's ambassadors; we know that God makes appeal through us. We beg you, for the sake of Christ, to be reconciled to God. For our sakes God made sin of him who knew no sin, so that in him we might become God's holiness (II Cor. 5:17–21).

When this text emphasizing man's role in cooperating with Christ in the reconciliation of all creatures is compared with the previous one from Colossians, 1:14–23, we see the urgency of proclaiming the gospel not only in word but in living deed. Christ's message must be proclaimed to the ends of the earth, in every generation. Even the non-human cosmos must come under the influence of Christ and his message. The cosmos is groaning until the fullness of time when human beings will live by the message of the divine Word and thus bring the whole universe to its fullness.

Letter to the Ephesians

Following the hypothesis of P. Benoit[2] that the letter to the Ephesians was written after that to the Colossians, we discover in Ephesians a doctrine of universal redemption much more developed and nuanced. He seemingly presupposes the universal cosmic primacy of Christ so strongly insisted on in Colossians and builds upon it. He writes in a calm, synthetic manner, with none of the polemical overtones so prevalent in Colossians. In the letter to the Colossians, Christ appears in his cosmic role as Head who effects the fullness of the cosmic universe, while in the letter to the Ephesians, Christ is shown to be the mystical Head of the Church. He brings about the close unity of all believers, both Jews and Gentiles, in himself, by vivifying them with his own life and elevating them to a oneness of Body with him as its Head. This doctrine follows since the cosmic aspects of Christ's universal dominion have been clearly established.

In this letter Paul wishes, therefore, to show the Church as the link between Christ and the cosmos. In Ephesians 1:10, Benoit sees in the "mystery of his will" (*mysterion*) the union of the Jews and Gentiles into the one Body, the Church.[3] Thus, Paul would say that God's good will, to gather all men into one Body, was "put into effect in Christ when the designated period of time had elapsed, namely, to gather all creation both in heaven and on earth under one head, Christ" (Eph. 1:10).

Later, Paul more clearly associates the Church with this

awesome mystery, touching the loving decree of God himself who wills our individual salvation: "This is a great mystery—I mean in regard to Christ and the Church" (Eph. 5:32). The clearest example of combining the cosmic primacy of Christ as illustrated in Colossians and the mystical primacy of Christ in his Church is found in Ephesians 1:20–23:

> The exercise of the might of this power was shown when he raised Christ from the dead and seated him at his right hand in heaven, high above every Principality and Power and Virtue and Domination, yes, high above every being, no matter by what title it may be called, no matter whether it is in this world or in the world to come. He has subjected every single thing to his authority and has appointed him sovereign head of the Church, which is truly his body, the complement of him who fills all the members with all graces.

Thus, Christ is the absolute Head of the physical, created cosmos, but his primacy will not be completely recognized until the parousia when he will return to subject all things to his dominion. He is also absolute Head of the spiritual Body, the Church, whose members have freely, through loving faith, submitted themselves to his absolute primacy.

After using the metaphor of Christ as Head of the members in the unity of one Body, Paul then moves to describe this bond of union between Christ and the Church by the metaphor of spouses. In this metaphor he strives to convey the duality of dominance and submission, through love, plus the added nuance of an intimate union resulting in a new life, the divine life brought about solely by Christ, the Spouse. Christ is the source of this divine life not only for his bride, the Church, but also—through his activity in the Church—for the individual members:

. . . Christ is the head of the Church and also the savior of that body. Thus, just as the Church is subject to Christ, so also let wives be subject to their husbands in all things. . . . Christ loved the Church and delivered himself for her, that he might sanctify her by cleansing her in the bath of water with the accompanying word, in order to present to himself the Church in all her glory, devoid of blemish or wrinkle or anything of the kind, but that she may be holy and flawless. . . . Now no one ever hates his own flesh; on the contrary, he nourishes and cherishes it, as Christ does the Church, because we are members of his Body (Eph. 5:23–30).[4]

Searching still for new pictures, metaphors, symbols that will convey the intimate union of Christ with the individual members in whom he lives by his own divine life, Paul seizes upon the analogy of a building:

You are an edifice built on the foundation of the apostles and prophets with Christ Jesus himself as the chief cornerstone. In him the whole structure is being closely fitted together by the Spirit to become God's temple consecrated in the Lord. In him you, too, are being fitted by the Spirit into the edifice to become God's dwelling place (Eph. 2:20–22).

Without Christ there would be no foundation for this life in the Spirit. Yet the Church has many members with different functions—apostles, prophets, and so forth—all individuals distinct from Christ, yet forming one single temple in which God dwells. We must leave to the second part of this chapter the discussion of growth in Christ; however, there remain three points still to be touched on in regard to the cosmic dimensions of Christ: his recapitulation of all things, the Pleroma, and the Parousia.

Recapitulation in Christ

St. Paul uses the word *anakephaloioomai* (Eph. 1:9–10) to describe Christ's role assigned in the decree of his heavenly Father, namely, that when the fullness of time had arrived, God would gather all creation both in heaven and on earth under one head, Christ. H. Schlier finds a great variety of possible meanings for this term as it is used in Scripture, but *reestablish* seems to be the best translation.[5] We can accept this to mean that Christ will restore the world's lost unity under his own headship.

Christ at the time of his death and resurrection, in microcosm as it were, reestablished or reconciled humanity in himself by destroying sin, death, and the distorted element in the flesh. In the second parousia he will also reestablish all things, "raising up the flesh of the whole of mankind" by spiritualizing it. He will bring all things completely under his dominion by bestowing the fullness of his divine life upon men for all eternity.

Yet, in a very true sense, this reestablishing of divine life in the individual soul need not wait for the parousia; the process has already begun in human souls through baptism and the increase of faith, as will be discussed in the following chapter. Again we see Christ's own bodily death and resurrection as the perfect type of our own individual dying to the "carnal" elements in order that we might be reestablished by Christ's grace into the new creation in him.

Ontologically, all created beings are through Christ and for him; all subsist in him. They have their reality, their full meaning, only in relation to Christ. He gives them unity, harmony, cohesion. Yet it is man alone among all created beings on the earth who is capable, by reflecting in the depths of his consciousness, of finding the nexus between Christ and the rest of creation. J. Huby has well synthesized how Christ gathers up all things to give them their fullest meaning in himself:

In Him all has been created as in a supreme center of unity, harmony, and cohesion, which gives to the world its sense, its value, and therefore its reality. Or, to use another metaphor, He is the focus, the "meeting point" as Lightfoot puts it, where all the fibres and generative energies of the universe are organized and gathered together. Were someone to see the whole universe, past, present and future, in a single instantaneous glimpse, he would see all beings ontologically suspended from Christ, and completely unintelligible apart from Him.[6]

Pleroma

To understand Paul's meaning of Christ's reestablishing all things in their fullness in the parousia, we must first look at his meaning of the word *pleroma,* fullness. Paul uses this word in five important texts in his two captivity letters, thus giving to it a specialized, technical meaning.

(1) "For it pleased God the Father that in him all *fullness* should dwell. . . ." (Col. 1:19). Here there is question of a fixed abode; God wills that the fullness be in Christ in order that he might reconcile and pacify all things. In this text *pleroma* could not refer to the fullness of the divine essence which Christ possesses as God, nor is there any question of it referring to the Church as the fullness dwelling in him. Paul is probably thinking of the terminology used by the Stoics who held that the whole cosmos was unified in its diversity by the divine Spirit that compenetrated all sensible things, filling them with its universal presence and being filled by them. Paul rejects the Stoic, pantheistic immanence while applying the

nuances in the Stoic concept to the transcendence of the monotheistic biblical concept of God.

Thus Christ, through his redemptive work and by means of his present glorious resurrectional life, assumes in himself not only regenerated humanity, which is his Body, but also the whole cosmos which becomes a new creation, at least potentially, to form the framework of this Body.

(2) "For in him is embodied and dwells the *fullness* of the Godhead" (Col. 2:9). Linking this up with what follows, Paul says that through the incarnation, whereby Christ has taken upon himself a body (*somatikos*), the fullness of the Godhead has been localized in this Body-Person, Christ. Christians have become filled because they exist now as new creatures in Christ who fills them with his divine life through his resurrectional life. They come into contact with his divine fullness when they become incorporated with Christ resurrected by means of baptism.

(3) ". . . that you may be perfected and bring to realization God's *fullness*" (Eph. 3:19). Paul uses the cosmic dimensions of the term *pleroma* to apply it to the one great reality that is ever before his eyes in this letter to the Ephesians, namely, the Church. Christians, by becoming more perfect, build up the fullness of God in the Church. God's fullness exists perfectly within the immanent action of the trinitarian life, but now it must be built up to a fullness in the Church on earth.

(4) ". . . [God] has appointed him sovereign head of the Church, which is truly his body, the complement of him who *fills* all the members with all graces" (Eph. 1:22–23). Here we see for the first time *pleroma* identified with the Church-Body. Some commentators, such as Voste, maintain that just as the head is completed by the rest of the body, so Christ is completed in his mission as Savior by the Church which con-

tinues and prolongs his work through time and space. He, in turn, supplies the members with all needed graces.

(5) "Thus we attain to perfect manhood, to the mature proportions that befit Christ's *fullness*" (Eph. 4:13). Again, the *pleroma* of Christ is coextensive with the Body of Christ, the Church. Christ individually, in his resurrectional, glorious existence in heaven, enjoys the fullness as Head of the Church. His Body, however, made of all men who are in the process of being saved, is still in the process of formation on this earth.

Thus, we can say that the *pleroma* for St. Paul, at least in his Epistles to the Colossians and the Ephesians, where he is especially concerned with presenting Christ in his cosmic dimensions, refers to a multiple fullness. Christ in his risen Body-Person, possesses the fullness of the Godhead. Yet precisely through the same glorious new existence of the Body-Person, Jesus Christ, is he able to communicate this same divine life to us human beings who are forming his Body, the Church. This formation goes on without ceasing in the universe until the end of time. Christ is conceived not only as the chief and Head that commands his Body, but also as the principle that nourishes this Body. Through his sacramental union of grace with the individual members who form his Body, the Church, Christ extends his influence to the entire universe. The cosmos or created world is being redeemed through Christ and thus is arriving gradually at its goal of fullness, which is God himself.

Parousia

The last feature of Paul's cosmic christology is his concept of the *parousia,* Christ's second coming in glory at the end of time. The usual meaning of the Greek word *parousia* is *presence*—hence, by implication, the arrival of some person. In the Hellenic period in which Paul was writing, this word had a technical meaning, both political and religious. It denoted the triumphal entry of rulers, kings, emperors, high-ranking magistrates, and religious leaders into a city. Because sovereigns were treated as gods and gods were treated as rulers, the two senses melded into each other. Paul undoubtedly had such a triumphal entry of a sovereign in mind in the description he gives of Christ's victorious return to earth at the end of time:

> At the given signal, at the summons of the archangel, at the blast of God's trumpet, the Lord in person will come down from heaven and the dead who are in Christ will rise first. Afterwards we who are alive, who survive, shall be caught up with them on clouds into the air to meet the Lord, and so we shall continue in the Lord's company forever (I Thess. 4:16–17).

Paul several times alludes to the parousia (I Thess. 5:2; II Thess. 1:7–12, 2:1–12; I Cor. 15:20–28; II Cor. 1:14). In nearly all these texts he borrows chiefly from the language and popular notions of Jewish eschatology. But his contribution is not to be found in these eschatological symbols, taken from Jewish conventional imagery, but in the innovations that he introduced into the Jewish traditional eschatology. We are concerned here only with Christ's cosmic aspects; the latter part of this chapter will seek to show the eschatological aspects of the growth of the individual and the community, or Church, "in Christ."

Christ, by his death and resurrection, as has already been pointed out, achieved victory over the cosmic powers of evil. It is a decisive victory, but requires extension in space and time in order to reach all men, in all places. Hence, even now, after the historical victory of Christ through his resurrection, the demonic elements of death, sin, and chaos are very much at work in the universe. At present, Christ's victory is being worked out in the process of reestablishing the universe under his dominion. Christians in whom Christ vibrantly lives are his beachhead, his foothold, in the movement to conquer the whole world. Thus, for Paul, the eschatological, cosmic process of reestablishing Christ in all things has already begun through the instrumentality of men in whom Christ applies the victory of his death and resurrection: first, to these men in their personal relations to God and neighbor, and second, to the non-human cosmos by their grace-informed activities in it.

Adam's rebellion against God affected both his descendants and the cosmos. A chaotic element was introduced into man that inclined him more readily toward evil than toward God. This chaotic element, concupiscence, also touched the cosmos that was meant to serve man in his loving submission to God. This cosmic enthralling of non-human creatures to demonic elements is allegorically brought out by the curse leveled on the earth in Genesis 6. The Jewish doctors of the Law taught that eventually this cosmic curse would be lifted by a universal annihilation of the material world held in bondage by this curse.

Paul's great contribution was to point out clearly that the whole universe, along with the individuals saved in Christ, would not be destroyed but would be transformed in the parousia or final coming of Christ. He was not concerned with how this final transformation would be effected. Nowhere does he portray the final end of this world in the traditional eschatological tones of the Jewish teachers, as does, for example, St. Peter:

Then the heavens will pass away in a roaring flame and its elements will burn up and be dissolved. . . . Since all these elements are to be dissolved in this way, what holy and pious lives you ought to lead, as you await and hasten the coming of God's day. By that coming the heavens will be set afire and dissolved, and the elements will be burned up and melted. Yet, in keeping with his promise we look for new heavens and a new earth, in which holiness dwells (II Pet. 3:10–13; *cf.* I Cor. 3:13–15).

Paul's universe is to be a creation renovated through the agency of Jesus Christ. This "new creation" will be the dwelling of the saints in God's kingdom. Isaias had centuries earlier prophesied the state of harmony that would exist between man and the non-human cosmos when they would be at peace with each other. Man would be master of the created world as God had intended him to be:

Then the wolf shall be a guest of the lamb, and the leopard shall lie down with the kid (Is. 11:6).

The baby shall play by the cobra's den, and the child lay his hand on the adder's lair (Is. 11:8).

There shall be no harm or ruin on all my holy mountain; for the earth shall be filled with knowledge of the Lord, as water covers the sea (Is. 11:19).

Ezechiel also hinted at the reconciliation of animal life with men.

I will make a covenant of peace with them, and rid the country of ravenous beasts, that they may dwell securely in the desert and sleep in the forests (Ezech. 34:25).

For Paul, man's redemption and glorification were intimately tied up with that of the world as a total unit. As man's fall had cosmic repercussions, so too his glorification into the "new man" would touch the cosmos. It, too, would somehow share in the "new creation." "All creation," St. Paul says in Romans 8:19–22, "awaits with eager longing the manifestation of the sons of God" and hopes that it (creation itself) "would be delivered from its slavery to corruption to enjoy the freedom that comes with the glory of the children of God . . . all creation groans and travails in pain until now." Thus, included in "all creation" would be the non-human cosmos that would also participate in man's glorification.

The Semitic mind—and Paul follows the same thinking—conceived man and the material world in which he lived as a unit, a community of interrelated beings on march in a linear process to their completion. The whole of creation, therefore, moved together in the attainment of fulfillment or destruction (in Paul, "corruption"—*phthora;* e.g., Rom. 1:23). In the final attainment of the end toward which all creation was moving there would be two distinct parts of Christ's victory that are even now *in via,* but only in the parousia will be complete: all creation that is now subject to "vanity," whose rule is corruption, will be liberated and transformed into harmonious submission of service according to the mind of God, contributing to the full glory of God that comes only from all created beings operating fully as God had intended. This will be the cosmic act of deliverance from corruption. It is intimately bound up with the first part of Christ's victory in the parousia, that is, the deification of human beings into sons of God "by participation" (II Pet. 1:4).

We have seen how Paul gradually formulated a doctrine of redemption through Christ's own death on the cross and his glorious resurrection that embraced all of cosmic creation. The cosmic dimensions of his christology unfolded slowly;

only under the pressure of combat with Gnostic and Stoic heresies in the Asiatic communities did he order his ideas into a more systematic teaching. Although he lacked the knowledge of the physical interdependence of all created material beings that modern science clearly demonstrates, divine revelation gave him, through a deep penetration into the mystery of the cross and resurrection of Jesus Christ, an understanding of the total redemption of the universe which would be completed in the parousia. Paul has shown not only that the universe is an instrumental means of man's redemption, but also that every created being itself is an object of Christ's redemption. This physical universe is in travail to be born to a new life. It is our Christian hope that God does not create for death, annihilation, or frustration, but rather to perfect his creatures unto the fullness of their participated being. Thus, our hope assures us that not only our God-created soul but also our God-created body will be touched by the glorious resurrected life of the Savior and be brought to the fulfillment God had planned in his original creation of man. But if our material body will be transformed and not destroyed, Paul tells us that so also will be the total cosmos. It likewise was created by God for a purpose intimately connected with the end God had in creating man, namely, that the whole created order be brought into the glorification of the full Body of Christ. Thus Christ, as Head of the created cosmos, can bring it back, complete and full, to its Maker and Final End. In First Corinthians 15:28, Paul summarizes concisely the relation of all things to Christ and of Christ to God:

Once everything has been brought into subjection to him, then the Son himself, in order that God may be everything to everyone, will be brought into subjection to the Father who subjected everything to him, in order that God may be everything to everyone and everything.

The glory of the risen body of Christ, or the completion of his created humanity through the full manifestation of divine life within it, was accomplished only when Christ left this world with his material modality of existence. He communicates this glory to men by bringing them into his own full divine life, thus reestablishing them in the fullness of God's plan of salvation for each individual. He imparts this glory to the non-human cosmos through the glorification of man, the total man, body and soul. Through his body, man makes contact with the cosmos. Through his activities and works, he makes the resurrectional glory of Christ shine upon all material creation "in order that God may be everything to everyone and everything" (I Cor. 15:28).

This section on St. Paul's cosmic christology can best be closed by quoting from Karl Rahner, who beautifully summarizes what we have discussed here at somewhat greater length, namely, how the world is not blindly hurtling itself into aimless expansion, a mass of heterogeneity, but is being moved by Christ to Christ that God may be "all in all":

Here we must remember that the world is a unity in which everything is linked together with everything else. When anyone grasps a portion of the world as a whole for his own life's history, at one and the same time he takes upon himself the world as a whole for his personal environment. Thus it would not be extravagant, as long as it was done with prudence, to conceive the evolution of the world as an orientation toward Christ, and to represent the various stages of this ascending movement as culminating in Him as their apex. The only danger to be avoided is the suggestion that such evolution is an ascent which the world accomplishes by forces which are wholly its own. If what St. Paul says in Colossians 1:15 is true and not softened by some moralistic interpretation, if furthermore the world as a whole, including therefore its physical reality, is actually in process of reaching in and through Christ that final state in which God is all in all, then the line of thought we are developing here cannot be entirely false.[7]

II

ST. PAUL'S MYSTICAL THEOLOGY

Mystical Union in Christ

One of St. Paul's most original theological contributions to the early Church was his doctrine of the dynamic growth of the individual soul, the Church, and the cosmos "in Christ." On these three planes he viewed Christ's incarnation as being prolonged in space and time and eventually touching all creatures; yet he never separated these three areas from one another. An individual who is growing in Christ is helping to build up the full Body of Christ, the Church, which, as leaven, is moving the universe closer to its completion of "all things in Christ Jesus." Having seen Christ's influence on the largest area of the three, the cosmic plane, we turn now to an examination of Paul's christology on a microcosmic level and see how, pondering a *christified* human being, he evolves a cosmic christology.

In Christ

Paul had received the central doctrine of Christianity concerning man's incorporation into Christ's own life, hence into his very being, from Christ himself. As the Apostle to the Gentiles, he boldly developed this key teaching that made Christianity essentially different from paganism. Through the cross Christ destroyed eschatological death and sin. By his own resurrectional life he brought to us this "new life." "The death that he died was a death to sin once for all, but the life that he lives is a life for God. Thus you too must consider yourself dead to sin, but alive to God in Christ Jesus" (Rom. 6:10–11). But for man to become "alive to God in Christ Jesus," he must be united with Christ; he must be *in Christ.*

The phrase *in Christ* is used 164 times by Paul; usually he means a very real, intimate union with Christ. We will see later how this union relates to the Church. Here we note its usual significance—the intimate, dynamic union between Christ and the baptized Christian.

The human being through baptism is made into a "new creation." "But in virtue of his mercy, he saved us through the bath in which the Holy Spirit regenerates and renews us" (Tit. 3:5). Baptism puts us into direct contact with the resurrected, glorified Christ who now, by his spiritualized Body-Person, can come and truly dwell within us. Christ becomes man's reconciliation with God (Rom. 5:10–11). He effects in us the discarding of the "old man" in order that we might live according to the "new." The "new man" is precisely this given individual, baptized in Christ, now living according to the new inner principle of life which Christ is. It is truly "Christ who lives in him" (Gal. 2:20). The baptized man becomes an adopted child of God (Gal. 4:5; 3:26) and is aware that he lives in a relationship similar to that which exists between God the Father and his only-begotten Son, Jesus Christ, because the same life of the Son is dwelling within him. Before man's change of heart and conversion to Christ, he was a child of wrath (*teknon*) by nature (Eph. 2:3). In baptism he becomes like Christ, a true son (*huios*) (Rom. 8:14, 19; 9:26; II Cor. 6:18; Gal. 3:26; 4:7) through divine adoption (*huiothesia*), by which he becomes an heir in Christ, of the Father (Rom. 8:15; Gal. 4:5; Eph. 1:5).

Transformation into the Image of Christ

The relationship to Christ brought about by baptism is more than a mere extrinsic, ethical model to be imitated by man. The Christian is in the most vital union with Christ who lives within him as the principle of his thoughts and operations. St. Augustine captured the meaning of Paul in the daring affirmation which Pope Paul VI (*Ecclesiam Suam*) applied to modern Christians:

> Let us rejoice and give thanks that we have become not only Christians but Christ. My brothers, do you understand the grace of God our Head? Stand in admiration, rejoice; we have become Christ.[1]

The Christian shares in Christ's own life, that life of the historical person, Jesus Christ, now gloriously resurrected. He is personally incorporated into Christ, without losing his own identity. Christ lives in the Christian, but he must always be further formed in him (Gal. 4:19). By yielding to the life-giving influence of Christ, the Christian is gradually transformed into the image of Christ. The first creation of man according to the image of God (Gen. 1: 26–28), as understood by Paul, is a mere shadow, a symbol, of the true likeness to which God has predestined him in the order of salvation. The only destiny God ever had conceived for man is his transformation into the image of the only-begotten Son, Jesus Christ. "For those whom he has foreknown he has also predestined to be conformed to the image of his Son, so that this Son should be the first-born among many brothers" (Rom. 8:29).

Paul declares that man, made to the image of God, was by the Fall made to the image of the first man and thus became capable of sin (I Cor. 15:46–49). But Christ is the "heavenly man," the true image of God, according to whom we must be transformed. There is no inconsistency in Paul's doctrine. He merely wishes to show that the "new man," Christ living in the Christian, is not of the created order, but is assumed into the divine life.

Therefore, for St. Paul, Christ is the image of God, both in his preexistence, and in creation. Created in his image, man can become fully a son of God. And, finally, Christ is the image of God, in his glorious resurrectional life which he is able to transmit to man in the order of salvation (Col. 1:15 ff.; II Cor. 3:18; 4:4). If we are to reach the fulfillment for which we have been created, we must be transformed into the new creation (*kaine ktisis*). "If then any man is in Christ, he is a new creature . . ." (II Cor. 5:17). This becomes a new life, a new way of existing, for Christians who are ontologically in a world apart from human beings in whom Christ does not dwell.

Paul's Mystical Realism

Today when we use the word *mystical* we usually imply extraordinary charismatic gifts and special religious experiences.

These experiences imply a large measure of subjectivity and by their nature are exceptional. Yet for Paul, the doctrine of the incorporation of the Christian in Christ and transfiguration into him through his grace and our cooperation, were nothing esoteric, no delicacy reserved for a few. For Paul, every Christian turning away from his sinful past in a true *metanoia* (conversion of one's whole being to God), enters into a permanent union of life in and with Christ. One is a Christian only as long as he lives in this union with Christ. He may or may not experience feelings and awareness of this union with Christ, but these are not essential to the reality. The reality was attained by faith as the Savior himself said before his ascension: "He that believes and is baptized, will be saved" (Mk. 16:16).

Neither the mere example of Christ, derived from the Gospels, nor his ideas operate on us in some vague, impersonal way. The very historical person of Jesus Christ who indwells in the baptized Christian as a spiritual, yet personal, power, this is the Christian dynamic. To be baptized in Christ is to be possessed by his person. Paul was "apprehended" by Christ (Phil. 3:12) so that the principle of his thought, words and deeds was no longer Paul, the natural man subjected to the laws of the flesh, but Christ "who lives in me" (Gal. 2:20). It is the Christ who died on the cross and rose from the dead, the Christ of history, who lives in him.

Paul seized on the reality of this relationship to Christ and never tired of seeking different metaphors to bring out its vivid truth. He speaks of the life of Christ within the Christian as a new life that must be put on, not by some few, but by all Christians.

You are, in fact, all children of God through faith in Jesus Christ, since all of you who have come to Christ by baptism have clothed yourselves with Christ. No longer is there Jew or Greek; no longer is there slave or freeman; no longer is there male or female. You are all one in Christ Jesus (Gal. 3:27–28).

To "put on Christ" is to become surrounded by him. This relationship to Christ is not merely moral: it is ontological. We have his being within us.

Growth in Christ

But Christ's presence within us must grow as an embryo grows in the womb. Paul wanted to spend himself in order that his Galatians might grow up into Christ.

My dear children, I am again suffering the pangs of childbirth for you, until Christ is formed within you (Gal. 4:19).

Christ's life admits of growth, dependent on our cooperation. From the embryonic life given to us in baptism we are to progress unto "perfect manhood, to the mature measure of the fullness of Christ" (Eph. 4:13). Again, Paul shows this growth as a progress in unity of faith and deeper knowledge of the Son of God whereby we come to know "what is the breadth and length and height and depth and to know Christ's love which surpasses knowing, in order that . . . [we] may be perfected and bring to realization God's fullness" (Eph. 3:18–19).

The effect of this ontological union with Christ is the activation in the individual's life of a piety and conduct of life like Christ's. The Christian, raised to a new life by possessing a new principle of activity, Christ himself, must not merely possess this life, but must "walk in the newness of life" (Rom. 6:4).

Many commentators have pointed out in Paul's writings the verbal paradox he employs in speaking about the progress to be made in the moral virtues. In many texts Paul speaks of the ideal effects of baptism, the Eucharist, the other sacraments, and man's own virtuous asceticism as though these effects were already attained in their perfection. In other texts, of more explicit moral exhortation, he speaks of these effects as imperfectly possessed and admitting of a greater degree of attainment.

One example will suffice to demonstrate the frequently repeated paradox. Paul speaks of the "old man" as crucified, put to death, the body of sin destroyed in him (Rom. 6:6; II Cor. 5:14, 17b), each as accomplished fact. In other texts of a hortatory nature, he enjoins his readers to put off the "old man" and his evil deeds as though, by baptism (he had asserted the contrary in the above texts), the old man and his deeds were not really put off (Col. 3:9; Eph. 4:22; Rom. 6:13). How explain this difference?

The explanation lies in Paul's concept of growth in Christ, through virtue, unto full righteousness or salvation. In the process of growing into Christ we are in a sense what we are growing to be. We can speak of our having already attained the goal because we shall attain it. Our nature is perfected because we have already put off sin in our lives, and yet our nature is in the process of being perfected because we must continue to do so. Some day we will surely arrive at being "sons of God and heirs of Heaven." Intrinsic to this process of putting on Christ is that we already possess, as a seed possesses the future tree, the final goal. Thus Paul, depending on his view of the process, which is defined by its goal, can say that we have been saved (Eph. 2:5, 8), while, looking at the dynamic *in via,* he can say that we are "in the process of being saved" (I Cor. 1:18; II Cor. 2:15).

Hence, the Christian life in Christ is precisely a continuous process of despoiling oneself of all self-love, of casting off the "outward man" in order to renew constantly the "inward man" (2 Cor. 4:16) so as to grow into the fullness of Christ. The differences in the degrees of virtues will be more evident when we view the community growth in Christ wherein exist simultaneously individuals of varying degrees of Christian perfection.

The Spirit: Principle of Life

Paul uses the phrase "in the Spirit" nineteen times and often the sense is "in Christ." But more specifically, we find Paul using the more specialized term of Spirit to apply to the divine Power, the Holy Spirit, sent by God through the merits of Christ and his intercession to effect the work of sanctification or christification of man. In Romans 15:18–19 he clearly distinguishes between the work of Christ and that of the Holy Spirit:

> I do not make bold to mention anything but what Christ has wrought through me to bring about the conversion of the Gentiles, by word and deed, with mighty signs and wonders, by the power of the Holy Spirit. . . . I have fully preached the gospel of Christ (Rom. 15:18–19).

To the Holy Spirit, Paul assigns the character, initiative, and salvific action proper to a person. Paul had discovered through a personal experience "in the Spirit," the world of the Spirit. It was a "new sphere of life" (Rom. 6:4) and the function of the Spirit was to create this new life. He explained that we had become alive by the Spirit so we must walk by the Spirit (Gal. 5:16, 26). Christians were *pneumatikoi,* spiritualized by the Spirit, because the primary function of the Spirit was recognized in the creation of this life in Christ. The possession of the Spirit was not the totality or the fullness of Christian perfection, but the Spirit was given as the "first-fruits" (Rom. 8:23) and the pledge or guarantee of its completion (II Cor. 1:22; Eph. 1:14). Here we see how the phrases "in the Spirit" and "in Christ" complement one another. The Spirit is given in embryonic form in baptism to bring about the fullness of Christ's life in men by conforming them gradually through progressive growth to a greater likeness to the image of Christ. "You are not in the flesh, but in the Spirit" (Rom. 8:9).

Christians are caught between two dynamic forces: the power of evil and the Spirit of Christ. They must live according to the Spirit, the new principle of Christlike operation within them. The Spirit that has created this new life in Christ fosters it and brings it to its fullness in the proportion that the same Spirit becomes the normative influence guiding men in the moral choices that determine their true growth in Christ. Ideally, the life of a Christian is to be a turning within, to be guided by the Spirit. No longer is there an extrinsic code of morality, a Judaic Law. The Spirit works individually with each given human personality. "But if you are led by the Spirit, you are not under the Law" (Gal. 5:18). Human personality takes on a maximum importance for Paul because the Holy Spirit is a respecter of persons, of God-given creatures, influenced by the several different factors of environment, heredity, self-improvement, and sins. In each individual he works to effect salvation and to accomplish the glory of God through the fulfillment of each.

Christian Moral Conduct

Man, as depicted by St. Paul, has been set free by Christ (Gal. 5:1). No longer bound by the slavery of sin nor by the extrinsecism of the Judaic Law, the Christian felt the freedom of serving not as a slave but as a son of God, according to the inner principle of the Holy Spirit. But the Spirit is not merely given once, but is being continuously bestowed by God and is constantly revitalizing and energizing the new inner man. As man corresponds to the Spirit, his inner life in Christ grows. This growth is in knowledge and holiness. One grows in the knowledge of "those things which God has prepared for them that love Him" (I Cor. 2:9): knowledge of the mystery of salvation; knowledge of the will of God which must become, in the concrete, man's guide for moral conduct.

Man is to respond constantly to the living Word within him: the Holy Spirit reveals to man God's will through the community or the Church; and, finally, in the participation of the Holy Eucharist, the perfect symbol and sign effecting what it symbolizes, the union of the one Spirit of Christ in the many members is achieved, and all seeking the unity of knowledge and holiness are formed into a unified community. These are three basic sources which man uses to form a norm for right conduct: response to the living Word within man, response to the Holy Spirit in the Church, and response to the union with others in the Eucharist.

Paul did not wish to construct a system of Christian morality. He was preeminently practical, seeking to give advice to meet pastoral exigencies. Thus, we find no theoretical presentation, in any abstract form, of ethics or a system of the virtues. What replaced any code or law of conduct was the "governing principle of the Spirit of life in Christ Jesus" (Rom. 8:2). And the "spirit yields a harvest of love, charity, joy, peace, patience, kindness, generosity and forbearance . . ." (Gal. 5:22–23, Knox Version). Charity or *agape* is the touchstone to the law of the Spirit. It was divine charity that moved God to send us his Son. That charity could be powerful enough in man to uproot inordinate self-love, which did not liberate man to act fully according to his God-given nature but destroyed him in his defiance of God's dominion over him.

Paul's emphasis was on the individual person's freedom to love God by loving his neighbor for love of God. Thus, he felt little need to detail the concrete acts of obligation proper to every Christian. Rather, he gave some important applications stemming from the ontological reality that the Christian man had become: the new creature in Christ. "If you are risen with Christ, seek the things that are above . . . Mind the things that are above, not the things that are on earth. For you have died and your life is hidden with Christ in God" (Col. 3:1–3).

In keeping with this inner dignity, Paul appeals to the principle of consistency. One in whom Christ lives must be consistent with his higher self and put away, or rather put to death, the actions of an earthly being. Paul exhorts the Colossians to give up immorality, uncleanness, lust, evil desires, and covetousness, not by appealing to an extrinsic law or an eternal sanction but by recalling to them that they are to put off the "old man with his deeds" in order to "put on the new one that is being renewed unto perfect knowledge 'according to the image of his Creator!' . . . Christ is everything in each of us" (Col. 3:9–11). He exhorts the Corinthians in a similar vein to put away all immorality and sins of the flesh: "Do you not know that your members are the temple of the Holy Spirit, who is in you, whom you have from God and that you are not your own? For you have been bought at a great price. Glorify God and bear Him in your body" (I Cor. 6:19–20).

Another principle that flows from the awareness of the inner Spirit as the force that sets men free to perfect themselves and the community in which they live is that which tells Christians to seek to do always the actions that please God, "so as to live worthily of the Lord unto all pleasing" (Col. 1:10). It is really God within us who produces through his Spirit "both the willing and the acting according to what pleases Him" (Phil. 2:13). In Second Corinthians 5:9 Paul says that the aim of all Christian living is to "strive . . . to be pleasing to Him." Yet he was not an unrealist, unaware of how easily many could be swayed by passions; even those with upright motives, seeking to please only God, sometimes end in sinful actions. Paul appeals to the teachings of the Master to correct any erroneous subjectivism (I Cor. 7:10; 10:14). According to his example (Rom. 15:7; Eph. 5:2; Col. 3:13), one is to "put on Christ" so completely that he thinks, acts, and, above all, loves as Christ does.

It would take us too far afield to show how Paul descends to particulars in applying this "inner law of charity" whereby the Holy Spirit teaches us to act always in Christ. The majority of applications of his moral principles concern the implications of a christified human being's relation to his social environment. Man's relations to civil government, to society in general, to fellow Christians, and to members within the family unit are the chief areas of Paul's social concern. But even in giving his practical counsel, Paul wants to keep before his Christians the basic principle of Christianity—that morality is to be based on an inner law of liberty and love. The individual, purified of any "carnal attractions" by putting to death the "old man," is thus free to hear the Holy Spirit. Each one's conscience, rightly informed by the Holy Spirit and guided by faith and true love for God and neighbor, was to be the faculty for discerning God's holy will (I Tim. 1:19; II Tim. 1:3; I Cor. 6:12, 8:7, 8:10).

Individual circumstances would change each situation, and hence no extrinsic law of conduct, such as the Jewish Talmudists worked out for every conceivable "case" that a practicing Jew could expect to encounter in his life, could ever be the ultimate criterion of the morality of a given act. The Holy Spirit, sent to us by the presence of Christ within us through grace, is not only to teach us what is right according to God's mind, but to give us the power to accomplish it. ". . . Let the spirit be our rule of life" (Gal. 5:25). ". . . learn to live and move in the spirit; then there is no danger of your giving way to the impulses of corrupt nature" (Gal. 5:16, Knox Version).

This morality of the Spirit guiding and empowering the individual to act always "in Christ" is not a special charism given to a few advanced Christians. Paul insists that "all of you" are in Christ through baptism. That all did not correspond, Paul was keenly aware. There were those who "grieved the Holy Spirit" (Eph. 4:30). Paul, however, was concerned not with a theology of bad Christians but with a theology of good and perfect Christians, with the normal evolution of the powers Christians receive in baptism which are to be climaxed in a full sonship of God and brotherhood with Christ in heaven.

A Christology of Individual Sanctification

Before we develop Paul's ecclesial christology, it would be well to summarize the chief points of his sublime doctrine of the individual soul's relation to Christ. Paul had been deeply impressed by the realization that the historical Christ who had been crucified on Calvary was raised from the dead by his heavenly Father and still lives in this world of ours, especially within individual Christians, through the new mode of existence that he acquired through his triumphal resurrection. This relationship of Christ to the individual Christian, begun in baptism, was one of organic union between two persons. Though we could live our so-called "natural" life, our physical, "carnal" life, without this union in Christ, nevertheless, for Paul, we are dead limbs as long as we live without union with Christ who is the only true life. Physical life was given us by God in creation and sustained in existence only that we might be "implanted in him" (Rom. 6:5). Paul meant it literally when he wrote that we are one being in him. "You are all one in Christ Jesus" (Gal. 3:28). "God brought you to life with Jesus" (Col. 2:13). We are "alive to God in Christ Jesus" (Rom. 6:11).

Thus, the life of a Christian was a *symbiosis,* a life with Jesus; all actions were not only to be done with him as the model but, through his Spirit, we would be guided in this imitation of Christ and empowered to accomplish God's holy will. The depths of the riches of the knowledge and wisdom of God were unfolded to man and accomplished in his being. God, out of his infinite goodness and his superabundance of life, created men, capable of responding through proper use of intellect and will to his initial and continued act of love for them. We are called to share in the life of God's divine image, Jesus Christ. We are to grow into his likeness so that even now (but more perfectly in the life to come), we are "participators" in God's divine nature (II Pet. 1:4). Jesus Christ is the center of our creation; we have our true being in being possessed by him, so that we share in his divine sonship.

In the Epistle to the Hebrews, we see summarized clearly the centrality of Jesus Christ: "Through him, too, [God] made the world. This Son is the radiant reflection of God's glory, and the express image of his nature, conserving all things by his mighty command" (Heb. 1:2–3).

With the life of Christ immanently present in our whole being, we are being transformed by his Holy Spirit into a greater likeness of him, our divine model.

> But all of us, reflecting in a mirror the Lord's glory, are being transformed into his very image from one degree of splendor to another, such as comes from the Lord who is the Spirit (II Cor. 3:18).

But this transformation into Christ takes place only through a constant, reflective act of faith and love. The Logos, the Speech of God, speaks and, through his Holy Spirit, we listen and recognize his voice. "I know mine and mine know me" (Jn. 10:14). The Holy Spirit enables us to act with Christ and gradually to become, to coin a word, "logosized," to become an image of Christ, the Logos of the Father. Each day, therefore, the Christian seeks to purify himself of everything un-Christlike. He must be renewed, interiorly, by a more intense *metanoia,* a change of heart, a conversion, a turning to God through Christ. Only a mature adult—Christian age is measured by the degree of correspondence to Christ's immanent activity—can reconcile the heady liberty from all extrinsic laws with the stringent demands of divine charity. For such an adult in Christ, personal initiative reaches its maximum in seeking to do good to others out of love of Christ. Because the interior law of charity (Gal. 5:14) draws and attracts the Christian to action, abuse of one's liberty is to be checked by the urgings of the Spirit in doing good to others. Paul himself gives us the perfect example:

> Independent though I am of all men, I make myself everybody's slave to win the more converts. . . . I become like a weak man for the weak to win over the weak. I become all things to all men, by all means to win over some of them. Whatever I do, I do for the sake of the gospel that I may have a share in its blessings (I Cor. 9:19–23).

Thus, from a christology of individual sanctification we are led easily to the consideration of our relationship to others in Christ—that of "building up of the Body of Christ." And, Paul asserts, this Body *is* the Church.

An Ecclesial Christology

Absorbed with this new life in Christ, Paul moved easily between the levels where he found this new life in process of dynamic, progressive growth, namely, the level of the individual, and that of the Christian community. He gives small attention to distinguishing *whose* perfection is being built up, the individual Christian's or that of the total Christian community, the Church. The reason is that he saw these levels, not as distinct areas of activity and life, but as two points of view of the identical reality, the life of the physical Christ, living in both the individual and in the united members of his Body, the Church. Further, he knew that no individual sanctity grew outside of the organism that he fondly called the Body of Christ. The Church grew in sanctity as the life of Christ developed in the individual being.

To understand more clearly this Pauline ecclesiology, let

us look at his conception of Christ's Church as the Body of Christ.

"*You Are Christ's Body*"

Paul uses the Greek word *ekklesia* about sixty times, and with a variety of meanings. A progression in the evolution of his ecclesial thought is clear from his letters. Most frequently, at least in his earlier letters, he uses this word to refer to a local church or a concrete assembly of Christian believers, for example, ". . . when you meet in the church [gathering]" (I Cor. 11:18). "The churches [congregations] of Asia greet you" (I Cor. 16:19). Again, he refers to the universal Church, transcending any local congregational boundaries: ". . . God has established in his Church some in the first rank, namely, apostles" (I Cor. 12:28); ". . . how beyond all measure I persecuted the Church of God and ravaged it" (Gal. 1:13).

The Church, whether local or universal, was conceived as a community (*koinonia*) of believers linked together by the bonds of faith, by the sacraments, especially baptism, which incorporated the members into the community, and especially by the Eucharist, which not only symbolized the union of the members with the physical Body-Christ but greatly deepened it. Not less, this community was bound by its obedience to the bishops and presbyters empowered by Christ to teach his word with his authority.

In stressing the living Christ as the source of the common, supernatural life within the believing Christian, Paul moved only gradually to a greater emphasis on the Church as identified in some manner with the physical, resurrected Body-Person, Jesus Christ. In his major epistles the concept of the Church as the Body of Christ was not fully developed.

For just as in one body we have many organs, yet not all the organs have the same function, so we, the aggregate, are one body in Christ, but individually to one another we stand in the relation of part to part (Rom. 12:4–5).

. . . just as the body is a unit, although it has many members . . . so too is the Christ. In fact, by a single Spirit all of us . . . were introduced into the one body through baptism and were all given to drink of a single Spirit. . . . You are Christ's body and individually its members (I Cor. 12:12–27; *cf.* I Cor. 6:12–20, I Cor. 10:17).

But in the letters to the Colossians and Ephesians, Paul clearly states that the Church is identified with the Body and Christ is the Head. In these two letters the doctrine of the Christian people as the Body of Christ now occupies a clear and central position. ". . . Christ is the head of the Church and also the savior of that body" (Eph. 5:23). He loves this Body, the Church, nourishing it and cherishing it. ". . . because we are members of his body" (Eph. 5:30), Christ is

. . . the head from whom the whole body is supplied with nourishment and strength by the joints and ligaments, thus growing with a growth that is divine (Col. 2:19).

The whole body is dependent on him. Harmoniously joined and knit together, it derives its energy in the measure each part needs only through contact with the source of supply. In this way the body grows and builds itself up through love (Eph. 4:16; *cf.* Col. 1:18, 24; Eph. 1:22, 23; 4:15; 5:23).

Modern scholars, such as Pierre Benoit, John A. T. Robinson, Lucien Cerfaux, Joseph Huby, and Alfred Wikenhauser have insisted strongly on the realism intended by St. Paul in the use of the term "Body of Christ" as applied to the Church. The Church is not merely a moral aggregate of members coming together to honor the historical person, Jesus Christ. The Church is intimately related to the resurrected Body-Person, Jesus Christ (Eph. 1:20–23).

We are dealing with something more than a mere metaphor. The term Body (*soma*) of Christ, as used in the New Testament and especially by Paul, can refer (1) to the historical body of Christ that the apostles knew so intimately during the public years of his life; (2) to the resurrected and glorious body of Christ, ascended into heaven; (3) to his body in the Holy Eucharist; (4) and, finally, to his Church. There is absolute identity between his earthly historical body and his glorified body that lives today, spiritualized and transcending all space and time. The Body of Christ that the Church is, is not ontologically identical with the historical, now glorified body of Christ. Yet in a very real sense there is a partial identity insofar as the life that infuses the Christians is identical with the divine life of the physical Christ. Although the Christians in baptism, and more so in the Eucharist, come into contact with the same divine life, they retain their own individual, human personalities and life.

Benoit describes this union "under the form of a physical [sacramental] union of the body of the Christian with the individual body of Christ."[2] It is the spiritual (pneumatic) body of the living, risen Christ (I Cor. 15:44) that is the carrier of the regenerated life of salvation to our souls. "Without a doubt," Benoit continues, "this 'physical' reality is of a very special type, completely new which is that of the eschatological era begun—while the old era still continues."[3]

Robinson comments that the term Mystical Body as understood by Western minds today has the connotation of an ethereal union; this connotation lessens the understanding of the physical reality of this union between Christ and the community of believing Christians in the Church. Surely one regrets the false concepts that the word "mystical" conjures for us, and we could perhaps desire an expression more apt for modern times to describe the very concrete, physical reality of this unique union with Christ's life. Yet the expression "Mystical Body" has a legitimate theological development that through the centuries has steered a clear course in describing this unique union so as to avoid a purely physical union on the one hand and a purely moral aggregate on the other. Further, it has received the sanction of papal teaching in the encyclical *Mystici Corporis* which contains all the elements that modern exegetes of St. Paul have been trying to elucidate.

Christ, living his glorified, resurrectional life is, through his physical body, still the causal means of contact and union with the members of his Church. He gives to them his risen life so that they, with him, forming the Church, are truly forming the Mystical Body of Christ. In order to see the points of identity and the points of difference we must see how the Body-Church can grow with Christ as its Head.

Christ, the Head of the Body-Church

In First Corinthians 12:12–27, cited above, the head is included as a member of the whole body with no conscious reference on Paul's part to Christ. Yet the idea of the head viewed as the director of the whole body is implied by Paul. In the captivity letters, Paul gradually reaches the final development of his teaching by designating Christ as Head of the Body-Church. In Colossians 2:10 Christ is pictured as

Head of all the Principalities and Powers, in the sense of superior, or sovereign, having complete authority over them and all other created orders of beings. But in Ephesians, especially, Paul develops this theme.

He has subjected every single thing to his authority and has appointed him sovereign head of the Church, which is truly his body, the complement of him who fills all the members with all graces (Eph. 1:22–23).

Christ is the Head of the Church, as having supreme authority of command. Yet Paul's is a deeper insight: the head of a body is conceived also as the principle of life, the mover, the nourisher and sustainer of life. Plato conceived the head as seat of the *nous,* reason, while the Greek medical physicans, like Hippocrates and Galen, held that the head contained the nervous center that directed all the other members. "In union with him who is the head of every Principality and Power you have been made complete" (Col. 2:10). "The whole body is dependent on him . . . it derives its energy in the measure each part needs, only through contact with the source of supply" (Eph. 4:16). This intuition of Christ as head, as the source of life and activity, is here only hinted at. We shall now see it stated explicitly.

Building Up the Body of Christ

Paul's clearest statement that Christ is Head of the Body-Church, and of how it grows, is found in Ephesians 4:10–16. Christ is pictured as filling the entire universe from the highest to the lowest reaches of the heavens and earth that "He might fully impart all graces" (Eph. 4:10). We have seen that

Christ "is filling [pleroumenou] all the members with all graces" (Eph. 1:23). The present participle here denotes that Christ's work of filling all the members with all graces is going on now. And Christ, the Head and source of this life, accomplishes this filling up both in his Body-Church and through it. This is why Paul immediately passes to a brief description of the hierarchical divisions in the Body-Church.

He established some men as apostles, and some as inspired spokesmen, others again as evangelists, and others as pastors and teachers, thus organizing the saints for the work of the ministry, which consists in building up the body of Christ, until we all attain to unity in faith and deep knowledge of the Son of God (Eph. 4:11–13).

For this reason Christ elects certain persons in the Church to dispense his gifts. Paul's enumeration of offices is not exhaustive, but he lists apostles, prophets, evangelists, pastors, and teachers because these are the instruments most frequently used for the building up of the Church through the gift of the three graces that he mentions in Verses 13 and 14: faith, knowledge of Christ, and solid doctrine. The image Paul uses to explain the purpose of Christ's filling up his Church with these gifts deserves our attention.

Paul says that Christ gives his gifts "to organize the saints for the work of the ministry which consists in building up the body of Christ" (vv. 12–13). The Greek word *katartismos,* which means the act of organizing and perfecting, is rich with nuances. The verb *katartizo* means to restore to a complete or correct condition. It implies, also, bringing a being to a completion which it has never attained before, but one that is in keeping with its given nature and its potentialities.

Thus, we could paraphrase this Pauline thought: the purpose of Christ's filling all the universe with his gifts is to perfect the saints (the Christians in whom Christ lives) in order that they may be able to accomplish the great work of service to be rendered in the Church, so that by their works they may build up the total Body of Christ. The hierarchical officials, appointed by Christ, are to organize all Christians for service in the Church. Every Christian has some gift to develop and contribute to the building up of the Church. The Church officials have the task of establishing the best conditions of Church life so that each Christian may be stimulated to live fully according to those gifts which are his.

Paul emphasizes the importance of the activity of each individual member in building up the Body-Church by his responsible cooperation with God's gifts. He does not employ a concept of natural growth, that is, growth that would result without much reflective cooperation on the part of the growing body. Here and now Christians are building up the Church (*oikodome,* the word St. Paul uses, means to build a house) by their conscious activities, in cooperation with its Head from whom flow the gifts of grace. This building up of the Body-Church has as its goal the achievement of "unity in faith and deep knowledge of the Son of God. Thus we attain to perfect manhood, to the mature proportions that befit Christ's fullness" (Eph. 4:13).

Therefore each Christian's activity is a vital part of a whole process that is progressing toward a goal which will assuredly one day be reached. The Body-Church has, in embryonic form from its very beginning, the fullness that God destined for it. But only through the individual efforts of each member inserted as vibrant parts of a living whole can this fullness be attained. Christians are immature if they do not let the full life of Christ "apprehend" them, are "children" (Eph. 4:14; I Cor. 1:3). Although living among people "tossing to and fro and carried about by every wind of doctrine" (Eph. 4:14), Christians will mature by acquiring a deeper faith and knowledge of Christ. The sign of their maturity will be measured by their degree of unity in the "new man" (Eph. 2:5, 4:24), Jesus Christ. They put aside the selfish egoism of children to grow into the fullness of the perfect man, Christ. Pope Pius XII phrased it thus in his encyclical *Mystici Corporis:* "The Mystical Head which is Christ and the Church . . . constitute one new man. We call Christ the Head—and the Body, the total Christ."

Now the emphasis is not on one's own individual perfection; one obtains his fullness in building up the corporate maturity, the extent of which is measured always according to the degree of conscious corporate unity with Christ, its Head.

This building up into the "perfect man," Christ, is a process leading to a greater consciousness of faith and infused knowledge about Christ, and it stabilizes the whole community against wicked men who spread doctrinal errors. The means of growing into greater unity and stability in Christ are expressed in Paul's phrase "by living the truth in love" (Eph. 4:15). We can paraphrase this as "living an authentic Christian life in an environment of love" (C. Spicq). Faith, as Paul says in Second Thessalonians 2:12, accepts the truth, but the truth is lived in love. Love makes the truth manifest. We live by the truth only when we are impelled to do so by love for God. "The truth shall make you free" (Jn. 8:32). This statement perhaps prompted St. Augustine's words, "Love and do what you wish."

The whole Christian life must therefore be guided by this

single aim—to live the truth in love, that is, to do at every moment God's will as read in a conscience informed by grace, guiding the total person to act only and always out of love for God. Paul passes easily to the thought that such acting out of love for God brings about the union of the members of the Body with their Head who is Christ (Eph. 4:15). But such a union cannot be achieved, nor can we act out of love for God, except through Christ, the source of all true growth.

All growth is from Christ, through and with him: yet he gives growth only where there is a conscious effort on the individual's part to make "contact with the source of supply." Paul's image, expressed by the words "harmoniously joined and knit together," is drawn from the science of architecture. The side of one stone was worked so as to fit into the corresponding side of another stone. This meant painstaking and exacting work to hew the rough edges, climaxed by the drilling of the unifying holes and the pouring of molten lead to bind the two stones together.

Through the exercise of charity toward others, the individual members would hew any obstacles to the perfect unity that builds up the Church as a new Temple in which dwells the God of Israel. Christ, the "source of the supply" of this unity among the members built by actions done out of love, produces a compact, unified Mystical Body, but only in the proportion that these members are in contact with Christ to receive from him his grace, and are ready to transmit this life-grace through service or love to fellow members.

Love proven by action is the propulsion that moves a Christian toward Christ. But the more a single member loves Christ through the love of his neighbor, the more the whole Body becomes "full" of the love of Christ, loving his Body, which is the Church.

Conclusion

We have seen the three areas of belief treated in Paul's christological doctrine. The logical order should have been to treat, from microcosm to macrocosm, the progression of Christ's life first in the Christian individual, then in the Church—the collection of Christian believers in the unity of faith and charity—and finally, Christ's recapitulation of all things—the total universe or cosmos—in their proper fulfillment in the parousia. But Paul never wrote an orderly treatise on christology. He developed his teaching as practical pastoral problems forced him to elucidate more in detail his understanding of Christ on these three levels. Had he envisioned a more orderly presentation, he would have insisted on our final topic, the interrelationship between the individual Christian and the other members of the Christian community, and the Church's relationship to the cosmos.

An individual human being through baptism receives Christ, divine life, within him. But man finds himself a citizen among other citizens. He finds himself a brother to other Christian brethren, united by the same Christ-life. He knows by the Christian revelation that this life grows by self-activity in love for others based on love for God. "Whatsoever you do to the least of my brethren, you do to me." Loving service to others becomes a symbol of one's self-oblation and submission in love to God. And such service not only symbolizes our desire to give up self-love in order to possess more of God's life within us, but it actually effects this greater growth in Christ's life.

Thus, for Paul, it was the same to speak of the growth of God's life in the individual and the growth of holiness in the Church. The Church was as christified as were the individual members. An increase in divine charity in one member enkindled the whole Body-Church to a new fervor, and all the members shared in this increase.

The cosmos, as Paul spoke of it (*cf*. Rom. 8:19–22; Col. 1:16–17; Eph. 1:10, 1:21–22, 4:10), was the mass into which the leaven, the Church, was introduced. In the design of God, the Church was the true Body of Christ which, through its fidelity to the revealed word, the sacraments, and the teaching tradition, permitted the physical, living Body-Person, Jesus Christ, to make contact and fulfill the plan for which he became incarnate, died on the cross, rose, and now lives. He is still inserted in this universe of ours through the life he lives in his members. It does matter what the individual members and what the total Church Community do. For they are the rational instruments used by Christ to attain his pleroma—the fullness of all creatures who thereby will have attained the end for which God created them.

Christ is the Alpha containing the fullness of all perfections, and through him the Father has created all things. He is also the Omega Point (Teilhard) toward which the whole world is moving, through the united efforts of christified human beings, to its fullness in Christ. Christ will return the whole created universe, with man at the center, to the heavenly Father in an eternal paean of glory to God in the highest and peace among all creatures in the cosmos, transfigured into the new Jerusalem.

For it pleased God the Father that in him all fullness should dwell, and that through him God should reconcile to himself every being, and make peace both on earth and in heaven through the blood shed on the cross (Col. 1:19–20).

III

THE COSMIC LOGOS OF ST. JOHN

A great many books and articles have been written concerning the so-called Johannine literature, comprising the Gospel of St. John, the three Johannine Epistles, and the Book of Revelation or Apocalypse.[1] From neither external nor internal evidence will we, perhaps, ever establish their authorship with certainty. Traditionally, at least after the latter half of the second century, they have been attributed to St. John the Apostle.[2]

New discoveries of Gnostic[3] and Jewish sectarian literature, contemporary with the Johannine writings, have weakened the theory of Rudolph Bultmann[4] that the Johannine Gospel (and Paul's Epistles to the Ephesians and Colossians) was written by authors who sought to reinterpret primitive Christianity according to the cosmology of second-century Gnosticism. Likewise, C. H. Dodd's theory, in his *Interpretation of the Fourth Gospel,* that the Fourth Gospel is an attempt to interpret the Christian faith in terms intelligible to pagan Hellenism, is weakened greatly by recent discoveries, especially the Qumran Scrolls. The Scrolls show that many of the elements in John's Gospel which Dodd attributed to pagan Hellenism are found in the Essene Community of Qumran and have much more in common with Jewish usage.

For our purpose, the question of the authorship of the Johannine literature is of little importance. What is important, especially for our presentation of cosmic christology, is that the Church has accepted these writings as an infallible witness to the Christian tradition. They contain many of the facets presented in the earlier New Testament writings concerning the personality and profound teaching of Jesus Christ. Their message was not new; it was a continuation of the Synoptic Gospels. But their unity, their emphasis, and the theological interpretation of the historical facts are of great concern for our purpose.

John had been captured by Christ as was St. Paul, but in a somewhat different manner. We find in his conversion no lightning, no voice revealing Christ to him in a flashing moment. There is only calm and peace. John's credentials are those of an eyewitness. And he wishes to pass on to us his acquired treasure—the union he has found with God the Father through Jesus Christ:

> We proclaim what was from the beginning, what we have heard, what we have seen with our own eyes, what we have gazed upon, and what we have embraced with our own hands. I refer to the Word who is and who imparts life. Indeed, this Life has manifested himself. We ourselves have seen and testify and proclaim that Eternal Life which was with the Father and has manifested himself. To you we proclaim what we have seen and heard, that you may share our treasure with us. That treasure is union with the Father and his Son, Jesus Christ. I write this to you that we may have joy in the fullest measure (I Jn. 1:1–4).

The historical person Jesus Christ, whom the author knew so well, is the same person living in us and revealing himself to us as the Logos, the Word or Speech of God, within us and in our universe. He reveals himself as Light and Life. Thus, through these three notions—Jesus Christ as Logos, Light, and Life—we can view John's theology of the cosmic Christ.

Logos

Much has been written about John's concept of Christ as the Logos and of the sources of his concept. For the Greeks, in general, the term *logos* meant "not only the side of God which is reflected in creation, which touches the finite world; it is the ultimate reason which explains all existence, the eternal principle that underlies phenomena."[5] Heraclitus (sixth century B.C.) theorized that everything is material and in flux. He posited the logos as existent in all matter, giving to each being, in its state of perpetual fluidity, order and regularity. The logos was the rationale behind the changes, the law of the world, the criterion of truth, the rule of justice.

In a reaction against Plato's dichotomy between the world of ideas and that of matter, the Stoics posited the logos as Reason. Man participates in this Reason, which is found in all being, both as the interior logos (*logos endiathetos*) or reason, and as the externalized logos (*logos prophorikos*), the spoken word, or reason expressed externally in speech.

Philo (44 A.D.), the Alexandrian Jew who tried to harmonize Hellenic Platonism with the revealed books of the Old Testament, made the logos God's instrument of self-revelation whereby the inaccessible God could make contact with the material world and man could be lifted into eternity. Philo was aware that his concept of logos was inadequate, for he had based it upon the Old Testament Logos. Under Hellenic influence the Logos of the Old Testament was expressed progressively as a separated, hypostatized creative principle that allowed God to retain his inaccessibility and independence, yet communicate with creatures.

But in view of the known influence of Hellenic literature on the sapiential writings of the Old Testament, we are inclined to think that John was only indirectly influenced by Hellenic or any other non-Judaic sources, and this precisely through the literature of the Old Testament. The Logos had become wisdom personified in Proverbs; for example: "The Lord made me the beginning of his ways for his works. He established me before time was in the beginning before he made the earth. . . . I was by him, suiting myself to him. I was that wherein he took delight" (Prov. 8:22). The Psalms had personalized the word or speech of God as the creating Word:

> The Lord's word is true, he is faithful in all his dealings; faithfulness he loves, and the just award, the whole earth overflows with the Lord's goodness. It was the Lord's word that made the heavens, the breath of his lips that peopled them. . . . he spoke, and they were made, he gave his command, and their frame was fashioned (Ps. 32:4–9, Knox Version).

Psalm 147 joins the creative Word with the Wisdom-Word to establish in the Old Testament a theology of the Word: the Word governs in the cosmos as a universal, guiding force.

> See how he issues his command to the earth, how swift his word runs! Now he spreads a pall of snow, covers earth with an ashy veil of rime, doles out the scattered crusts of ice, binds the waters at the onset of his frost. Then, at his word, all melts away; a breath from him, and the waters flow! This is the God who makes

his word known to Jacob, gives Israel ruling and decree (Ps. 147:4–8, Knox Version).

The Judaic inspiration for John's doctrine of the Logos is evident in the Prologue to his Gospel, since he explicitly connects his account with Genesis. We need not explore in detail the parallelism that is so evident. Both accounts begin with the phrase "In the beginning," which takes us back to the same moment of creation. In Genesis (1:1–4) there is a contrast between emptiness and solitude, with darkness covering everything, and the light that God "saw was good," whereupon "He separated the light from the darkness." In John 1:3–4 there appears a similar contrast of "nothingness" as opposed to "life," since all things are created through the Word of God, which Word was the "life that was the light that shone in the darkness."

From the very first word of his Prologue, John wishes to establish the Word's role, not only in human salvation but also in the entire cosmos. He first establishes the eternal preexistence of the Logos. At the beginning of time, when the material world first came into existence, this Word already was. The world of becoming became when the Word already was in full existence. The contrast between the changing, becoming, material, finite world and the unchangeable, ever-existing Divine Being, who is the Logos, could not have been produced more succinctly and effectively.

John presents the same idea of the preexistent Logos in other writings. In the Apocalypse, Christ is called the "beginning of God's creation" (Apoc. 3:15). He is "the Alpha and the Omega, the beginning and the end" (Apoc. 21:6; 22:13; I Jn. 2:13–14). But the difference of emphasis between John's preexistent Logos and the Logos of the sapiential literature which gradually became the Torah (the Jewish Law personalized) is one of complete distinction by opposition. This Law was the speech of God: "Thus says the Lord." But it remained an extrinsic expression of the mind of God. John's choice of the word Logos is made to show precisely God's relationship with the created world through the creative function of the Word. John is not interested only in telling us the nature of the Word; he wishes to tell us that the Word is preexistent, abiding with God, hence of the same nature as God; therefore, "the Word was God." But this is to show us the function of the Word as a creating Word. "All things came into being through him, and without him there came to be not one thing that has come to be" (Jn. 1:3).

John establishes immediately a breathtaking perspective that covers the whole universe that ever was, is, or ever will be. It is in the presence of the perfect possessor of all being that we watch the created world slowly begin to move from the coldness of nothingness into the warmth of being. It is the Word that brings the universe from its existence in the mind of God into actual existence. Thus for John, Logos is applied to Jesus Christ in his role of creating the total universe. It is not a static role that began and is now finished; wherever created beings are coming into existence or moving to a greater degree of existence, there the Logos is operative. For there can be no progression in being except through the Logos who is the source of all being.

> In him there was life, and that life was the light of men. And the light shines in darkness, a darkness which was not able to master it (Jn. 1:4–5).

He gives life only because in him is the fullness of life. Here we make no distinction between God's supernatural life and man's natural life, but rather view life as the fulfillment of man's creation: the eternal life for which man was created.

Following a more ancient and perhaps better reading of John 1:4, we should translate it as did Irenaeus, Tatian, Theophilus of Antioch, Clement of Alexandria, Origen, Athanasius, Eusebius, Cyril of Jerusalem, Hilary, Ambrose, Jerome, Ephrem, Theodore of Mopsuestia, and many early exegetes: "that which was made was the life in him; the [Logos] and the life was the light of men." The whole cosmos therefore has life in the Logos. But for men, because of their intellects, he is the light, as will be pointed out later. Such a translation gives greater force to the cosmic operative role of Christ, the Logos, today. True, as the Prologue points out, through his incarnation he makes it possible for us to become truly the sons of God. But we become sons of God through an insertion into that "life" that the Logos is. He gives us and sustains in us this life in order to bring to its full completion his very life as the Logos, *the* Son of God.

But to as many as welcomed him, he gave the power to become children of God—those who believe in his name; who were born not of blood, or of carnal desire, or of man's will; no, they were born of God (Jn. 1:12–13).

The Logos Became Flesh

John contrasts man's birth as a son of God through the Logos with the birth of the Logos, God himself. In a few words filled with meaning he says: "And the Word became flesh and lived among us" (Jn. 1:14). By his choice of the word "flesh" (*sarx*), John is not thinking of Paul's contrast between spirit and flesh, the new and the old man. By use of this word, John strongly emphasizes the lowliness, weakness, and temporality of man as opposed to the transcendence, power, and eternity of the Logos, who is God. Isaias uses this contrast between the flesh and the glory of God in a similar way.

Then the glory of the Lord shall be revealed, and all mankind shall see it together; for the mouth of the Lord has spoken. . . . All mankind is grass, and all their glory like the flower of the field. The grass withers, the flower wilts, when the breath of the Lord blows upon it. So then, the people is the grass. Though the grass withers and the flower wilts, the word of our God stands forever (Is. 40:5–8).

Flesh is everything that passes away, whereas the Logos *is* from all eternity, "before the beginning." There is no question in John's mind here of distinguishing between the divine nature of the Logos and the human nature that he assumed in the Incarnation. Rather, John is emphasizing the conditions of the incarnational existence of the total, concrete person of Jesus Christ, the divine, eternal Logos, who humbles himself to become "flesh"; the eternal becomes temporal, the unmoveable becomes changeable, the Infinite becomes, before God, nothingness. We recall Paul's paean of praise to Christ who, being God,

. . . did not consider his equality with God a condition to be clung to, but emptied himself by taking the nature of a slave, fashioned as he was to the likeness of men and recognized by outward appearance as man. He humbled himself and became obedient to death; yes, to death on a cross. This is why God has exalted him and given him the name above all names, so that . . . everyone . . . should publicly acknowledge to the glory of God the Father that Jesus Christ is Lord (Phil. 2:6–11).

Resuming John's Prologue, the Divine Logos left his heavenly state and took up his dwelling among us. John's thought here may have been inspired by the Logos personified in Sirach:

In the highest heavens did I dwell, my throne on a pillar of cloud. . . . Over waves of the sea, over all the land, over every people and nation I held sway. Among all these I sought a resting place; in whose inheritance should I abide? Then the Creator of all gave me his command and he who formed me chose the spot for my tent, saying, "In Jacob make your dwelling, in Israel your inheritance" (Sir. 24:4–8).

As God stayed among his chosen people in the tabernacle of the Lord, so the Divine Logos pitched his tent or tabernacle and dwelled among the newly chosen people of Israel. John seems to follow, even in his choice of words, this cited passage. The Word that was with God from the beginning, that was active in the creation of the universe, now centers his presence in the tabernacle of human flesh. John identifies here the preexisting Word that created the universe and rules it by his power with the man of flesh that began to exist and whom John personally "had seen and touched."

And we have looked upon his glory—such a glory as befits the Father's only-begotten Son—full of grace and truth (Jn. 1:14).

The glory of his divinity shone through the frailness and lowliness of his humanity, by manifesting itself in his teachings and miracles. In his humanity there glowed the grace and the life of God. He touched men, looked upon them, spoke to them; his humanity was the point of encounter through which the life of God could flow into their lives. His sublime teachings, giving men the very mind of God himself, were the light that turned men from the darkness of the ungodly and the perverse. The Incarnate Logos led men back to their Father by sharing with them the life and truth that was his.

John returns in his conclusion to the thought of Moses and the Law. The Israelites received God's life and truth through the Jewish Law given them by Moses, but it was not the fullness of life and truth. Now life and truth have become incarnate in the person of Jesus Christ. "And of his fullness we have all received a share—yes, grace succeeding grace; for the Law was granted through Moses, but grace and truth have come through Jesus Christ" (Jn. 1:16–17).

The transcendent glory of God that Moses had begged to see has been seen in the only-begotten Son of the Most High God. It makes an interesting comparison to place Exodus 33 beside John's Prologue in order to see the two glories compared, the Mosaic Law to Christ who replaces it:

	Exodus 33		*John 1*
7	Now Moses used to take a tabernacle and pitch it outside the camp.	14	And the Word became flesh and pitched his tabernacle among us
9	And the pillar of cloud [the Shekinah] descended.		
10	And all the people saw the pillar of cloud.		. . . and we beheld his glory.
18	And Moses said, Show me, I pray thee, Thy glory.	17	For the Law was given by Moses; grace and truth came by Jesus Christ.
20	And the Lord said, Thou canst not see my face; for man shall not see me and live.	18	No man has seen God at any time: . . . the only-begotten Son . . . has declared him.
22	. . . when my glory passes by . . .		
23	. . . thou shalt see my back.		

Thus, St. John opens his Gospel with this moving Prologue that has captured in a few words the cosmic dimensions of God's creation and redemption, not only of mankind but also of the whole universe. Jesus Christ stands at the beginning, the center, and the end of history. It is he who gives meaning to the universe. He creates, sustains, perfects all creatures, bringing them to their full completion. To understand better how he fulfills his role in regard to the created world, we must see how he is the Light and the Life.

Christ, the Light of the World

Throughout the Old and New Testaments, including the writings of St. John, the theme of *light* is used in three ways. First, *light* designates an essentially moral reality, a manner of upright living. John rarely uses the image of light in this sense. Except for a rare text, such as John 3:20, he is much too occupied with Christ as the Light. Second, *light* designates an extrinsic rule of conduct, a norm for human actions. This is the usual way of referring to the Mosaic Law in the Old Testament. Third, *light* designates Christ as the Messias bringing salvation to those sitting in darkness or death. This third theme John employs in his frequent use of the word *light;* he applies it to Christ in his function as Savior of the world.

Christ calls himself the Light of the world clearly, without any equivocation.

I am the light of the world. He who follows me will not walk in the dark but have the light of life (Jn. 8:12).

I have come into the world as a light, so that no one who believes in me might remain in darkness (Jn. 12:46).

We have already seen in discussing John's Prologue the contrast between light and darkness. The world was created by the Word who is Life that gives light (salvation). But sin has disrupted the plan of God, and not only mankind but the whole world is immersed in darkness. Darkness is used symbolically here by John to describe the world, deprived of God's life, destined to eschatological death. "The light shines in the darkness" (Jn. 1:5). The universe was lying in darkness, "groaning in its travail" as Paul says, until the coming of the Light.

Surely one cannot understand John's use of the term *light* to apply to Christ's function in the universe unless he studies its use in the many ancient prophecies concerning the Messias, especially in Isaias. Isaias' main prophecy describes the Messias descending into a world of utter darkness. "The people who walked in darkness have seen a great light; upon those who dwelt in the land of gloom a light has shone. . . . For a child is born to us, a son is given us. . ." (Is. 9:1–5).

But what, in fact, happened when the Light came upon men who should have been waiting with joy is told with great sadness by John: "The light has come into the world, but men loved the darkness more than the light, because their lives were bad" (Jn. 3:19). Men should have rejoiced in the Light, Christ, giving men true happiness in eternal life, the one goal they should have been hungering for. But they chose to continue their lonely stumbling in the darkness.

Still, the fact that men did not receive the Light did not lessen Christ's activity. He still remained the "true light" (I Jn. 2:8; Jn. 1:9). John the Baptist "was not the light, but was to bear witness to the light." It was Jesus Christ who was the "true light" that illumines all men. Christ is, therefore, the true light because he is the Messias who brings life and truth to all men.

The five Jewish provinces held in bondage by the Assyrians were promised liberation, through the symbol of light, by the prophet Isaias: ". . . [say] to the prisoner: 'Come out!' To those in darkness: 'Show yourselves!' " (Is. 49:9). John applies to Jesus Christ the messianic function of leading those who live in darkness to the light, the true salvation which he is: Christ illumines their minds with the truths revealed by his Father, truths unknown by any other way of "flesh or blood." By use of the rich symbol of light, John pictures Christ not only as an illuminator, a teacher, but as the one who actually effects salvation. "He who follows me does not walk in darkness but will have the light of life" (Jn. 8:12). The Light is at one and the same time the effect and the cause of the "life." Matthew had said in his Gospel that "the just will be resplendent like the sun in the kingdom of their Father" (Matt. 13:43).

But not only will Christ's light or salvific action fall upon men, but he will save the whole universe, bathing it in a new light which will transform the world into the New Creation envisioned by St. Paul. In the Apocalypse, St. John describes this universe that will be transfigured by Christ's salvific action into the Heavenly Jerusalem:

> The city has no need of the sun or moon to shine on it, because the glory of God lights it up, and the Lamb is its lamp. The nations will walk by its light and the kings of the earth will offer their tribute of recognition to it. . . . Night will be no more, and so they will have no need of the light of lamp or of sun, because the Lord will shine on them, and they will reign for ever and ever (Apoc. 21:23–24; 22:5).

This symbolic view of Christ as light, viewed primarily as leading men to eschatological salvation, was most common in early Christian literature. The Byzantine Vespers still retains a beautiful hymn called "Joyful Light" (*Phos Hilaron*), addressed to Jesus Christ, the Light that bestows life.[6]

Thus, we see that John uses the metaphor *light* to apply primarily to Jesus Christ in his salvific role in the universe. The Synoptic Gospels, especially the early and simple Gospel of St. Mark, portray Christ's work according to the central idea of Jewish apocalyptic literature; for example, the book of Henoch presents the Messias as he who overcomes the Evil Powers that held not only the minds of men but even the non-human cosmos in darkness. Mark begins his Gospel portraying Christ as a warrior engaging the demonic forces in battle. Power over unclean spirits was a popular sign of the long-awaited Messias whose advent would finally break the hold of the demons over the whole of nature. John does not begin his Gospel in the same way as Mark. The latter seeks, by narrating miracle after miracle, to show Christ's universal, cosmic powers over all nature. John, however, by showing Christ as the Logos with a universal relation to all creatures and sent as the light to lead them out of the darkness of sin and the power of Satan, equally affirms Christ's relationship to all creatures in the entire cosmos. We must now see how John demonstrates this cosmic christological aspect even more profoundly in his constant portrayal of Christ as the Life of the world.

Christ, the Life of the World

All four Evangelists treat of the life and death of our Lord. And one can find in each of the four Gospels a distinct unifying theme around which aspects of the inexhaustible personality of Christ are presented to us. Even a cursory reading of St. John's Gospel and the other Johannine writings will reveal that his central theme is *life:* Jesus Christ is the Life of the world. While the Synoptic writers use this term in reference to Christ only sixteen times, John uses it in his Gospel alone thirty-six times. The Synoptic authors, on the contrary, present Christ and his mission on this earth under the image of the kingdom of God, using this phrase eighty-two times while John uses it only once. St. John Chrysostom indicates the reason, commenting upon John's Gospel:

Christ makes mention so often of life because life is one of the things most ardently desired by men and there is nothing more pleasant than the thought of never dying.[7]

Christ describes himself as life. "I am the resurrection and the life" (Jn. 11:25). But John is less interested in presenting Jesus Christ as subsistent life, whose nature is to be absolute, uncaused life (which, of course, he is), than he is in showing him as the giver of this life to the world, a life that the world does not otherwise possess. Christ is "the way, the truth and the life" (Jn. 14:6). In his First Epistle John calls Christ the "Word who is life and who imparts it" (I Jn. 1:2). "This Life has manifested himself" (*ibid.*). He has revealed himself in order that we might share in his life. "I have come that they may have life and have it in abundance" (Jn. 10:10). In him is the life (Jn. 1:4), and no one can have this life except through Jesus Christ.

Yet John comprehends the notion of life according to the traditional Semitic concept, developed over centuries of speculation. This, we will see, John incorporates into his understanding of Christ's relationship to the human world; upon this understanding he creates his original point of emphasis.

In the Old Testament we find but a very gradual development of the idea of life, culminating a few centuries before Christ in a full idea of an eternal life, of immortality, with God. In the rudimentary notion, life was conceived by the early Jews as this present, terrestrial life, full of activity, movement, the joy of being. It is conceived as the greatest gift given by God. "All that man possesses, he abandons in order to save his life" (Job 2:4). Those consigned to Sheol still have existence, but no life; thus life must be more than simple existence. Yahweh is the God of the living, the living God, the source of life. He gives life and takes it away. The Jew prayed to God in the words of the Psalmist: "Thou wilt not leave my soul in the place of death, or allow thy faithful servant to see corruption. Thou wilt show me the way of life, make me full of gladness in thy presence" (Ps. 15:10–11). Thus, life for man is the greatest of goods to be desired and possessed. To the just, God promises a long, full life; to the wicked, a premature death. But it is only in the second century before Christ's coming that a clear idea of an eternal life after death emerges in the Jewish tradition. Temporal life is considered a testing period for the life to come. But the future life is considered a continuation of this present life, free of everything painful, like death, injustice, sufferings.

The Christian era built upon this Semitic tradition. It is seen more clearly in the translations of such ideas as life, to live, to be saved, to be healed, to be fully happy, which in Syriac are all equivalent to the word "hj" (to live) or "haje" (life). The Christian writers of the (Semitic) Syriac language were convinced, as was St. John, that "theology of life" was an accurate Semitic description of Christ's message. Thus, we see strong Semitic influence in the idea of salvation conceived as new life, with Christ as the life-giver; faith as the seed or germ of life; the sacraments as carriers of this divine life, which is fostered through asceticism or purification of the obstacles to further growth and a virtuous life.

But in the New Testament, generally, we find this Judaic concept of a future life stressed in its eschatological literalness. The present life is conceived, not as the same life, but as a distinct period of probation. The moral aspects of this present life are stressed as only important in view of the future, eternal life. Christianity is a new life only by the new manner of living imposed as a preparation for the future, eternal life. It is the eternal life now possessed and lived in anticipation, in this life, of the resurrectional life of Christ. Life now has reference to the Spirit, partially now participated in but only eternally in its fullness. Eternal life, as the resurrection, remains in its fullest degree an object of hope.

One of John's original contributions is that he builds around the Semitic eschatological hope of a future, eternal life the dynamic concept of life that is here and now eternal. This new, paradoxical life admits of degrees of development, as does all life, but John's striking insight is that it is *already* eternal life. Keeping to the primitive Semitic concept of life as the attainment of complete health, joy, happiness of man, John emphasizes the continuity between this present life in Christ and our future life after death. There is no clash between "natural" and "supernatural" because for John there is only one life, the eschatological life of God already lived by Christians in this earthly existence. The manner of enjoying this life now differs from that of the future life, but the life itself is one and the same, continuous. To appreciate John's originality with its existential emphasis on the unity of present and future life, let us turn to his writings to explore the richness of the meaning of Christ as the Life of the world.

Life—A Present Reality

The central purpose of John's Gospel is to foster a deeper faith among Christians "that Jesus is the Messias, the Son of God, and that, through your belief, you may have life in his name" (Jn. 20:31). This life is to be possessed *now*. It comes to us by hearing the Word and believing in him. Faith in Christ allows us to pass, even now, from eschatological death, the death of God's life in us, to his life:

> He who heeds my message and believes him whose ambassador I am, *is in possession* of eternal life, and is not liable to judgment. On the contrary, he *has* once for all *passed* out of the realm of death into that of life. It is the truth when I tell you that a time is coming, in fact, it is already here, when the dead will hear the voice of the Son of God, and those who heed it will have life (Jn. 5:24–25). (Emphasis added)

A similar passage indicating the present reality of this life, now possessed by the faithful, virtuous person, is found in John's First Epistle:

> We know that we have passed from death to life, because we love our brothers. He who does not love abides in death. Everyone who hates his brother is a murderer, and you know that no murderer has eternal life abiding in him (I Jn. 3:14–15).

John often makes no distinction between this life and eternal life, thus he merely drops out the adjective. From his frequent joining of the adjective *eternal* with *life,* there can be no doubt that the two are synonymous in his mind, even when he uses the word *life* alone. "He who believes in the Son possesses eternal life" (Jn. 3:36; cf. Jn. 5:24–39; 6:40–47). "He who eats of my flesh and drinks of my blood has eternal life" (Jn. 6:54). There is only one life that is the healthy, full life of man, and that is to live the same life that he will live eternally. In a word, we are *now* living the *eternal* life. Death is a mere passage of man from the state of *becoming* to *being,* but he remains the same person and the life in him after death is still the same life that was in him during his earthly period, but now fully developed. Early Christians, like Origen, understood John's emphasis. In commenting on John's use of *life,* Origen notes:

> Those who share in Christ live the true life. Those others, however, who seemingly enjoy life, yet do not really possess the life of which Christ is the source, do not really possess the true Light and hence do not have, any longer, the true Life.[8]

For John, then, death has its true meaning only in relation to this eternal life. Bodily death with the separation of the soul from the physical body is not important or is important only in reference to the presence of true, eternal life already lived in this earthly existence. Christ hinted at this in a scene recorded by John (8:48–59). He told the Jews who refused to believe in his divine mission that "if anyone treasures my teaching, he will not see death in all eternity." The Jews challenged this eternal life that Christ was claiming to bestow on his followers. Abraham, they retorted, was greater than he, yet Abraham and the prophets died! What did Christ mean by never dying? For Christ, the physical death was meaningless in itself. The moment between *becoming* and *being* is not the all-important event that the wages of sin made death out to be.

What is important is that *Being,* the *life* of him who is, is present in our lives.

Jesus, in answer to Martha's protestation that Lazarus would rise on the last day, simply states:

I am the resurrection and the life. He who believes in me will live even if he dies. No one that lives and believes in me shall ever die (Jn. 11:25).

Even though man dies, and everyone will surely die, this is not important. The possession through faith and charity of the life that Christ alone can give during this lifetime becomes eternal life, in spite of physical death. Thus, the basic human concept of death as an end has no true meaning compared to the light of faith that tells us that we possess the same Jesus Christ who is our true life during this earthly life and after it. This has always been the Christian faith as phrased in the Preface of the Roman Mass for the Dead: "For those who have been faithful, O Lord, life is not ended, but merely changed." The manner of the life possessed even now changes, but life is not taken away.

Elsewhere, too, Christ stressed the present enjoyment of eternal life and promised we would never taste eternal or eschatological death, as when he referred to the Holy Eucharist, one of the chief means of nourishing this life within us:

I am the bread of life. Your fathers ate the manna in the desert and they died. The bread which I speak of, which comes down from heaven, is such that no one who eats of it will ever die. I am the living bread that has come down from heaven. If one eats of this bread, he will live forever, and, furthermore, the bread which I shall give is my flesh given for the life of the world (Jn. 6:48–51).

The Israelites in the desert had died a physical death. The manna that they ate did not overcome this death. But Jesus in substance says that those who eat of this "Bread of Life," himself under the Eucharistic species, will never die but will continue to enjoy the eternal life they *now* possess.

Christ—The Way, the Truth, and the Life

At the Last Supper, St. Thomas, the hard-headed realist, asked the Lord: "Lord, we do not know where you are going. How do we know the way?" (Jn. 14:5). Jesus simply answered: "I am the way, the truth, and the life. No one goes to the Father but through me" (Jn. 14:6). In order to go to the Father, in order to obtain complete happiness, in order to be saved, one must go through Christ, the intermediary. He is the truth, not merely in the metaphysical sense of absolute truth, but because he perfectly reflects the true objective relation back to God. Thus, no one is in a genuinely true relation to God (according to God's finality in creating man) except in and through Christ, who not only effects our proper filial relationship to God, but also is the exemplary cause, the standard according to which our fulfillment is measured. We measure our sanctity, our salvation, according to our likeness to Christ.

Christ is the life, as we have already said, because he brings us true life that knows no corruption, that will endure forever. This life is manifested in the humanity of Christ that was seen and touched by other humans (I Jn. 1:1–2). Jesus Christ replaced the Mosaic Law. Through his resurrection he is able to bring us himself as a vital principle of new life. No longer is there the Law, an extrinsic force, guiding man. Now the Law is replaced by a Person who dwells within us and guides us to fuller life. Not only must we be eager to receive this life, but we must yield ourselves to this intrinsic principle of vital operation and live according to his wishes. We must listen to and fulfill his message (Jn. 5:24; 8:43, 48). His teaching must find room in our hearts (Jn. 8:37). But to hear the message of Christ and to know that it is life-bearing, we must have faith. "He who believes in the Son possesses eternal life" (Jn. 3:36). One must believe in the revelation Jesus Christ came to give us. Chief among these revealed truths is that Christ is from the Father and he is the true Son of the Father. He is in the Father and the Father is in him (Jn. 14:10). He has come so that "they, too, may be in us" (Jn. 17:21).

The faith John demands of Christ's followers is not a purely speculative assent to a truth, but a total surrender of oneself in love to the person of Jesus Christ. To possess this life that comes through faith we must keep his commandments. The great commandment that proves our true love for Christ is our love for one another, loving each other as he has loved us.

Unity in Life

We are individually united to Christ through his same life. The life he gives us is the life of the total vine which he is. We are the branches, but we have no true life except in possessing his life. By our common faith and the exercise of charity, we become united with the other members as all branches are united by the one life of the whole vine (Jn. 15:18). All human beings are destined by God's salvific will to be united together in the same life of the Trinity.

> All are to be one; just as you, Father, are in me and I am in you, so they, too, are to be one in us (Jn. 17:21).

The fullness of all truth, power, life, and love that is in the Father flows to the Son through the Holy Spirit and passes into us. John moves away from the individual's union with the Holy Trinity through the indwelling life that Christ has brought us to perspectives of universal dimension. Christ in his Last Supper discourse prays for all his followers who would form a unity of faith and charity that would be called his Church. In these members Christ would live "that the love with which you love me may dwell in them as I dwell in them myself" (Jn. 17:26). The worldly wise would see a mere conglomeration of humans banded together by a set of beliefs and liturgical practices. The faithful, through faith and charity, would be aware of the same eternal life uniting them into close unity.

In this way individual Christians, aware of the Divine Logos as life and light living within each one individually, move through a vibrant faith to the Logos living in others and enlightening all. Too, they must so live that they reflect the unity in love that exists between the Father and Son through the Holy Spirit in the Trinitarian life. The unity that exists among the three Persons of the Trinity becomes the basis of the unity among all men through the life that Christ brings us. Christ the Logos is the true life of the individual Christian and of the community of believers, in this present life and in its full consummation in the life hereafter. It is he who effects, through the life he gives us by his Holy Spirit, the divine adoption by which we are incorporated into the Divine Family and live, even now, as befits children of God.

The conclusion to John's First Epistle can serve as an apt summary of our reflections on Christ as our *present* life, incorporating us into himself according to his image and through his grace, in growing charity, the bond of union that reflects the unity of the Trinity:

We know that we are born of God, but the whole world is under the influence of the evil one. We know, moreover, that the Son of God has come and has given us understanding that we may know the True One. In fact we are incorporated into this True One, God's Son, Jesus Christ. He is the true God and Eternal Life. Little children, guard yourselves from idols (I Jn. 5:19–21).

Conclusion

John presents Christ under three central aspects: *Logos, Light,* and *Life*. From one point of view, John's focus seems much farther removed from this present world than that of Paul or even the Synoptic writers. Paul's epistles spell out practical lessons of charity, zeal, purity, obedience, ecclesiastical unity. We live "in Christ" and must zealously reconstruct this world into a "New Creation." But John's writings breathe a simplicity that on the surface alarms us as "mystical," removed from present realities. On deeper reflection, however, we find that John is writing a synthesis which deals with the most basic reality. Like an arrow, he goes straight to the center of all earthly beings and there he remains. He insists that the practical applications in the transfiguration of this universe into the heavenly Jerusalem would follow easily enough once human beings were transformed by the reality of God's eternal life within them.

John chose three main images to present Christ's presence in our world. All three deal vitally with Christ's relationship to man and his world. He does not speculate about the abstract nature of the Second Person in the Trinity. Jesus Christ is the Logos, the light, and the life whose mission is to bring all men to eternal salvation. As Logos, Christ is the creative cause of all finite beings, "without him nothing was made."

But not only is he the beginning, the source and principle of all finite existence; he is the *raison d'être* of the universe, the Omega towards whom reality is moving and through whom it attains its fullness.

By the Incarnation, the Divine Logos has physically inserted himself into our created world. He is now a part of us in order that we may become a part of him, the source of all reality. He will come at the end of time as the executor of God's plan, "riding a white horse. . . . his name is the Word of God" (Apoc. 19:11, 13). He will overcome Satan and establish the kingdom of God for those who have done his will. Those who have refused their own fulfillment in and through him have refused to accept reality.

Humanity will converge around the Logos as around its center of recapitulation. Every human being who willingly refuses to cooperate towards his own perfection creates for himself a fire of frustrated spiritual powers, yearning by nature to be fulfilled by the Logos, yet unable by free choice to possess him.

But in the present world Christ prolongs his earthly activities. He illumines the minds of men to see him as the source of all life and reality. Through his free gift of faith, Christians see how Christ bathes the whole universe with his active presence. The eternal life that begins with faith begins also with a knowledge that will be perfected in heaven by a direct intuition whereby men will see Christ in all things and all things in Christ. We see now in a "darkly fashion as in a mirror," says St. Paul, but we do see! Christ is our light, enabling us to discern the traces of the Trinity in his created world. But this light is drawing us closer to himself where the illumination and the Illuminator, light and life, will be known in a direct vision that will allow us to see all things in their source and ground, Jesus Christ.

Beloved, now we are children of God, and what we shall be has not yet been manifested. We know that when he appears, we shall be like him, because we shall see him just as he is. Everyone who cherishes this hope in God strives to be holy, just as he is holy (I Jn. 3:2–3).

John's original contribution, however, lies in his consistent emphasis on Christ as life, not merely as the goal to be attained in the future, eschatological life, but in his stress on that eschatological life now enjoyed by us in this present life through faith and charity. We stretch out towards the full Life that will be revealed to us only after our physical death, but we even now possess this same Life in us. We look forward to the final parousia, aware that an inchoative parousia of Jesus Christ makes him present today. He is not separated from this present life by death. John insists that our relationship to God is a dynamic process of growth in this life that remains constantly the same, except in degree. Thus, above all New Testament writers, John links this present life in us with the life of the Trinity.

In the Last Supper discourse John highlights this Trinitarian union within us. Through the simple experience of eating and drinking bread and wine, we enter into the most intimate union with Jesus Christ, the Logos-Life. When we partake of the Eucharist, his physical presence, his life within us, brings us a new experience of the Trinity. As the living Son ever bespeaks a real relation of Son to a present Father in the union of love that is the Holy Spirit, so this same Son extends this same Trinitarian action within us. The Word does not come to us alone: "I am in the Father and the Father in me" (Jn. 14:10). Where Christ, the Divine Son, is, there also is the Father. "He who sees me sees the Father. . . . the Father who dwells in me" (Jn. 14:9–10). Where the Father and Son are present, there also is the Holy Spirit, who loves the Father and the Son within us and with us. The three Persons are not inert in the communicant. Within him, the Father utters his Word, generates his Son, perfect Image of his Father: the divine Logos, by a perfect response of love, jointly with the love the Father reciprocates, breathes forth the Holy Spirit.

The Logos-Life brings about this Trinitarian union within us, not only through his living presence, but by his activity within us. He speaks to us of the Father. He not only teaches us about the Father and the Holy Spirit, but he joins his activity as Son with our innate urge to respond, likewise in union with him, with a similar act of sonship towards our heavenly Father. He teaches us how to adore, praise, love, divest ourselves of every element that is an obstacle to true sonship in God by repeating his words: "Behold, I come to do thy will." He asks the Father that we be admitted into the mystery of divine love. "Father, I pray for them also . . . that they may be one in us" (Jn. 17:20–21). He begs of the Father our participation in the love he receives from the Father. "Father, may the love with which you love me dwell in them" (Jn. 17:26).

John stresses that this union in life continues beyond the presence of the Eucharistic species within us. The Logos-Life within us continues to speak to us of the Father's great love in every creature of our experience. Each moment can be an encounter with life as we pass from the life dwelling within us to the activity of the same life working dynamically in each creature. Jesus Christ, says St. John, is the Alpha and Omega (Apoc. 21:6), the Image of the Father according to whom we have been created to become "sons of God" (I Jn. 3:2; Jn. 1:12). Through an increased faith in the eternal life that is within us we can move out into the universe to find the Logos, for everything "moves and breathes and has its being" in him.

Conversely, through a more intense, expanded consciousness of the transcendent presence of the Trinity living and acting in all material creatures out of love for us, we can enter into a more vivid act of faith in the Trinitarian life living within us. The everyday world will not impede us but will be a sacrament, a true symbol, both signifying presence of the Trinity and effecting that presence in us. Everyday experience becomes a personal encounter with a Father loving us as he loves his only-begotten Son, with a Son loving his Father in union with the Holy Spirit, the bond of mutual love between the Father and the Son.

IV

COSMIC CHRISTOLOGY IN THE ANTE-NICENE GREEK FATHERS

There are many areas in the history of the evolution of dogma that could serve to illustrate how the Holy Spirit brings about a gradual increase in the Church's actual consciousness of the mysteries revealed by Jesus Christ. The growing awareness and articulation of the Greek Fathers concerning the role Christ is *now* playing in the universe, in man and in the sub-human cosmos, illustrates concretely how the understanding of a given dogma grows as the Church, the Spouse of Christ, yields herself more and more over the centuries to him and to his activity within her.

But important to the central theme of this book is this: the contribution of the Greek Fathers to the theological development of a cosmic christology is so fundamental and extensive that its mainstream has since been significantly enlarged rather rarely, and that principally by two towering freshets, both notably modern, *The Mystical Body of Christ*

(Pius XII, 1943) and the *Dogmatic Constitution on the Church* (Vatican II, 1964). Such pronouncements, we note again, are but culminating currents that stir within the ancient waters—here, largely Pauline tides that mounted under the slow pressure of long reflection by the Church upon herself as (respectively) Body of Christ and People of God.

The early Christian writers had inherited from the Semitic fonts of Christian revelation an understanding of the activity of Christ in the universe as a story of divine conflict and victory, with Christ fighting against and triumphing over the evil powers of the world in a final victory in the parousia. But when the Greek Christian writers sought to defend Christian revelation against the Gnostics and Stoics, they used the basic language and concepts of these pagan philosophers to rephrase the Semitic victory-struggle of Christ over the personal demons who held the world in bondage. The new formulation was not in contradiction to the earlier description; rather, it strove to state more literally what the Jews had left unexpressed in rich but vague symbols.

Irenaeus was the first to introduce the principle of "recapitulation" as an integrating structure by which he could explain, both to the Gnostic heretics and to his own flock at Lyons, the immanence of Christ in the material world. We shall see how Clement and Origen of Alexandria add to this concept; then Athanasius, the Cappadocian Fathers, Cyril of Alexandria and, finally, Maximus the Confessor. (Extensive quotations from these Fathers will be found in the Appendix.)

I. IRENAEUS

In the early Church there developed two distinct lines of emphasis in presenting Christianity as a way of life to the new converts. One line, centered in Syria chiefly around

Antioch, continued the strong Semitic emphasis of St. John and St. Paul who presented Christ in existential, dynamic terms, as *Life*. Christ was experienced in the totality of his person as the source of God's life in our souls.

The other line of emphasis was centered chiefly around Alexandria. This school, highly influenced by Middle and Neo-Platonism, presented Christ as the object of intellectual contemplation. He became the Teacher of morality, a model of virtuous living, to be contemplated and imitated.

Irenaeus was of the first school.[1] He came from Smyrna in Asia Minor where he had been the disciple of the martyr St. Polycarp, who in turn learned of Christ as *Life* from St. John, the Beloved Disciple himself. Irenaeus moved to Lyons, in Gaul, where he became the bishop and pastor of souls. His chief work, five volumes entitled *Adversus Haereses,* was an attempt to combat the heresy of Gnosticism that had infiltrated the Church in the West from Persia.[2] The Gnostics were mostly eclectics who borrowed from assorted philosophies, theologies, sciences, cosmologies, and world histories to fashion a pseudo-Christianity. They held that Earth resulted from the fall of a dissatisfied spiritual "eon" who refused his place in the harmonious unity of eons governing the divine spheres. He sprinkled Earth with sparks of divinity which, immersed in matter, became the source of all evil. Christ was the Divine Son sent down from heaven to immerse himself in evil matter and thus bring the other divine sparks back to heaven. Christ effects his mission by bestowing upon the elect the special gift of a "gnosis," an enlightenment about the world above and how to regain it. For the non-Gnostics or the *hylics,* those immersed totally in matter, there was no possibility of regaining heaven. Thus, the mission of Christ was to save only a portion of mankind.

Irenaeus bases his refutation of Gnosticism upon his development of Paul's Christic *recapitulation* and of man as image of God. Our Western minds, used to centuries of refined theological speculation, may find his basic concepts vague, inexact, poetic. Yet there has been a remarkable scholarly re-examination in the Church today of the early Greek Fathers in an attempt to recapture the rich insights they expressed in a genre of theological speculation practically unknown to us: the use of symbolic language. Irenaeus' study of two symbols —man-as-image-and-likeness-of-God and Christ-as-the-Recapitulator-of-all-creatures—are superb examples. Both convey deeper insights than a denotative, scientifically accurate statement about man's redemption.

Such symbols transcend space, time, and definitive conceptualization to transport us, still careful of mystery and of Revelation, into a vision of the history of salvation so sweeping as to approximate the Divine.

Image and Likeness

Irenaeus was the first theologian of the East to base a theology of redemption and grace on the doctrine of image and likeness. His polemic against the heretical Gnostics includes an anthropology drawn from God's own revelation.

Attempting to reconcile God's transcendence and perfection with his creating and conserving immanence, Irenaeus builds his theology of man upon those words of God: "Let us make mankind in our image and likeness" (Gen. 1:26). It is God who decides to create man out of his own bountiful goodness. This conception of God's self-communicating love must be kept in mind to understand Irenaeus and the other Greek Fathers. It is in man's relationship of total dependence on God that we can properly understand the relationship between nature and grace as we find it presented in these writers.

While God always retains his perfect transcendence over all creatures, the whole created world, Irenaeus insists, is a manifestation of his power, wisdom, and goodness. The action of the Trinity is the perfecting of creation, at the center of which stands man. Man, drawn by God, slowly progresses and gradually becomes perfected in the image and likeness of the Uncreated Lord (cf. Appendix, No. 1).[3]

In the Trinitarian activity in man's regard, it is the Son and the Holy Spirit who are, to use Irenaeus' favorite expression, the "two hands" of God. They are to draw from the image, rooted metaphysically in man's nature, the divine likeness. Man was created not a finished being but one destined to grow daily more open to the providential workings of God the Father, who would perfect man through the exemplarity of his Son. In his image man was created, and through the Holy Spirit the divine life within man would be nourished, ultimately reaching its fulfillment in man's likeness to the Son of God.

Irenaeus ultimately centers his anthropology on Jesus Christ. Man is not really the image of God; the true image that mirrors forth perfectly the Father is the Son. Irenaeus succinctly says: "The *image* is the Son of God in whose image man was made."[4] But the perfect prototype of man as image is the Logos Incarnate. The Incarnate Image, Jesus Christ, possesses three necessary elements, and therefore all "full" human beings must also possess these three constitutive parts: body, soul, and spirit. Christ, taking upon himself a human body and a human soul, received his fullness and entered into his glory when he received the Spirit, the life of God dwelling in him.

Irenaeus gives us a keen insight into the patristic understanding of nature and grace. Man's total nature (*phusis*) is made up of three constitutive elements: *body, soul* (intellect and will), and *spirit* (divine life dwelling within man). The "plasma" or image in man is made up of his body and soul. This cannot be destroyed, for we are dealing with the embryonic constituents in man out of which the full man, man perfected by divine grace, will develop under the activities of the "two hands" of God, the Son and the Holy Spirit. Although the gift of spirit is a gift of God that can be lost, it is considered by Irenaeus as an essential part without which man is not complete. The two (in Western categories, nature and supernature) are for Irenaeus distinct; one is not the other, yet they are not separated as, for example, two floors of a house can exist independently of each other.

Rahner says of the excessive separation of these two orders that it is as though "two layers were laid very carefully one on top of the other so that they interpenetrate as little as possible. And accordingly, nature's orientation towards grace is thought of as negatively as possible."[5] Irenaeus, on the contrary, sees the supernatural as a more advanced stage of man's development when, after purification, he allows himself to be acted upon by Jesus Christ and the Holy Spirit so that the Spirit may be the fulfillment of the undeveloped image implanted in him.

Irenaeus' insistence that the *body* of man is also made in the image of God has particular interest for modern man. Ladner rightly interprets Irenaeus' thinking: "The apparent paradox that the corporeal part of man should be according to the image of God, Irenaeus explains beautifully from the fact of the Incarnation."[6] Irenaeus strongly defends the goodness of matter against the Gnostics, for whom matter was the intrinsic principle of evil. Matter is holy because God had taken upon himself in the Second Person of the Trinity a body of flesh. For Irenaeus, Christ took upon himself a human body not only as an instrument of redemption but rather (and here we see Irenaeus' dynamic view of redemption as a fulfillment of man's nature through deification into the likeness of Jesus Christ) so that his human body would be also the image according to which man was created. Jesus Christ, the Incarnate God-Man, is the perfect image of his Father. But he is the perfect image according to which man is created precisely because he possesses a body and a soul, and through his lifetime of human openness to the Holy Spirit he attains to the perfect likeness of the Son of God (cf. Appendix, No. 2). Wingren thus interprets Irenaeus: "While the earth was being formed, Christ was in the mind of God and matter took shape in the hands of God in accordance with this future pattern."[7]

The Incarnate Word was exercising his exemplarity even before the Word actually became flesh in human history. Transcending space and time, God always had the perfect image of Jesus Christ, God-Man, before him. St. John had clearly said that all things were created in and through him, the Divine Logos, who was made flesh and dwelt among us (Jn. 1:1:14). Irenaeus writes:

> For in times long past, it was said that man was created according to the image of God, but it was not actually shown; for the Word was yet invisible, after whose image man was created.[8]

Therefore, we can say with Irenaeus that man is created according to the image of God, and this image is Jesus Christ, in his full humanity, body and soul. The body of man should not be a hindrance but a help to man's fulfillment. Yet this fulfillment looks to the likeness of God which the Incarnate Word possesses doubly; first, by his very nature as the subsistent Logos, the Son of the Living God; and second, by his assumed humanity, body and soul, from which a *created* likeness to his uncreated likeness—his divinized human nature—is born.

Thus, for Irenaeus, man viewed merely as body and soul is imperfect and incomplete. His nature needs to be completed through the acquisition of the higher likeness. The first man, Adam, was created with the higher likeness (God's grace) within him.

Still, he was a child (*pais*) as far as possessing the perfection of the Divine Life is concerned. By submitting his whole being to God as to his final end, he would move to greater maturity, the adulthood of the spirit. The spirit grew to maturity; the total human person, body and soul, lived fully. Such, for Irenaeus, was the glory of God: a human being living fully according to all his powers, under the influence of God's grace (cf. Appendix No. 2).

Effects of Sin

Adam rebelled against God. The virus of self-idolatry entered into the human family. Man lost the likeness to God insofar as he lost the living relationship of a loving son towards a loving Father. By a willful act of refusal to love God, Adam was turned away from the dynamic growth process that would have made him, by each good act, an adopted son of God according to the likeness of Jesus Christ. He became corrupt and dead, not in the physical sense, but in the eschatological sense; life within him was extinguished. Irenaeus takes pains to show that God was not at fault in man's self-inflicted disaster. The likeness to God in man was dependent on a willed friendship between man and God. God would not force his love upon any man (cf. Appendix, No. 3).

Christ's Role of Recapitulation

To describe the role of Christ as the Second Adam, the restorer of a cosmos grown sick with self-love, Irenaeus uses the Pauline word *anakephalaiosis,* recapitulation. Many commentators of Irenaeus have labored to define his precise use of the word, for Irenaeus uses it as a framework within which to construct the first articulated Christian theology of redemption, as well as an anthropology.[9]

His theory of recapitulation structures his theological system. It signifies a re-beginning of the human race, whereby Christ reverses the process that had turned earth away from true Light, Life, and Incorruption towards sin, chaos, and death. God gathers up in his Logos his entire work by fulfilling it according to his original plan through an intimate association with the living Logos in the individual human being, made according to the image and likeness of God which is Christ. The "logosized" creature, in union with the other creatures of the universe, is restored in Christ to reach the pleroma in Christ's glorious second coming, his parousia.

The term, therefore, can mean a resumé, a taking up of all since the beginning, a recommencement, a return to the source, a restoration, a reorganization and incorporation under one head. Included in this comprehensive, imaginative concept is the idea that Christ the redeemer underwent all the trials of Adam, but with total success. Nor does Christ merely undo, detail by detail, all that Adam had done to bring mankind into its fallen state. Basing his theology of Christ's restoration of man on a dynamic concept of growth and conflict, Irenaeus presents Christ as the champion of the human race who enters into the fray to do battle with the Evil One. Yet Christ the victor does not merely restore creation to what it was in the beginning; he completes it through a process of growth as a human person grows from embryo, through childhood, to full manhood.

The term *anakephalaiosis* (recapitulation) springs initially from Ephesians 1:10: ". . . [God decreed] to gather [anakephalaiosasthai] all creation both in heaven and on earth under one head, Christ." [10] But Irenaeus advances the content of the term:

> Christ has therefore in his work of recapitulation summed up all things, both waging war against our enemy and crushing him who at the beginning had led us away captive in Adam . . . in order that, as our species went down to death through a vanquished man, so we may ascend to life through a victorious one.[11]

Christ's birth and maturing is the first creation of man brought to its perfection. Christ is man in his fullest completion, as God had originally planned man to be. In the Incarnation a single human being came into existence but he contained and developed to its fullest all the purity and life that the whole world had lost. Christ is fully all that man ought to be. There is in him nothing of sin, of aversion from God through Adam's sin. In Christ's humanity, God lays hands on man again. Those hands, the Divine Logos and the Holy Spirit, will effect a "new creation" through the humanity of Christ, making all men one with him.

But the main work of Christ's recapitulation is to overthrow Satan and the works of sin. All the universe lay under the bondage of sin, "groaning in its travail," as St. Paul writes, until the fullness of time should appear. When Christ appears, his chief work is to wage battle against sin, death, and the devil. Christ's victory will start a new creation, will set mankind free from their dominion and give men again the source of divine life which, through growth, can culminate in mature sons of God.

To show how Christ effected this restoration Irenaeus uses exact analogies between the activities of Christ and those of Adam. Here we see Irenaeus' existential approach to Christ's redemptive action, for it includes not only the Incarnation and the cross but every action of his human life. There was no aspect of human life that was not experienced somehow by Christ: infancy, childhood, adolescence, adulthood, a lifetime of human experiences sanctified by obedience.

By his total obedience Christ undoes the disobedience of Adam. Both were virgin-born—Adam was born of the virgin earth, not of human parents; Christ was born of the Virgin Mary by the Spirit of God. Adam sinned through the disobedience of a woman; Christ recapitulates the Fall through the obedience of the Virgin Mary (cf. Appendix, No. 4). Christ's temptations in the desert and in his passion are paralleled by those of Adam, but Christ always prevails, thus overcoming Adam's disobedience (cf. Appendix, No. 5).

But Christ's actions are not mere mechanical reversals of the actions of Adam, through perfect obedience to his heavenly Father, in contrast to Adam's disobedience. While he does break the dominion of Satan over mankind and the cosmos, this alone does not assure the fulfillment of God's plan. Christ's activities, through his divinely instituted Church commissioned to teach his word and to administer his sacraments, are still being prolonged in the universe. It is in the Church above all that man encounters Christ the fulfiller. Through the Church, Christ restores to man the Divine Life lost through sin. Through this Divine Life by which man re-creates the world around him in accordance with God's original plan of creation, the whole world enters into the "new creation" of St. Paul.

Irenaeus explains the purpose of the Incarnation, effected now by the Holy Spirit in the Church, with words that would inspire Origen, Athanasius, and the other Eastern Fathers: "God became man in order that man might become God."

Christ, the Incarnate Word, brings to man the possibility of a new creation, one that is built upon the natural, physical life of man but which transforms the natural into a new life that makes man truly according to the likeness of God. The Lord, by his coming, "brought all newness, by bringing himself . . . For this was announced, that a Newness would come, to renew and give life to man."[12] God's created world is not intrinsically evil, according to Irenaeus, but it must be "absorbed by" the immortality and incorruptibility of Christ (cf. Appendix, No. 6).

Man's temporal life by which Christ brings about the "new creation" determines whether he will possess the gift of incorruption. His deeds, informed by grace, decide his eternal destiny. No being is neglected by the grace of Christ, by which he takes up all creatures and heals them. His work is one of renewing, of solidifying, of uniting.

Time is seen by Irenaeus, not as a measurement of a period of degradation through which man must pass in order, finally, to return to a lost perfection,[13] but as the measurement of the unfolding of God's gifts in a constant act of creation. The fullness of God's creative action is tied intimately with the fulfillment of his purpose in creating man "according to God's image and likeness." Man's true growth and that also of the entire cosmos are dependent completely upon the power of God who bestows upon man inexhaustible gifts. Man is the "receptacle of God's goodness" and, through the reception and proper use of these gifts, man becomes the instrument whereby God's plan, his "glory," is achieved (cf. Appendix, No. 7).

The Holy Spirit

God sends his Spirit to men through the Church. For it is "the Spirit of the Father who purifies man and raises him up to the life of God."[14] If the Holy Spirit brings "incorruptibility," which is Irenaeus' way of describing God's life within man, the question arises: does Irenaeus hold more than a verbal distinction between the Holy Spirit and the spirit in man? Is the Holy Spirit simply the likeness of God in man? By using the analogy of a wild olive branch that is inserted into a fruit-bearing olive tree, he clearly wishes to show the intimate relation of the Holy Spirit and "the man grafted in [who] receives the Spirit of God." But he is careful to add that such a man "does not lose the substance of flesh," any more than "the engrafted wild olive . . . lose(s) the substance of its wood" (cf. Appendix, No. 8).

Again, Irenaeus clearly shows a distinction between the "breath of life which renders man an animated being" and the "vivifying Spirit which causes him to become spiritual."[15] The Holy Spirit is not the likeness of God in man but it is he who "has formed man to the likeness of God."[16] Without using the theological terms "uncreated" and "created" grace, Irenaeus teaches the same clear distinction between the Giver of grace and the gift given. The Holy Spirit lives and operates within man; through his energizing activities along with man's co-operation, the Spirit produces an effect distinct from himself, a created gift which renders man more and more *like* God. The created gift, a relationship in love of a divinized child of God towards the heavenly Father, transfigures man more and more into an adopted son of God. This relationship is not conceived by Irenaeus as a merely external declaration that man has found favor with God. It is viewed as an intrinsic, ontological change within man. The life of the spirit in which the created likeness of God is found in man and the Holy Spirit, the uncreated life of God, along with man's human nature, his body and soul, created to the image of Christ, these are all distinct but closely related in a new dynamic growth process.

God's presence within man is one of activity as he unfolds and fulfills in his Providence, through the instrumentality of man, the plan that he has conceived from all eternity. Man's activity is his response to the new life within him. In a unique partnership, man cooperates with God to effect in the world about him the harmony that now is his through his loving submission to God. Conflict and tribulation are necessary in order to effect this new creation.

The "apostasy" of self-love must be put aside, and this precisely through suffering. Irenaeus shows the presence of the Son and the Spirit within man working to effect, especially through a death to self, a more vibrant image and likeness in man (cf. Appendix, No. 9).

Man's growth as well as that of the cosmos is a process of constant maturity into the greater fullness of being. This fullness will not be reached in this life but in the life to come. The present world will not be destroyed or annihilated but only transfigured into a new manner of existence. "For neither is the substance nor the essence of creatures annihilated . . . but the 'fashion of the world passes away.' "[17]

> Then there shall be the new heaven and the new earth in which man shall continually remain, always holding fresh converse with God.[18]

The cosmic dimensions of salvation in Irenaeus' teaching and the fundamental orientation of his *Adversus Haereses* are summarized in our closing quotation. In the completion of all things in Christ, saved humanity will contemplate God and all created beings in him. Yet man will spend eternity probing the mysteries of God's personal love for each individual human being and still never fully comprehend:

For there is the one Son, who accomplished his Father's will; and one human race also in which the mysteries of God are wrought, "which the angels desire to look into" (I Pet. 1:12) and they are not able to search out the wisdom of God by means of which his handiwork, conformed and incorporated with his Son, is brought to perfection; that his offspring, the First-begotten Word should descend to the creature, that is, to what had been moulded (plasma) and that it should be contained by him; and, on the other hand, the creature should contain the Word and ascend to him, passing beyond the angels and be made after the image and likeness of God.[19]

II. CLEMENT OF ALEXANDRIA

Clement is one of the Greek Fathers who would understand the "New Breed." He was a Christian optimist, seeing the goodness of God in every created being. For this reason he was attracted to all types of philosophies and natural theologies, searching for a possible "natural" revelation made by God to searching man, outside of his Judaeo-Greek inheritance. Above all, the beauties of Hellenic culture attracted him:

Why should I not enjoy them? For whom have they been created if not for us?[20]

he writes in his *Paedagogos*. And again, in his *Stromata:*

One true God is the sole author of all beauty, whether it is Hellenic or whether it is ours.[21]

Clement takes, therefore, a different stance before the pagan philosophies of his day than did Irenaeus. He is not the rabid apologist eager to refute heretics. Rather, he seeks by a rational process to understand the truth perhaps contained in other views.

In short, fuller knowledge was to be found by dialog with one's adversaries. Like Socrates, Clement avoided any systematic doctrinal presentation to his disciples. He taught by stirring up questions in the minds of his listeners. Truth was an "encounter," and a good teacher prepared the environment for this event. Clement demonstrates more than any other early Christian thinker an optimism toward the world, its institutions and people. Though his life bore traces of the "bon vivant" or modern Bohemian (as Campenhausen pictures him), yet his openness towards the world stemmed from his basic belief in the unity of all human history as rooted in and permeated by the Logos, the Second Person of the Trinity, Jesus Christ.

Role of the Logos

One of Clement's key ideas is the unity of all history in the Logos, the Second Person of the Trinity, the Incarnate Word, Jesus Christ. All human history, whether pagan, Old Testament, or New Testament, had its significance in and through Christ. Christ was the Divine Pedagogue, sent by his Father to teach us the perfect way to heaven. Christ's activity as teacher was going on before he ever became man, and is still going on among even those who do not recognize him.

Clement's Logos, as described by R. B. Tollinton, is the "Creator, the Advisor of Deity, and Supreme Executor of the Designs of God."[22] He is the "archetypal light of light."[23] He is the Mediator between the eternal Godhead and the created cosmos. "No one knows the Father except the Son and him to whom the Son chooses to reveal him" (Mt. 11:27).

Clement places great stress on the abiding intention of the Godhead to create man and bring him to eternal life. Thus he stresses the continuity of man's nature and his supernatural destiny. Although we can find in Clement's writings clear distinctions between man's natural orientation towards this eternal life and the actual Divine Life already in him through supernatural grace, in general, unlike Irenaeus, he does not stress a natural affinity to the Logos by reason of the body and soul (image) and the state of divine likeness through grace.[24] His approach and choice of language were determined by the purpose he had in mind and the audience for whom he was writing. Clement combats Gnosticism, as did Irenaeus, yet he uses the very language and concepts of those systems. A Christian gnosis, therefore, is at the heart of Clement's doctrine. Divinization of man begins first through faith but is perfected by knowledge about God given as a special gift by Christ the Teacher (*cf.* Appendix, No. 10).

Like Irenaeus, Clement affirms that the Divine Word is the Image of God and that man has been created according to this Image. But unlike Irenaeus who held that man is made according to the Image, Jesus Christ, in that man possesses a human body and soul, Clement insists that the Image is the pre-existent Divine Word alone, according to which man is created (*cf.* Appendix, No. 11).

In his *Stromata,* Clement insists in a similar way that the Divine Word is the Image of God and man is "the image of the Image" insofar as he has a human *mind*. Through his mind man is drawn into communication with, and a likeness to, God (*cf.* Appendix, No. 12).

Man possesses the image of the Divine Image and hence the possibility of growing into a divine likeness, not through the body but through the mind. True to Platonic principles, this is the manner of assimilation into Divine Life (*cf.* Appendix, No. 13).

After having studied the rather thorough and systematic presentation of christology by Irenaeus, one may be dissatisfied with the sketchy doctrine of Clement. But Clement was a teacher who strove to meld the traditional teaching of Christianity with the philosophical structure of Greek philosophies. Thus the role of the Cosmic Christ of Clement is conceived primarily as a function of the Divine Logos manifesting himself to the minds of men, and thus assimilating men to the mind of God.

The historical Incarnation is supremely important in his thought, but it is not the only manifestation of the Logos among men. The Logos is communicating himself in various degrees to all men, at all times. The details of how the Logos speaks are not of primary importance: what matters are the principles and the ontological reality of divine assimilation with man that is effected through the various "theophanies" of the Logos. Whether the Logos was being manifested through the philosophers of old and the Old Testament prophets, or in the humanity of the historical Jesus Christ or in the Church, the important point for Clement is not the manner in which the Logos speaks but that the Logos is revealing the mind of God to men and giving them the opportunity of being assimilated into that Divine Life.

The purpose of the action of the Logos upon man and the

cosmos remains the same for Clement as for Irenaeus, and here we see the influence of the latter on the Alexandrian School. Clement writes: ". . . the Word of God became man, that thou mayest learn from man how man may become God."[25]

Clement is the first to use the word *theopoiein* (to divinize) to express in an unbiblical term a very biblical reality. Hellenic pagan literature spoke of a divinization by "association," but after Clement all Greek Fathers would use the term *theopoiesis* (divinization).

Divinization of man by the Logos was conceived by Clement as a process of assimilation into God's life by knowledge. Unfortunately, Clement's doctrine along with that of his disciple, Origen, has too often been interpreted as a moral intellectualism. Through a person-to-person revelation by God to the individual, God's infused knowledge assimilates the individual to God through love. Far from being a static knowledge or one of conceptualism, Clement's knowledge is the self-revelation of God by his very ontological presence living within man and drawing him into a similar ontological likeness to God. Its bestowal would depend upon God's gift, but man would have to purify himself from all self-centeredness by a vigorous asceticism (*praxis*) which would lead man to the state of "impassion" or freedom from inordinate passions. Briefly, Clement depicts this individual Christian Gnostic as one who imitates God as far as possible by practicing self-restraint, by ruling over his passions, and by living as virtuously as he can in word and deed (*cf.* Appendix, No. 14).

But the imitation of Christ was to proceed from the presence of the Divine Word living within us and revealing his *gnosis* or the inner meaning of things in reference to God's plan of creation. Because Clement's audience often was composed of non-Christians, we find this inner presence of Christ through grace rarely expressed with the realism of St. Paul or St. Ignatius of Antioch. Using the terminology that would be understood by his listeners, Clement describes this special gnosis or knowledge (which presupposes faith).

This (advanced) gnosis makes a man a perfect Christian and assimilates him to the likeness of God himself, even in this life. It is a gift that comes through Jesus Christ, that leads to moral and intellectual activity. It is an infused contemplation or knowledge of all creatures in their proper hierarchy under God. From this knowledge, man is led to moral activity which befits a son of God, indifferent to all inordinate movements, since the passions have come under the influence of this divinely regulating knowledge or wisdom.

Irenaeus had placed the emphasis on the presence of the Spirit, the giver of Divine Life, who effected the gradual transition in man's being from image to likeness of God. Clement, addressing himself to pagan thinkers, couches his christology in terms of Christ the Teacher of right moral conduct, and emphasizes man's initiative in imitating the virtues of Christ.

Clement's approach has singular relevance today, especially his doctrine of the mystical presence of the Divine Logos speaking within us, and his stress upon free, intelligent response by self-guided, morally good actions to make this presence grow within us by a constant increase in divine love.

Thus, through an assimilating knowledge, man loves God and all things in God. God gives him the power of creating a synthesis of all things in himself:

> . . . [Man has the] power of well-doing and of comprehending the whole creation and administration by the Lord, that, becoming pure in heart through the knowledge, which is by the Son of God, he may be initiated into the beatific vision face to face. . . .[26]

Clement realizes that one cannot describe this final process of assimilation of man to God which takes place through infused knowledge. This may be the reason why he never finished the third book after his *Protrepticos* (aimed at the heathens) and his *Paedagogos* (directed to the newly converted). It was to be called the *Didaskalos* (Teacher) and was to be directed towards the Gnostic Christians. Clement probably saw that the topic centered on the person-to-person relation of man to God in the higher flights of the unitive way, and that universal laws were therefore impossible to frame. He is content to describe this higher degree of assimilation to God in terms of contemplation and prophecy (*cf.* Appendix, No. 15).

Of all the Greek Fathers, Clement of Alexandria is the most unsystematic. Study of his ideas of the cosmic dimensions of Christ will yield no set doctrine. He was content to stir up questions and thus allow the individual to reach newer and richer insights. We conclude this section by quoting from one of the great authorities on Clement, R. B. Tollinton:

> Both in love and in understanding there is a certain identification of man's individual nature with the external fact or person, insofar as this is loved or understood. We are what we see. There is a certain kinship between the mind and what it apprehends. The final stage of vision, as Clement seems to conceive it, is the fulfillment of this principle in its completest term. We have already seen how the increasing likeness of the soul to God issues, at last, in a condition in which man *is* rather than resembles, the divine. It is the most intimate phase of his being's contact with supreme reality. It is more than knowledge, though it is less than ecstasy: "communion," perhaps, is the nearest equivalent in English, though the conception never loses a certain intellectualist tone. Man has intercourse with the divine and shares its holy nature. "The apprehensive vision of the pure in heart" is consummated in fellowship

with God. "We close with all we love," and with all we know. It is the Pauline conception of "seeing face to face," the entire accord and harmony that unites the soul to its kindred environment. Language is a poor medium for portraying the final intimacy of the soul with God. There is more, Clement knows, than he can say: it is significant that he can only conduct the spiritual traveler up to the vestibule of the sanctuary. The great High Priest must do the rest.[27]

III. ORIGEN

When Clement left the *Didascaleion,* the famous school of Alexandria founded by Pantaenus, to escape persecutions during the reign of Septimus Severus in 203, Origen, then only eighteen years old, assumed charge and began a scholarly career that produced one of the greatest minds early Christianity knew.[28] He was the Church's first great biblical exegete. He is considered the first speculative theologian who attempted to evolve the traditional doctrine of the Creed into a total system. He was the father of Christian asceticism and mysticism who greatly influenced Gregory of Nyssa, Evagrius of Pontus, and Pseudo-Dionysius. Through the last-named he greatly influenced St. Bernard, St. Bonaventure, Master Eckhart, Tauler, St. John of the Cross, and St. Teresa of Avila.

His great doctrinal synthesis is the *De Principiis* (Peri Archon). Here we find his fertile mind freely speculating on the data of Revelation, on "open questions" which at that early date of Christian theological development seem to us to touch some very basic doctrinal issues. Other works include his *Contra Celsum,* an eight volume apologetics in defense of Christianity against the pagan Platonist, Celsus; *De Oratione; An Exhortation to Martyrdom;* and *De Resurrectione.*

It is important in considering Origen's theology, therefore, to remember that many of his views represent his own personal way of articulating undefined questions. His system of theological thought was formulated in the free-thinking tradition of the Alexandrian school where pagan concepts, especially those drawn from the philosophies of Neo-Platonism, Gnosticism, and Stoicism, were used to express the Christian revelation.

We do not have his original texts since most of his works come down to us through the Latin translation (greatly revised) of Rufinus.[29] Also noteworthy in examining Origen's views is his constant use of myths, symbols, and metaphors. In regard to his cosmology, we must recall that the Church has officially condemned many of his views as heretical.

Still, we must remain open to the richness of Origen's insights, often locked within his Platonist usage of symbolic language. In his effort to render the non-phenomenal in phenomenal language, to express experiential facts of history such as the Fall and the effects of sin in terms of intellectual content, he often failed to do justice to his own thought. Platonists and Gnostics spoke of a pre-terrestrial existence. The author of the Book of Genesis spoke of fallen angels and fallen men. Origen, too, felt entitled to use such symbolic language (his theory of the Fall has been called a "Platonic myth") to express man's creation by God, his aversion from him, and his desire to return to him. To distinguish the literal from the metaphorical in his theory of the Fall and Redemption is a task which continues to tax the finest scholarly effort.

Regardless of his evident errors in treating certain questions not officially settled when he wrote, Origen assures us of his burning desire to be faithful always to the traditional teachings of the Church:

I would want to be known as a son of the Church, not as the founder of some heresy, but as one who carries the name of Christ. I would desire to bear this name which is in benediction on our earth. Here is my desire: that my spirit, as my works, give me the right to be called a Christian.[30]

Godhead and Logos

Origen begins his christology by treating the Logos in relation to the Divine Godhead. God the Father is the uncreated, eternal, transcendent source of all being. The Father eternally begets his Word who mirrors forth his own perfect wisdom (*cf.* Appendix, No. 16).

From his doctrine of the pre-existent Logos, Origen develops a relationship between the Logos and the created order. Recalling Paul's statement in Colossians 1:15 that "He is the image of the invisible God, the first-born of all creation, for in him all things were created," and also in Hebrews 1:3, "He reflects the glory of God and bears the very stamp of his nature, upholding the universe by his word of power," Origen shows that "it is through wisdom which is Christ that God holds power over all things, not only by His own authority, as Master, but also by the voluntary service of His subjects."[31] The Divine Logos is the perfect and immediate Image of the Father but mediates the creation of this world. All things are created through him.

Creation

If all things are created in and through the Logos, how could there ever be a time when God who is all powerful was not exercising his supreme dominion? Origen realizes that he is trespassing upon a mystery but is content to affirm: "We can therefore imagine no moment whatever when that power was not engaged in acts of well-doing; whence it follows that there always existed objects for this well-doing, namely, God's works or creatures."[32] He does not wish to affirm an eternal creation; unable to solve the dilemma, he insists on the immutability of God who could not begin to act and hence undergo a change (*cf.* Appendix, No. 18).

Origen sees the necessity of an eternal creation not only in order to preserve the immutability and dominion of God but also his divine justice. God is no "respecter of persons," and the inequalities and discrepancies in gifts and talents of individual human beings, Origen thought, could be explained only by the free choices of individuals.

Ultimately he was led to posit his theory of a Double Creation by his exegesis of the creation account in the Book of Genesis. Instead of seeing two accounts of one creation, he conceived them as two distinct creations: the first and eternal creative act whereby man is made according to the image of the Logos (Gen. 1:26–27), and the second and temporal creation, whereby man, as a result of a personal fall, is confined to a material body-existence (Gen. 2:7).

Apokatastasis

To describe this process of return to the original state of man-spirit, Origen uses the word *apokatastasis,* a restoration to a former condition. The role of Christ in bringing about the redemption of mankind is conceived primarily as that of a teacher. Evil, conceived as the lack of due perfection in a being, hence intimately associated with matter, the principle of potency, would eventually disappear. All men would finally reach their destined goal since Origen views sanctity as a matter of sufficient knowledge. God uses the whole material world, with the evil inherent in it, to educate us away from our fallen selves back to the dignity that once was ours, as sons of God.

Origen regards our redemption under a double aspect: Christ by his life of obedience to his heavenly Father, especially in his death on the cross, has conquered the evil powers; secondly, Christ, the Divine Logos, instructs us in our radical insufficiency before the heavenly Father. Considering God's infinite love for mankind and man's free will, Origen taught that the complete fulfillment of God's purpose in creating human spirits according to his Image, Christ the Logos, would be attained only when all created spirits eventually acknowledge his supremacy and love him for himself. The time will come, as Paul insisted, when God will be all in all (I Cor. 15:28), when the whole of creation will reach its fulfillment, or, as Origen reads the Divine Mind, be restored to its original integrity.[33]

Quoting St. Paul's phrase that "the whole creation shall be delivered from the bondage of corruption into the liberty of the glory of the sons of God," Origen describes the recapitulation process as the liquidation of all corruptible bodies (*cf.* Appendix, Nos. 18 and 19).

The Fifth Ecumenical Council, Constantinople II (553), condemned the doctrine of *apokatastasis* in these words: "If anyone teaches the mythical doctrine of the pre-existence of the soul and the *apokatastasis* that follows from it, let him be anathema" (Canon I). This canon condemns two assertions: that human souls existed before human bodies, and that all human beings must eventually be saved. Clearly, the teaching of St. Paul and St. Irenaeus that Christ will recapitulate all things in the parousia (Eph. 1:10) was not condemned. *How* this will be done remains a mystery, but Origen, stressing the mercy of God, posits the salvation of all men with the eventual disappearance of evil.

Christ's Role

At the basis of the writings of Origen, as of Clement, is the theory of gnosis. His aim is to bring about a deeper understanding of the faith, to look beyond the sensible appearances of material phenomena in an effort to penetrate to the inner reality. He placed little stress, compared to Irenaeus, on the Incarnation, mainly because the visible is no more than a sacrament of the invisible. Christ has been working in the entire universe from the beginning of time. The temporal appearance of the humanity of Christ provides simply one of many ways in the history of salvation to contact the Logos. We find the Logos revealing himself to us on different levels according to our capabilities, and these are actualized by the purification of our sense knowledge. Everything in creation begins and ends with Christ, hence Origen does not limit Christ's activities only to his historical incarnation. He postulates three analogous "incarnations" of the Logos: in the historical Christ, in Sacred Scripture, and in the Church.

In all three manifestations of the Logos, men apprehend him in a threefold manner: some judge only by the literal, external, phenomenal appearances; others see beyond to the moral implications behind the sensible that lead them to a more intense life of virtue; but the man of faith, whom the Holy Spirit instructs, pierces beyond mere appearances and moral implications to encounter the mind of God revealed through the inner *logos* or principle of harmony, ordering a given creature back to the first creative act of God. Origen illustrates this by his doctrine on scriptural exegesis which he builds up according to the threefold division of literal or somatic, moral or psychic, spiritual or pneumatic, interpretations (*cf.* Appendix, No. 20).

The somatic is the literal sense of phenomena which manifests God revealing himself, either through the written literal word or through nature or through our individual sense experience. The psychic sense is the moral sense that we derive beyond the literal interpretation. The highest, the pneumatic, is the spiritual sense, the mind of God hidden beyond the phenomena. Through an infused gnosis, one's speculative and practical intellect is brought to resemble the mind of Christ. Christ is virtue, and by living virtuously one lives in Christ. The gnosis brings about a resemblance and imitation of Christ. To be in Christ means to be immersed in Christ in a very real and concrete way, though difficult to describe. It is not simply to model ourselves on the example of Christ, but it is to allow the Master, the Teacher (*Didaskalos*), present within us to teach, to reveal himself, the Logos, as the summation of all reality.

Origen develops a whole spirituality of the Logos around Christ as the intermediary between absolute unity of the Trinity and multiplicity of creatures, at times to the extent of apparently subordinating Christ to God the Father.[34] Redemption lies in Christ's victory over the powers of evil that hold mankind in captivity. The world is regarded by Origen as the scene of the great educative process carried on by the Logos, the Master and Healer who gradually illumines free creatures to return to the good. Everything in life is a means of education. The universe is a vast *didaskaleion* in which everything contributes to the education of free human beings.

Final Transfiguration

Through prayer and good works man cooperates with the Holy Spirit, the *dynamis* or power of God working within man to draw him into the likeness of the Logos. The process of man's divinization is only complete in the last resurrection. The thought of Origen on the future of the human body in man's final transfiguration has been disputed by scholars through centuries, beginning with Jerome, Epiphanius, and Theophilos, each of whom denied that Origen held the resurrection of the body or at least berated him strongly for his confused doctrine on this subject. In the preface to Book I of his *First Principles* (*De Principiis*), Origen clearly confesses: "Further there will be a time for the resurrection of the dead when this body which is now 'sown in corruption,' shall 'rise in incorruption' and that which is 'sown in dishonor' shall 'rise in glory.'"[35]

There is no doubt that Origen uses the word *body* and *flesh* in quite ambiguous ways. We have already shown that he considers matter as pure potency, a receptacle for receiving individuating qualities but with no quality of its own. This potency is ever undergoing change; yet a substratum remains to give us continuity and identity. This he calls the "corporeal form."

Thus, besides matter or potency (and in this sense Origen is correct; eventually all matter, i.e., potency *will* cease to exist) there are "corporeal forms." Even angelic spirits possess these forms, their principle of individuation. Origen maintains that in the final resurrection the terrestrial form, subject to unruly concupiscence, self-centeredness, potency, and indetermination, will cease to exist, or rather will be transfigured into a "celestial" form while the "corporeal" form, giving identity and continuity with the earthly being, will continue to exist.

In baptism man has been buried with Christ and reborn by the Spirit. In the final resurrection all disordered self-love will be purged from man, and in perfect conformity to the will of God, imitating Jesus Christ in his humanity, man will participate, body included, in the resurrection of Christ. The Logos' work of teaching men to see God in all things will reach its perfection. In Paul's words, I Corinthians 15:28, repeated constantly by Origen, God will be "all in all," but we will be individuals who will know God as an individual Person in all individual things (*cf.* Appendix, No. 21).

Thus the end follows the pattern of the beginning as outlined in the paradisal state of the Book of Genesis. Evil will no longer exist, for man's will shall be drawn so strongly by the magnetism of God's goodness as no longer to turn away from him. Yet man will enjoy maximum freedom for it will be he who determines himself to choose only God as his final end and to choose all things in him.[36]

Origen describes the beatific vision in terms of contemplating and understanding God but within the framework of an unfolding process (*cf.* Appendix, No. 22).

No longer will the Logos function as our teacher and mediator with the Father, but through a mysterious willed-offering of ourselves in knowledge and love we will be assimilated into him without at the same time losing our own identity. All the potencies of our first creation "according to the Image," that is, Jesus Christ, will then be realized in our likeness to him.

Then all of those who will have reached God through the Word who is near him, will engage in a unique activity—to comprehend God so that they, so formed in the knowledge of the Father, all together will become exactly one Son as now only the Son knows the Father.[37]

Man's destiny will then be fulfilled—constantly to say "yes" to the heavenly Father as his Only-begotten Son did perfectly during his earthly existence and does throughout eternity. Man will then mirror forth the *mind of the mind* of the Father in his own regard as the realized image that he is through an assimilation to the Logos. Then St. Peter's words will be fulfilled:

See how all the gifts that make for life and holiness in us belong to his divine power; come to us through fuller knowledge of him whose own glory and sovereignty have drawn us to himself! Through him God has bestowed on us high and treasured promises; you are to share the divine nature, with the world's corruption, the world's passions, left behind (II Pet. 1:3–4).

IV. ST. ATHANASIUS

St. Athanasius was considered by the early Church as the Father of Orthodoxy who, in his witness to the truth at the great Councils, and through his innumerable writings, brilliantly limned the mind of the traditional Church.[38] He breathed a holy zeal to teach in strict accord with tradition; we find in him the pristine doctrines of Ignatius and Irenaeus living again. He sought only the revealed truth and used Greek philosophy as a means to convey that truth accurately. His theology was far removed from the speculations of an Origen, so eager to put all dogmas into a metaphysical system.

Archibald Robertson evaluates Athanasius as theologian and thinker and finds his greatness in his all-pervasive view of Christ's redemption:

Athanasius was not a systematic theologian; that is, he produced no many-sided theology like that of Origen or Augustine. He had no interest in theological speculation, none of the instincts of a schoolman or philosopher. His theological greatness lies in his firm grasp of soteriological principles, in his resolute subordination of everything else, even the formula *homoousia* [identical in nature, consubstantial], to the central fact of Redemption, and to what that fact implied as to the Person of the Redeemer. He goes back from the logos of the philosophers to the Logos of St. John, from the God of the philosophers to God in Christ reconciling the world to Himself.[39]

Perhaps no other early Christian writer focused his particular point of view upon the exigencies of the Church of his day as closely as did St. Athanasius. For forty-five years every word he wrote was a zealous defense, against the heretical Arians and the non-Christians, of the divinity and equality of Jesus Christ with the Father.[40] He shows that Christ is the Divine Logos, the Image of the Father (Col. 1:15) but a likeness of absolute equality, a perfection mirroring the total being of the Father. The Logos is begotten, "engendered," but not extrinsic nor foreign to the Father. The Father rejoices in his Image because he finds himself entirely reflected there. Creatures, including man, participate in existence received from God the Creator. To participate in being is to bespeak a relationship to the Divine Logos. The Logos, on the contrary, does not participate in but *is* the *ontos on,* the really real, the true one, from whom all other creatures have their being and their reality, their truthfulness. The Logos unites all things in a harmony, one with another, and brings them all back to God. The Logos is the raison d'être of all created beings. In his *Contra Gentes,* Athanasius expressed this harmony and unity by using the example of a musician blending on his lyre low, high, and medium tones to produce a single melody (cf. Appendix, No. 23).

In order to see more in detail the cosmic dimensions of Christ in the writings of St. Athanasius, we must examine his doctrine of creation, sin, and divinization. It can be said that the concept of grace in the Greek Fathers is inseparable from their ideas on creation, sin, Christ, and the Holy Spirit. Grace, for Athanasius, is the condescending love of God for man, showing itself in creation and redemption or restoration. Regarded at its source, Grace *is* the Logos, operating constantly within man's universe. Only if we remember this dynamic concept of the Logos-as-Grace will we penetrate somewhat into Athanasius' rich views of incarnational theology.

Creation

Athanasius witnesses to the immanence of God in creation by showing how actively God is involved in the creation and fulfillment of man. We have already seen that Athanasius protects the transcendence of God by insisting that God alone does not participate in existence but *is* existence, without beginning or end, by reason of his very Being, infinite and perfect.

Yet it is through his Logos that God creates, as after a pattern, giving all creatures their proper place in relation to the Logos. And the causality of the Logos exercised upon creation is more than exemplarity. The Logos is present *in* his creation by his activity, sustaining and directing all creatures to their fulfillment (cf. Appendix, No. 24).

The world can never be without the immanent presence of

the Logos, for each creature, by participating in existence as a finite, contingent being, is dependent upon his activity for its continued existence and growth in perfection. The Logos' support of creatures in their existence is a grace (*charis*), the uncreated energies of God throbbing through all creatures and thus sustaining them in being. Without this sustenance, creatures would fall into non-existence:

> For they could not have endured His absolute, unmitigated nature, and His splendor from the Father, unless, condescending with the Father's love for man, He had supported them, and brought them into subsistence.[41]

Added to each created nature (*phusis*) is the grace of God's inner presence and activity supporting each being and drawing up "the whole circle of creatures into divine adoption," as Cardinal Newman describes it.[42] But God is present to and acting in creatures, in different ways, according to each one's degree of participation in being. Man, the crowning point of God's creation, participates in the Logos' sustaining power through the highest grace of God given to creatures—here Athanasius introduces his doctrine of image.

Athanasius' doctrine of the creation of man differs somewhat in emphasis from what we have seen in other Greek Fathers, due to his absorption in combating Arianism. Man is not the image of God. Athanasius uses the image doctrine to prove the divinity of Jesus Christ. Thus, the Son alone is the perfect Image of the Father. If he mirrors forth the Father perfectly, he also must be divine. As the Father is invisible, so the Son, *qua* Image, is invisible. The Logos-Image is eternal and transcendent, as the pre-existent Second Person of the Trinity. As Image of the Father, the Logos is outside any time-space relationship that touches his incarnational mission. This is clearly highlighted in Athanasius' *De Decretis* (cf. Appendix, No. 25).

Thus, for Athanasius, the Logos is the Image of the Father, without immediate relation to the created order. Having firmly established the *homoousia,* identity of nature, between the Father and the Son, Athanasius considers the Logos' relationship to human beings.

Man is created by God "according to the Image" (Divine Logos)—*kat'eikona.* Athanasius fixes firmly this terminology that had been used, as we have already seen, by Irenaeus, Clement, and Origen. Man participates in a relationship to the Logos that grows by man's perception of the divine presence of the Logos living within him. In two striking passages Athanasius shows that here lies man's greatest perfection, having been created *kat'eikona,* namely, according to the Image (which is Jesus Christ). Man is logical (*logikos*) when he corresponds to the idea in the mind of God by living in imitation of the Divine Logos. This is brought about by grace (*charis*), which is a living relationship of man to the Logos (cf. Appendix, Nos. 26 and 27).

There is an equation among these concepts of *kat'eikona, logikos,* and *charis.* The gift of grace that God gives man as a rational being allows him to grow by knowledge of God to a greater assimilation "according to the Image" of Christ. Following Origen, Athanasius affirms that for a man to be a true man, a logical being, living to the limit of his rational nature, he must possess Grace, that is, the Logos dwelling within him and teaching him the Wisdom of God and all creatures in relationship to God. The *kat'eikona* given to the first man is more than the indestructible image that Irenaeus and Origen affirmed.

For Athanasius it is a gratuitous gift that includes not only the ability of man, possessing an intellect, to open himself to God's truth and to live accordingly, but also it embraces all we understand by supernatural. Man has been given a portion of the power of God's Word which allows man with his reason to reflect on the Word within himself (cf. Appendix, No. 29).

Sin

Sin is one of the greatest realities for Athanasius and he shows the cosmic effects of man's refusal to live "according to the Image." The impress of the divine is lost. Man lives without grace in a cosmic condition that Athanasius calls *phthora,* corruption. A process of disintegration takes place as a result of sin which is described by Athanasius as a state wherein man loses the divine life of eschatological incorruptibility within him and becomes mortal, corruptible, and is "liable to the affections proper to nature."[43]

We merely note a minor inconsistency. In discussing the fate of the *kat'eikona* after sin has entered into man's life, he states that the "according-to-the-Image" is not lost but is covered over by sin as dust covers over the lineaments of a picture. This seems to us inconsistent—surely the man in sin is not merely a "dusty" image of God; he is simply *not* God's image, and when Athanasius wishes to stress the absolute gratuity of redemption, he insists that sin has *completely stripped* fallen man of grace *kat'eikona.* He insists upon the radical opposition between sin and grace, death and life, corruption and incorruption.

In another passage that will call to our mind the images used by Plato in his allegory of the Cave in the *Republic,*

Athanasius compares sin to idolatry that *drives out of our being* the Image of God according to which we have right reason to judge other creatures with the wisdom of God (cf. Appendix, No. 29).

Athanasius has a highly developed sense of the corporateness of the human race and can offer us a much needed corrective to our faulty understanding of the Tridentine canon on original sin. Adam's sin clouded his own vision of God present in his soul as well as in all of creation and finally in the *kat'eikona*. ". . . as Adam had transgressed, his sin reached unto all men,"[44] but not in the sense of a concrete sin attributed to the offspring of Adam. Adam's sin brought about the state that Athanasius succinctly calls *phthora* (corruption). Into this state every man is born. All men suffer, therefore, the sin of Adam. Yet each man is guilty for his own sins. Each man's yielding to self-idolatry brings more of "corruption" into the world. Life according to the Image, the Logos, is diminished, not only in the individual, but through him in the sub-human cosmos, which now is no longer harmoniously moving back to God. Athanasius summarizes the state of humanity and the absolute need for the Incarnate Word:

> The nature of man did not change. The difference is that man has clouded the light, hindered the plan of God and now the Son must come to replace man in the correct, logical path to beatitude and immortality.[45]

Christ the Restorer of Man

Into a world turned away from God through self-love, the Logos enters and takes upon himself the same condition as the rest of man. He submits his human nature to the same phthora or general corruption that infects man like a deadly virus. He inserts himself into the cosmos as a living enzyme, giving Divine Life through his grace. He comes to restore man to the *kat'eikona* and thus to raise up true sons of God.

For Athanasius, Christ is the Life, as expressed so often in St. John's Gospel. It is this that constitutes his main argument against the Arians who denied the divinity of Jesus Christ. If Christ is not consubstantial with the Father, we are not deified in him. But because he divinizes us, gives us God's own life, he must be God. Again we see the scope of the Incarnation, succinctly expressed in Irenaeus:

> He took a created and human body in order, as Creator, to renew it, to deify it in Himself, and thus to lead us all to the Kingdom of Heaven in imitation of Him.[46]

The Redemption that Christ came to effect is a work of unity. The world was planned by God as a unity and Christ inserts himself into this universe precisely to bring it back to its unity. By their contact with Christ, all material things take on a new dignity. This unity is supernaturalized, intensified, and strengthened by Christ's Incarnation. The hypostatic union, the meeting of the divine with humanity, is applied through the Incarnation to us. Christ's activities are being prolonged among us. But Christ's activities are viewed exclusively in the area of restoring us humans to the dignity from which we fell away through sin. This is the sole purpose of the Incarnation, Athanasius tells us: God the Son became man in order that men might become the sons of God (cf. Appendix, No. 30).

Thus, on nearly every page in his work against the Arians

St. Athanasius presents his doctrine of the divinization of the faithful. We are changed, raised up, adopted, deified, through the union of grace which the Incarnate Word gives us.

No Father before Athanasius so clearly and with such prolific and strong insistence preached the physical concept of man's divinization through Christ. Irenaeus, as we saw, developed this Johannine and Pauline stress on Christ as a physical life living within man, "re-created" through baptism and a conversion of heart by a constant yielding to the Logos speaking within man. But Athanasius makes it a synthetic principle that provides for an integral theology of the work of the Trinity in relation to man. He identifies divinization of man with man's filiation towards the heavenly Father. This gift proceeds from the Father as the source of all good and is conferred by the Logos through the operation of the Spirit.

A beautiful summation of what Christ accomplished by his physical insertion into the stream of human life is presented by Athanasius in his treatise against the Arians (cf. Appendix, No. 31).

The Divine Word takes upon himself a human body and thus is able in a perfect human nature to overcome the "corruption" that was due it through the corporate sins of men. He brings about a radical change, making it possible for man to receive again the life that is proper to God's own nature, namely, immortality and incorruptibility. The activities of Christ in the world are viewed almost exclusively as effecting a new incarnation within each man so that every human being can be divinized "according to the Image." H. Sträter summarizes this thought:

In the very existence of the Man-God, the redivinization of humanity is accomplished in its source. It is in the make-up of the person of Christ that for Athanasius the Redemption has its center of gravity. The fact of the inhabitation of the Logos in humanity has made it possible for humanity to penetrate into the divine life. Such is the fundamental thought of his soteriology in which he evidently depends on St. Irenaeus.[47]

Athanasius stresses so strongly the power of Christ and the change he produced in mankind by the Incarnation that at times he gives the impression that Christ has automatically redeemed us by restoring us to what man was before he fell into the state of "corruption." Such an impression is created by his emphasis on the uniqueness of the incarnational act, but it does not render Christ's sacrificial act of redemption of no avail, nor does it render man's cooperation no longer necessary.

Christ restores mankind to the *kat'eikona* relationship that man possessed before sin but he adds a new grace, a new incarnational relationship between man and the Word-made-flesh, a grace that was not given to Adam and the rest of mankind before the Incarnation. But this grace of deification by physical contact with the resurrected Jesus Christ presupposed also man's cooperation. The continuance and growth of this relationship to the Incarnate Logos living within man through grace are dependent on man's openness to his presence and readiness to live according to his commands. The life of virtue in imitation of the actions of Jesus Christ is man's proper response (cf. Appendix, No. 32).

Man must purify himself of all self-love and then give witness to the knowledge derived by contemplating the Logos living within him through a life of constant virtue. In his *Vita Antonii,* a classic of Christian asceticism, Athanasius outlines the way of asceticism that every serious Christian must follow in order to live "according to the Image." Typical of the synergy of divine operations and human cooperation is the following text:

> Truly the Lord worked with this man—He who for our sakes took on flesh and gave to His body victory over the devil. Thus all who fight in earnest can say, "Not I, but the Grace of God with me."[48]

In this work, addressed primarily to dedicated souls to stimulate them to Christian perfection, we can find passages that seem to indicate that man, by merely willing it, can become sanctified. But Athanasius here emphasizes the role that man must play by cooperating with God. Neither he nor his readers forgot for a moment that God begins the process of our deification and continually directs it.

The Work of the Holy Spirit

One final point needs to be discussed in order to have a well-rounded picture of Athanasius' theology of man's restoration in Christ: the role assigned in man's sanctification to the Holy Spirit. However, we can hardly present here Athanasius' full pneumatology. It is in his four letters to Serapion that Athanasius seeks to prove the divinity of the Holy Spirit against the heretical *Pneumatochoi*. He appeals to their belief that the Holy Spirit brings about man's divinization. If this is so, he cannot be a creature, argues Athanasius, but must be God since he gives God's life to men. Athanasius draws a parallel between the activities of the Holy Spirit in the first Incarnation of the Logos through the Virgin Mary and the divinization of men. The Holy Spirit formed the Logos in the womb of the Virgin. It is through the Spirit that the Logos deifies men, makes them sons of God (cf. Appendix, Nos. 33 and 34).

The Holy Spirit, Athanasius argues from Holy Scripture, is the stamp or seal of perfection, who completes and perfects the work begun by the Logos. "The Son condescends to the imperfect, but the Holy Spirit is the seal of the perfect."[49]

But for Athanasius, the God who creates and effects man's fulfillment is the total Holy Trinity. All creation and fulfillment of creatures are the work of grace, God's condescending love toward men; hence it is the total Godhead, God Triune, who acts (cf. Appendix, No. 35).

In conclusion, we have seen Athanasius' consistent emphasis on the Incarnation of the Divine Logos who is the perfect Image of the Father; according to this Image we have been created and are destined to reach our fulfillment. We are somewhat shocked at his little interest in the material world as such. Yet we understand this because of his overwhelming absorption with the Divine Logos. Athanasius is not concerned with the sub-human cosmos in itself, or how it participates in the Logos, but he is concerned, among finite creatures, only with human beings created according to the Logos. The rest of non-human creation is only subordinate and instrumental in helping man to be restored to the *kat'eikona,* lost by sin and restored and increased through grace.

Less interested, therefore, than Irenaeus in the total recapitulation of the whole material universe in Christ, Athanasius emphasizes the presence and activity of Christ immersed in this universe, but working through his divine immanent life in human beings to restore them to the divine filiation destined for them in the first moment of their creation.

The whole earth is full of Christ, his doctrine permeates everywhere, his actions transcend our concepts. By his hidden, immanent power, Athanasius affirms, Christ's action has transformed the multitude of barbarous people into a God-fearing race, replacing savagery with temperance, virginity, and charity:

> Since the Savior produces such effects in men . . . can anyone still doubt that Christ lives, yes, that He is Life itself?[50]

Christ's work in the cosmos is conceived by Athanasius as a continuance of his resurrection. His victory in his own resurrection marks the beginning of his present work in the world of men, which he, through his Spirit, ever triumphantly continues in order to break down sin's power and to deify men. By his emphasis on the *kat'eikona* as man's true nature, Athanasius joins the natural and the supernatural into a unity of salvation history as seen from God's viewpoint. Other Fathers, especially Cyril of Alexandria, would take Athanasius' doctrine of the centrality of the Logos, not only in restoring but in fulfilling man, and would develop more in detail a theology of how Christ's Incarnation still exerts its power to unite the entire regenerated human race with God in Christ. But it is St. Athanasius more than any other Father who has shown us that man's perfection lies in *Another,* according to whose Image we have been created and in whom we are fulfilled.

V

COSMIC CHRISTOLOGY IN THE POST-NICENE GREEK FATHERS

I. ST. GREGORY NAZIANZEN

The transition from the existential "life-theology" of Athanasius and Hilary to the final stage of early Christian christology was effected primarily by the Cappadocian School under the influence of Basil the Great (c. 330–379), Gregory of Nazianzus (c. 329–389), and Basil's brother, Gregory of Nyssa (c. 355–394). St. Basil stressed in his spiritual and theological writings the ascetical efforts involved in the process of sanctification. Written largely for monks, we find very few new insights into the life and activity of Christ on a cosmic scale. St. Gregory of Nazianzus, Basil's friend who later occupied the See of Constantinople but resigned in the face of political intrigues and retired to a monastery, does give us new insights into a personalism, an I-Thou relationship, with Christ, truly living within us.[1]

St. Gregory of Nazianzus, alone, of all the early Greek Fathers is accorded the title of "the Theologian." Despite the fact that he had given no systematic presentation of Christian doctrine, his theological works enjoyed the highest authority by 400 A.D. in the West as well as in the East. Possessing a delicate, even poetic nature, which he used as a powerful oratorical tool, he received a broad and deep education in Hellenistic humanism and had a rare ability of expressing in concise formulas the most abstruse Trinitarian and christological truths. Unlike his great friend, the practical-minded St. Basil, Gregory loved solitude and was easily dismayed by conflict in the world. Yet he had his share of human vanity, particularly in regard to his oratorical powers, which moved him to accept ecclesiastical positions of great responsibility, especially the See of Constantinople, for which he was little suited.

These characteristics help us to understand his approach to Christ. From now on, except for St. Maximus the Confessor, most of the Greek Fathers would follow much of St. Gregory's approach to Christ—a deep personalism, an I-Thou relationship with Christ living ontologically within the individual through grace. But eclipsed for a time is the strong cosmic dimension that was seen in the Fathers before Gregory, especially in the writings of Irenaeus.

Gregory merits the title of theologian for his clarity in exposing the orthodox doctrine of the Trinity and of Christ against the three prevalent heresies of the second half of the fourth century: Eunomianism, a form of Arianism; Apollonarianism, a christological heresy that denied Christ a full rational human soul; and Macedonianism, which denied that the Holy Spirit was truly divine. He clearly fixed the terms *essence* and *hypostasis* so that theologians could discuss the nature of the Godhead as clearly distinct from the properties of the three Persons. "We use," he writes, "in an orthodox sense the terms one essence and three hypostases, the one to denote the nature of the Godhead, the other the properties of the three."[2] Within the Trinity, beyond motion and time, a unity in essence is achieved within a diversity of persons (cf. Appendix, No. 36).

The Trinity has created man according to the Divine Image and has placed him in the material world as a "microcosm," possessing everything that the material world possesses, and yet he is destined for a life in God. Man stands between God and the rest of material creation (cf. Appendix, No. 37).

The Fall of Man

True to his Platonic training, Gregory describes man's greatness in terms of contemplation, an assimilation into the likeness of God through an infused knowledge given by God himself. He describes, also, man's fall as one of anticipating too soon the fruits of contemplation. Man unjustly anticipated, as though already attained, his assimilation to God (cf. Appendix, No. 38).

Man was given a composite nature, a material and a spiritual part. He has been given a free-will (*autexousia*) "in order that God might belong to him as the result of his choice, no less than to him who had implanted the seeds of it."[3] Thus, man was to develop his divine potentiality gradually through his free choices. Man was not to anticipate the degree of his evolutionary process as he grew slowly into a son of God. But, in the Fall, man refused to submit himself to God's plan of development. Though fallen, man gains God's mercy and the history of his salvation begins.

Recapitulation in Christ

God guides man "by word, by law, by prophets, by benefits, by threats, by plagues, by waters, by fires, by wars, by victories, by defeats, by signs in heaven and signs in the air and in the earth and in the sea, by unexpected changes of men, of cities, of nations,"[4] and, finally, the most sure remedy to call man back to God, the Word of God himself becomes Incarnate. Gregory is overwhelmed by the mystery of the Word-become-flesh. He cries out in wonderment, ". . . O strange conjunction! the self-existent comes into being; the uncreated is created, that which cannot be contained is contained, by the intervention of an intellectual soul, mediating between the Deity and the corporeity of the flesh . . ." (cf. Appendix, No. 39).

In order that man might be elevated to the destiny predetermined for him by God, God had to condescend to man's world. The gulf was spanned between the unapproachable Divinity and finite, sinful man by the Word Incarnate. Man's elevation is never completed in this life; it remains but partially fulfilled, capable of greater completion, yet to come, when "we shall know even as we are known." From God's ineffable condescension to men, Gregory draws the principle that he used against the Apollonarians, and which other Fathers would constantly echo: "What is not assumed by Christ is not saved; that alone is saved which is united with God."[5]

This was the source, for Gregory, of Christian optimism and the basis for an intimate union with Christ, not merely spiritual, but total, in every part of our being. The work of Christ in the world begins in the depths of man's being, by his gradual transformation into a son of God. The Incarnation is dynamically viewed (not simply as an historical event in time and space) as Christ's activity, now continuing even in the interior life of man as Christ renews the face of the earth.

Gregory expresses in vigorous, forceful language this reality of incorporation of the individual with Christ through a most personal, intimate union. "My Christ," he constantly repeats, "is my constant companion. To live with Christ is to act with Him."

I must be buried with Christ; I must rise with Christ; I must be a co-heir with Christ; I must become a son of God; I must become God.[6]

Finally, be crucified-with-Christ, be put-to-death-with-Him, be buried-with-Him, in order to rise-with-Him, to be glorified-with-Him, and to reign-with-Him."[7]

The events of Christ's life on this earth, even his miracles, are being renewed in our souls. The Passion of Christ is taking place today. He is suffering today in his members suffering with him. He sustains them by his divine life. The image of Christ is "recovered" in us by our actions *with* Christ. To live *with* Christ is to act as a new creature with him (cf. Appendix, No. 40).

Finally, after man has relived Christ's mysteries, or better, after Christ has relived his mysteries in man, man's final fulfillment, as Gregory portrays it, is to "lastly, be crucified and share His death and burial gladly that thou mayest rise with Him and be glorified with Him and reign with Him."[8] That such an introspective mystic as Gregory neglects to develop in detail the activities of Christ in the cosmos is not surprising. Through the cross man is purified, and shares to some degree the visions of God and his created world that Christ in his humanity possessed.

Indwelling of the Holy Spirit

Through asceticism man prepares himself for this illuminating vision, the putting on of the "mind of Christ," but it is the Holy Spirit who effects it. Like Athanasius, upon whom he relied heavily for his doctrine on the Holy Spirit, Gregory is only secondarily concerned with the Spirit's influence within the world. His primary interest is to defend the divinity of the Holy Spirit against the heretics, and this he does chiefly by adducing the effect of the Spirit upon man—a quasi-deification. In a highly rhetorical passage that mingles a great deal of counter-pointing, Gregory describes the role of the Holy Spirit as "sanctifying, not sanctified, measuring, not measured, shared, not sharing, filling, not filled, containing, not contained, inherited, glorified, reckoned with the Father and the Son. . . ." It is primarily in Baptism that the Holy Spirit, through the Church, begins the process of restoring man to his proposed fullness. Baptism gives a man a new creation (cf. Appendix, Nos. 41 and 42).

Gregory follows the general doctrine on Baptism in the Eastern Church of the 4th century, that the elevation to a new, divine life is chiefly an enlightenment produced by the Holy Spirit. Of course, it is presupposed that Baptism is being received by a mature adult who can accept the illumination and thereafter live according to the newly acquired vision.

To conclude, we have seen that Gregory of Nazianzus, in concise, even poetic, formulas, has expressed the work of God in restoring and fulfilling mankind in a vibrant man-to-

Trinity personal relationship. Through the consciousness that the Trinitarian presence brought to him, man moved through virtuous living from a partial vision of God in the world to a fuller vision that led to an assimilation, realized completely only in the eternal vision to come. By relating his fundamental soteriological principle ("nothing is redeemed unless Christ has assumed it") to not only man's composition of body and soul but to all facets of human existence and activity, Gregory opened the way again for an incarnational presence of Christ within man's cosmic world, though he did not himself produce a systematic theology of Christ's cosmic presence.

II. ST. GREGORY OF NYSSA

Of the three Cappadocian Fathers, St. Gregory of Nyssa brings to his writings the best speculative mind, equipped with an exact, encyclopedic knowledge of the sciences of his day.[9] He was a thinker, a philosopher, and had a talent for systematizing abstract thought. He drew heavily upon Platonic and Stoic writers and was an ardent disciple of Origen, though he rejected the latter's extreme form of *apokatastasis*.

Gregory joined his brother, St. Basil the Great, in a lifetime doctrinal struggle against Arian and Sabellian heresies. He distinguished himself in the Ecumenical Council of Constantinople (381) through his clear and orthodox presentation of the doctrine on the Trinity and the Incarnation. "In the roll of the Nicene Fathers, there is no more honored name than that of Gregory of Nyssa. Indeed, such is the esteem in which he has been held that some have not hesitated to call him 'the Father of the Fathers.' "[10] His writings made him the central authority in the Eastern Churches of the fourth and fifth centuries.

Eternal Now

St. Gregory of Nyssa has special interest for modern theologians because of his unified, synthetic vision of the history of salvation. Depending heavily on the ideas of Origen and yet correcting many of his more evident errors, Gregory gives us a valuable insight into God's relationship with mankind.

He first establishes the absolute, transcendent position of God, declaring that "God is essentially He who transcends all knowledge and is outside the grasp of the mind."[11] God freely determines in his "eternal now" to create the whole cosmos with man in the center. In the divine plan there is a unity between the beginning, the unfolding through time, and the final consummation. God's all-seeing knowledge and power and the actual fulfillment of his plan through the gradual evolution of creation are not separated but interdependent. Gregory sees the reality of God's creation as primarily present in his transcendent eternal decree. We might call it a fourth-dimensional view that allows him to view the beginning (not chronologically but in the order of God's finality) as coterminous with the end, the *eschaton.*

Measured history, therefore, is a dynamic process, a fulfillment of the divine unified idea of the cosmos, wherein the end coincides with the beginning; God's idea of the created world, which he possesses from all eternity, will be realized in the pleroma exactly as he has conceived it, outside of time. Thus, one of the great hurdles of Western theological thinking is cleared, namely, the union of nature and supernature. Man is viewed *in toto* and is never outside of God's redemptive plan.

Roger Leys comments on Gregory's thought:

> Gregory is unaware of a state of pure nature. The world has been created in grace. But it is also certain that this grace was not part

of the essence of creation . . . that it is conferred on him as a pre-existent subject, without doubt not according to a temporal succession but according to an ontological consideration.[12]

This "ontological consideration" permeates Gregory's anthropology. He finds recorded in the Book of Genesis the reality of creation, as viewed by God. "God created *man,*" for Gregory, means not the first man, but the ontological "everyman." In his comment on the Genesis account, we see the influence of Origen, in this first instance, not as an historical event, but rather as an ontological presentation of man, as seen in the creative decree of God. The first man in the Genesis account, Adam, stands for universal man, everyman, who has been made by God to his image and likeness. Thus, the first man and the final, perfected man are alike (cf. Appendix, No. 43).

We see, therefore, that this first man of Genesis, in Gregory's thinking, is not an individual but is the ontological nature of man, man as willed by God; and hence the "beginning" man is identical with the fulfilled, completed man. Gregory continues in his same work on the "Creation of Man," insisting that before Adam, historically the first man, man's nature in the mind of God was already perfect and realized (cf. Appendix, No. 44).

In the Book of Genesis, God determines to create man, and the total nature of man in his perfect form coincided with the concrete, perfected individual human being. In commenting on the six days of creation, Gregory makes much of the Hebrew phrase *bereshit,* "in the beginning." The Septuagint translates it *en arche,* but Gregory finds in the Aquila Greek version a stronger argument for his view. The Hebrew phrase is translated in Greek as "en kephalaio," meaning, "in the total ensemble." The unity of God's creation, brought out by Gregory's phrase "in the total ensemble," indicates the simultaneity of all creation in the mind of God (cf. Appendix, No. 45).

The unity between God's plan conceived in eternity and the fulfillment of this plan through the gradual activities of God and man in the created world gives to Gregory's vision a very dynamic aspect. Man's nature can never be removed from the order of salvific grace. In fact, human nature (*phusis*), for Gregory, demands the supernatural life of God within it, not as attainable in any mechanical way or flowing intrinsically from man's essence, but as attainable, according to God's decree, by man's free, loving, cooperation with God.

Jean Daniélou has expressed Gregory's understanding of nature as embracing both orders which in Western thought are too often conceived as separate entities:

> This notion of nature is totally different from that which is understood in Western theology. The latter understand by nature the intellectual life and the animal life of man—and opposed to this is the supernatural life which is added. Gregory on the contrary understands by nature the intellectual life and the supernatural life—and it is the animal life that is added. This explains why the Greeks can say that man is good by nature.[13]

Body and Sex

Like Origen, Gregory found in Genesis a "second creation" at the point where the Genesis story switches from the universal idea of God's destined man to the actual, existing man. In the first creation, in God's mind, the perfection of man's nature consisted in being made, by God's decree, to his image and likeness. In the second creation, which begins man's march in space and time to the fulfillment of God's plan, man is brought into existence as a complex, divided being. Diversity not found in the first creation rules throughout all of God's actual creation (cf. Appendix, No. 46).

God knows no such distinction as male and female. Nor can man, made to his image, in his perfect state know of this distinction. Our Lord himself had promised us that in the life to come, man's fulfilled life, when historical man will "return" and be identical with God's "beginning" creation in his eternal decree, we will know no distinction based on sex. There will be "no marrying nor giving in marriage" (cf. Appendix, No. 47).

Gregory knew Origen's obscure statements that had led Methodius, Epiphanius, and Jerome to condemn his view that man's body was a result of sin. He avoids this error by showing that the human body with its basic distinction of male and female sexes is not the result of sin. Sex was given man in order that he might make the proper choices in loving submission through virtuous living. Love for God was the energy in man which would unify the diversity within man. Through love for his Creator, man will actualize the image of God within himself. But in order that love be possible for man, God made man capable of choice: to say *yes* or *no* to God. This choice necessitates, and hence God decreed, composition in man's imperfect nature.

Hans von Balthasar attempts to reconcile Gregory's ideas on body and sex as a part of God's eternal plan with man's perfect nature which knows no such distinctions as materiality and sex. He insists that Gregory views these as both a punishment and as a gift from God. Drawing upon the example of the Jewish institution of kings in the Old Testament, von

Balthasar shows that the Jewish king-ruler was an institution that God willed as a means, in the light of the Hebrew's infidelity, to call them back to his convenant. In a similar way, God, foreseeing man's self-seeking and sinful infidelity throughout human history, decreed the human body, sex, matter, contingency, change, and even corruptibility as means whereby man could freely opt for God instead of self-love, and hence could reach his fulfilled nature which would experience no material body, no change, no corruption, no sexual passion.

Gregory expresses this idea by the simple Genesis image of the garments of skin. Man is now immersed in a condition that is the total result of united mankind's turning away from God. But the garments of skin decreed by God were created by God as a means whereby man could regain (thus reaching fulfillment) the original state of perfection that was primary in God's mind (cf. Appendix, No. 48).

In God's eternal decree, therefore, man's nature was conceived in its fullness; yet in God's vision of man's perfected nature there was contained also the imperfect state through which man would pass to reach perfection. The body and sex, the whole material cosmos through which man would move to his perfection, were willed by God as the means whereby the seed would grow through greater complexity and perfection, until man would achieve the ideal, complete state of eternal immortality.

Christ the Perfect Adam

Yet man could not, unaided, respond positively to God's ideal plan. A greater, more perfect being, one who already had attained the state to which man was aspiring, was needed, who could not only inspire by his example but also by his activity effect in man this "return." This more perfect being had to be none other than the very Lord of man's nature, for he had given to man his existence, and only he could restore man to participation in his own divine likeness (cf. Appendix, Nos. 49 and 50).

Redemption is described by Gregory mainly in terms of restoration by Christ of the image according to which man was created. Christ was "transfused by our nature in order that our nature might by this transfusion of the Divine become itself divine."[14] Being united to a Divine Person, Christ's humanity was perfectly divinized. Hence his human nature "returned" to the state before the Fall; Christ's humanity, through his human oblation of self to God, became deified. He was the perfect man according to which model God conceived the full *nature* of man. Man, by his nature as conceived in the *eternal now* of God's decree, signifies, of necessity, a relationship to Christ. Christ is necessary if man is to be fulfilled as perfect man.

Christ's humanity still lives inserted in our universe, drawing men to the "return" or fulfillment in accordance to his own image. His redeeming, restorative activity extends to all men (cf. Appendix, No. 51).

Using an example already used by St. Paul to illustrate the intimate bond of union between Christ and his Church, the mystical Body of Christ, Gregory describes the resurrectional activity throughout all mankind.

Just as, in the instance of this body of ours, the operation of one of the organs of sense is felt at once by the whole system, as one with that member, so the resurrection principle of this Member, as though the whole of mankind were a single living being, passes through the entire race, being imparted from the member to the whole by virtue of the continuity and oneness of the nature.[15]

It is through Christ's activities in man that he can touch and change the universe into glory to the Father. Christ is the Living Word in men, suggesting their good thoughts, working in them to do good deeds. The individual begins by contemplating the divine activity of Christ within him. This activity of the prolonged Incarnation in man extends to the universe. Yet Gregory is rarely concerned with the rest of material creation. Man is the masterpiece of this universe; for him Christ became incarnate and assumed, as St. Gregory of Nazianzus earlier had said, a full, perfect human nature in order to redeem the whole being. Man is saved only if his whole being is recapitulated by the whole being of Christ. With Gregory, as with the early Fathers, there was no merely extrinsic application of the merits of Christ to the individual soul; rather, salvation was dependent on the organic, real nexus existing between Christ and his life in us. Through the same life in us we become one with Christ's Body (*cf.* Appendix, No. 52).

A community of newly resurrected beings in Christ (the Church) is formed by the initiating act of Baptism. Gregory of Nyssa is outstanding among the early Greek Fathers for his dynamic sacramental theology. The sacraments were points of encountering the glorified resurrected Savior, living and activating within men the potential divine image. We glimpse something of this dynamism as Gregory depicts the union effected between Christ and the baptized Christian. Not so much by Christ's precepts are we saved as by the deeds that he accomplishes within us after Baptism through the dynamic union between him and ourselves (*cf.* Appendix, No. 53).

It is especially in the sacrament of the Holy Eucharist that the recipient opens himself to the activating energies of Jesus Christ which effect Paul's "new creation." In Chapter XXXVII of his *Great Catechism,* Gregory shows how Jesus effects in man the restoration to the divine image and thus brings mankind to true immortality. Christ's resurrected Body comes to man in Holy Communion. Like a leaven that "assimilates to itself the whole lump, so in like manner that body to which immortality has been given by God, when it is in ours, translates and transmutes the whole into itself."[16] Gregory argues that Christ, through his Eucharistic Body, can vivify the whole of mankind just as the same divine power changed the physical bread that Jesus Christ ate into the Body of God. Instead of the consumed food becoming part of the person eating it, the eater is transformed into the divine nourishment (*cf.* Appendix, No. 54).

Continued prayer and the practice of virtues, especially faith and humility, foster the Divine Life obtained through the sacraments.

Epectasis

But Gregory develops his doctrine of *epectasis* (straining out towards) as one of the most necessary virtues, or rather, as an habitual state of soul, to keep the divinization process ever moving towards a greater assimilation into God's life. St. Paul had exhorted the Philippians: "Brothers, I do not consider that I have reached it [salvation]. But one thing I do: forgetting what is past, I strain toward [*epekteinomenos*] what is ahead" (Phil. 3:13).

Daniélou has indicated that around the Greek word for straining we can see the double polarity that forms the foundation for Gregory's mysticism. The Greek prefix, *ep(i)*, indicates a pouncing upon, a surrounding and possessing of a good. The prefix, *ek,* stresses the outgoing movement, an élan towards the infinite, transcendent God. Gregory is not derogating matter in this upsurge towards spirit. He is placing the stress on the dynamic process of the inner élan in man, a partly material being and immersed in a material cosmos, but who finds his true meaning and fulfillment in Another who is at one and the same time within and without him. Never in this earthly life does man reach complete growth or perfection.

Though initially it causes the individual soul affliction, this inner urge to possess the Unpossessable is at the very root of man's greatest dignity and happiness:

> But the veil of her grief is removed when she learns that the true satisfaction of her desire consists in constantly going on with her quest and never ceasing in her ascent, seeing that every fulfillment of her desire continually generates a further desire for the Transcendent.[17]

From Glory to Glory

This is the goal of Gregory's anthropology as well as his cosmology. Man "returns" to his original state by a gradual process of ever profounder contemplation of God in all things, so that eventually man will arrive at the end destined for him by God in the "beginning." Then God will be all in all, the Alpha from whom man has flowed out into existence and the Omega towards whom man has reached out in this life with longing. In this earthly life as well as in the eternal life to come, Gregory points out to us, every end is a new beginning, a further initiation by transformation into a greater likeness to God. Man will never cease discovering new heights of perfection, new wondrous goods to possess.

The image of God in man, for Gregory, resides not only in man's intellect whereby he knows God, but in man's whole being, moving him to possess God ever more completely. Man's being, or person, grows through desiring. When man will have been purified so that all earthly desires will be fused into one burning act of love of God, man will possess the whole world in and through the vision of God. To see God is to know him; but to know him is to experience him in all the manifestations of his inner nature, that nature characterized succinctly by St. John, "God is love."

We can best close this section on St. Gregory of Nyssa by a brief passage of his that links up the transfigured world and the transfigured man:

> When such, then, have been purged from evil and utterly removed by the healing processes worked out by the fire, then everyone of the things which make up our conception of the good will come to take their place: incorruption, that is, and life, and honor, and grace and glory and everything else that we conjecture is to be seen in God and in His Image, man as he was made.[18]

III. ST. CYRIL OF ALEXANDRIA

St. Cyril (+444) lived in a time of turbulent theological upheaval when the early Church was groping to express in human concepts the awesome mystery of divine nature uniting with human nature in the sole Person, Jesus Christ.[19] His crusade against Nestorius, who claimed two persons in Christ (the Blessed Virgin being the mother of only the human

Christ), climaxed in Nestorius' condemnation at the Council of Ephesus (431) and the adoption of Cyril's formulation. Although Cyril did not consider himself an original thinker, he was the first Father to emphasize the theological importance of the "Apostolic Fathers" as cited authority, independent of the Bible, for the interpretation of dogmatic truths. This was now the royal way of theology, to quote St. Cyril: "To inquire into the beliefs of the Holy Fathers which came about through the inspiration of the Holy Spirit, to keep firmly in mind the train of their thoughts."[20] This meant that the ground-breaking age of theological speculation of the early Christian era was nearing its end. Campenhausen calls Cyril the "first of the Byzantine scholastics."

Cyril brings christology as well as the related doctrine of the image and likeness of God in man to its highest point of articulation; and in his doctrine the immanence of Christ reaches its highest development. This is the golden era of christological theology. Why it remained eclipsed for centuries, especially in the West, why particularly the question of Christ's cosmic effect was neglected, is an interesting question in the history of dogma. No doubt, in the West the reaction against mediaeval Teutonic Arianism, and in the East a hidden Monophysitism, both of which exalted the divinity of Christ to the virtual exclusion of his humanity, largely account for a one-sided emphasis on his divinity.

For Cyril, the emphasis, always strong in the Alexandrian school, was on the unity of operations in Christ. The human and divine formed a real, intimate unity, one "nature," not in the philosophical sense of the term (the Monophysite error), but one objectivized, total existing subject. He carries this same realistic unity over to the union of Christ with us.

Here we see the influence of his favorite patristic writer, St.

Athanasius of Alexandria, whom Cyril quotes profusely in all his works. One third of his Thesaurus is made up of excerpts from Athanasius' *Orationes.* Following those guidelines, Cyril works out his christology. The Word took flesh so perfectly that one can no longer think of the divine in Christ without his accompanying humanity. Christ's humanity is one with the Word. The Word is Life, incorruptible, eternal, subsistent. But his humanity is still flesh and blood, still living united with the divinity, still giving life. As in his temporal lifetime, the Word gave life-giving power to his humanity, so now, in turn, his humanity is exercising the same power, as well as illuminating individual beings. Christ's work will continue until he shall have made us by grace what he is by nature.

In refuting the Nestorians, Cyril insisted on the "physical" reality of the two natures in Christ. Equally he applies this term to express the intimacy of the union effected by Christ with the individual soul through Holy Communion. According to Cyril, Christ makes those who believe in him "concorporal with himself" (*cf.* Appendix, No. 55).

Nor does Cyril restrict the union with Christ achieved in Holy Communion to moments of union with the Sacred Species within us; but a real unity continues in grace. He admits it is not a hypostatic unity, but he objects to the traditional words *union, contact, inhabitation* as not strong enough to express his thought. Our union with Christ is a "physical" union, according to flesh; i.e., by means of Christ's humanity, this mysterious but nonetheless real union takes place whereby our total human "nature," meaning our total person, is incorporated into his Body.

Cyril is the only Greek Father who ventures an explanation of this union, although no explanation can be adequate as we are dealing here with a revealed mystery. His explanation involves his teaching on the image and likeness of God in man and the relationship of so-called "nature" (in our Western concept) and "supernatural."

As Walter Burghardt, the American Jesuit patrologist, has painstakingly shown, Cyril's doctrine of the image of God in man derives from the idea that this "image" is implanted, by his creation, in man's intellect. This is the faculty that makes man *man,* with a "natural" resemblance to God, prescinding from the question of his supernatural elevation. His faculty of understanding, like his very being, is possessed in virtue of a human participation in something that is radically divine. Man through his reason shares in him who is Light by nature, the Word of God. The Word alone is properly Light, alone able to enlighten, alone not in need of light. Man participates in his illumination and can never lose this basic participation in the Logos through his reason. Hence, he is *logikos,* a person able, if he cooperates, to be illuminated by the Logos. In this sense, reason is a gift of the Creator as is man's entire existence. It is already, in a sense, in the "supernatural" order, as it is freely given by God as radical orientation towards God. But the Logos continues giving his gifts, if man cooperates through the proper use of his reason, by actuating the faculty which enables man to become the image of God. And the proper use of reason, for Cyril, means faith and the increase of faith through virtuous living. "Faith," says Cyril, "is the beginning of understanding."[21]

Cyril sums up his doctrine, and the common doctrine of his patristic predecessors:

Man's formation to God's image has other meanings—meanings on the surface and meanings deep within; for man, alone, of all the living creatures on earth, is rational, with a capacity for all manner of virtue, and a divinely allotted dominion over all the creatures of earth, after the image and likeness of God. Therefore, it is inasmuch as he is a rational animal, a lover of virtue, and earth's sovereign that man is said to have been made in God's image.[22]

By restoring the lost image to man according to which he was created, Christ regained for man some degree of that dominion over creation which Adam had lost. It will be complete only in the next life when the whole universe will be given back to man's dominion. But even in this life, Cyril believed, by participating in the life of God, by which he meant putting on God's holiness, man is transformed to a new life, a holy life. Union with Christ means putting on God's mind, a likeness to Christ's action brought about by virtuous living, with a limited dominion over creatures, using them according to the mind of God. Christ's work of recapitulation in man consists in the actuation of man's radical potency to become an adopted son of God through his relation to the physical life of Christ within. This was the work Christ came to do by his Incarnation, and here Cyril repeats what Irenaeus and all the Fathers unanimously had to say: "The Son of God became man in order that men might become sons of God."[23]

Christ Our Brother

Again, we see the rich personalism of the Greek Fathers synthesized in Cyril's doctrine of our divine filiation. He avoids the highly juridical, legalistic concepts of redemption often found in standard theology manuals by stressing the solidarity that exists between Christ and human beings, both as brothers in a common humanity and as sons of God in a divine filiation.

Cyril, citing Luke 2:7 (the Virgin Mary "brought forth her first born Son"), distinguishes clearly between the Only-begotten Son (*monogenes*) and the First-born (*protogenes*). Divine by nature, the Second Person of the Trinity as Son of the Father could not have brothers, for they would then be co-equal and identical with the Logos. But through the Incarnation Jesus Christ takes upon himself a full humanity, thus forms a bond of union with other men, making us also sons of God, not by nature but by participation in his sonship (*cf.* Appendix, Nos. 56 and 57).

Cyril envisions the restoration of man to his true dignity, lost through sin, as an elevation of man to the sonship of God by participation. By the fact that God took on himself our nature, a unity, a oneness, is formed between Christ and each human being. God, becoming a human creature, became a brother with every other son of the human race.

But is this sufficient for sanctifying all men? Is the human race, and through it all other creatures, then restored to the fullness destined for it by this bond of human unity? Cyril sees that the world is not mechanically saved by the insertion of God into the human family. He distinguishes between man's sonship *in* Christ and man's elevated sonship by adoption *through* Christ. Christ, by becoming man, has given to every human being a radical sonship, an orientation towards God the Father in a new, ontological sonship through a participation of Christ's divine sonship, which is his by nature. This potency becomes actualized through the mediation of Christ's glorified humanity, especially through the sacramental encounter with the physical, resurrected Christ in Baptism and the Holy Eucharist. Then the radical sonship is actualized into a real, ontological transformation whereby the Son sends his Spirit who operates within man to bring about not a mere extrinsic divine adoption, in name only, but a "genetical" (if we may so speak) adoption. Remaining human as Jesus did in the hypostatic union, we become united to his Spirit so that we become truly assimilated by participation into the very nature of God:

> Therefore is he man, made like unto us, that we might also be like unto him . . . that we might be gods and sons.[24]

In his divinity Jesus Christ was God by nature. But the humanity that he assumed was not divine by nature and hence had to be, as ours, raised to divine adoption by participation. During his whole temporal life, every conscious act done by Jesus Christ out of love for his heavenly Father produced, through the Spirit, a divine filiation of his humanity that imaged (without losing its own identity) the image that the Logos was as the Only-begotten Son of God by nature.

Man's Sanctification

For Cyril, an increased filiation with the Father is another way of saying that we grow in sanctity; another way would be to say that man's potentialities were being fulfilled. Our filiation and sanctification, which for Cyril are synonymous, are effected by Jesus Christ through his Spirit. By an encounter with his resurrected humanity, especially through Baptism and the Holy Eucharist, we become truly transfigured into sons of God.

By taking human flesh upon himself, Christ unites us physically with himself by a kinship of the flesh; yet being God, he unites us as sons of the same Father. Baptism gives us the communication of his Holy Spirit whereby we are given God's own life in us. The Holy Eucharist allows us to participate in the Flesh and Blood of Christ in a physical union, thus participating not only in his humanity but also in his divinity, as they are hypostatically united (*cf.* Appendix, Nos. 58 and 59).

The Holy Eucharist is the most perfect means of effecting this insertion into Christ. Christ comes to change us, to vivify us with his own life, uniting us all in himself and to one another and to God. Christ is no less truly personal, no less real, no less alive for coming to us in this Eucharistic "modality" than he was during his earthly life. The faithful, too, lose nothing of their individuality, being raised to a higher life in Christ and joined in union with other members of Christ's Body in whom Christ likewise lives by grace.

The effects which the humanity of Christ produced by his visible activity during his historical life, he now produces invisibly but no less really in the Eucharist. We are transformed into what is "proper to the Eucharist, that is, into life" (*cf.* Appendix, No. 60).

Following his master, St. Athanasius, Cyril insists that it is the Holy Spirit who accomplishes with man's cooperation the divinization of man. "The Holy Spirit works through Himself in us, truly sanctifying us and uniting us to Himself."[25] Like St. Athanasius, Cyril depicts the Holy Spirit as the true image of the Son who then makes us true images through participation. The Holy Spirit effects within us a new form of existence, human, yet pulsing with God's life.

Transfigured World

The presence of the indwelling Trinity within man transfigures man's nature without destroying it, and through this transfiguration a special dominance over the cosmic creation is given to sanctified, deified man. As Genesis depicted the ideal man, God had given him power to dominate, rule, order, all sub-human creatures. To man was given a share in God's image. Sin, for Cyril, wiped away the image of God in man, destroying the incorruptibility that man participated in by possessing the indwelling Divine Life. Christ's role, through his Church, especially by her sacraments and the preaching of the Divine Word, restores by his Holy Spirit the lost image and gives back to man a certain degree of dominance over the rest of creation. This dominance effects also a degree of incorruptibility in the non-human cosmos, but it will be complete only in the life to come.

Man retains his own human nature, but Christ and the Holy Spirit bring man to his fulfillment in making man immortal and glorified (*cf.* Appendix, No. 61).

For St. Cyril, as well as for all his patristic predecessors, the concepts of incorruptibility and immortality served as the best way to describe an incorporation of man into God's own life. Only God by nature is incorruptible, possessing no matter or substratum of potency that would need a process to move itself from a state of imperfection to perfection. Only God by nature is immortal, knowing no death, no change in his manner of existence. And these two characteristics are possessed by deified man. A new order is established through Christ and his Spirit, bringing to finite, corruptible, and mortal man a participation in the incorruption and immortality of God himself (*cf.* Appendix, No. 62).

We have seen how Cyril wanted to hand on only what the most orthodox patristic writers before him had taught. Recalling that he spent most of his theological career fighting for and clarifying the christology enunciated by the Council of Ephesus (431), we understand why Cyril stressed so greatly the quasi-consubstantiality of Jesus Christ with all members of the human race through his Incarnation. No Greek Father stressed, as he stressed, the restoration of man as steady growth in a conscious filiation with God the Father. To be called and to really *be* sons of God—here, for Cyril, is man's greatest dignity and the fulfillment of all of his God-given powers. As he expresses it:

They who mount to God's adoptive sonship by faith in Christ are baptized not into some created being but into the Holy Trinity itself through the flesh which is united to Him, and who is linked naturally to the Father inasmuch as He is God by nature. This is how the slave rises to sonship: through the sharing in the true Son, he is called, and, as it were, ascends, to the dignity that belongs by nature to Him. That is why we are called, and are, begotten by God; through faith we have received the regeneration that comes through the Spirit.[26]

IV. MAXIMUS THE CONFESSOR

Although St. John Damascene is usually considered the last of the great patristic Greek writers, it is Maximus the Confessor who marks the end of the patristic theological development.[27] Born in Constantinople in 580, he received a well rounded classical education that proved a fine background both for the imperial service and for that of the Church. After serving as secretary to the emperor, he entered a monastery in Chrysopolis opposite Constantinople where he made great progress in the ascetical life and wrote prolifically on theological matters.

Because of the Persian invasion in 626, or in order to combat the growing heresy of Monothelitism,[28] he left his monastery, traveled to Africa, and finally to Rome. In 649, at his suggestion, Pope Martin I convened a Lateran synod which condemned the heresy of Monothelitism. However, Maximus, along with Pope Martin I, was tried in Constantinople by order of the emperor, Constans. He was twice exiled and condemned again in 662. He had his tongue and right hand amputated because of his defense of the Chalcedonian christological doctrine. He died the same year in exile near the Black Sea.

Although he is best known for his staunch defense of the orthodox teaching on the two natures in Christ as defined in the Council of Chalcedon (451), Maximus interests modern readers more because of the cosmic dimensions of his synthesis of the whole created order, a harmonious unity in union with God through Christ.

He renews and develops the central idea found in the second century writings of St. Irenaeus on the recapitulation of the whole universe in Christ. He sees the whole world in the light of the Incarnation. Polycarp Sherwood finds that this is the key to Maximus' speculation:

> For the coherence of Maximus' thought . . . does not derive from the systemization of the Church's teaching in function of some humanly-posited principle or philosophy, but from a vision of divine things in the light of the Incarnation of the Son of God, in the light therefore of that mystery by which alone we know the Father and our salvation.[29]

Maximus speaks for himself in stressing the centrality of the Incarnation. Only a proper understanding of the purpose of the Incarnation of Christ and his Resurrection would yield a true understanding of the cosmos as it was created and destined by God. From this mystery he derived his fundamental law that would provide the keystone to his synthesis of the universe (*cf.* Appendix, No. 63).

The Council of Chalcedon had defined as infallible dogma: "Jesus Christ, God's Logos made Man, is a single Person in two natures which exist in this one Person without confusion, without change, without division and without separation."[30] Just as in the person Jesus Christ there existed two distinct elements, the divine and human natures united without destroying the distinct identity of the two component elements, so too, Maximus argued, the created cosmos is composed of distinct elements, yet the whole is also fashioned into a unity. Both as the preexistent Divine Logos and as the fullness of existing human nature, Jesus Christ is the bond providing the unity of intelligibility and of cosmic energy (love) that are hidden beneath the surface of the material appearances of creatures.

Maximus sees all existence polarized into various antithetical categories. God planned the whole world to be united in his own Divine Life, but man turned away from the plan of God. Through sin, the world is groaning in disharmony. All existence is splintered into antipodes of the created world and the uncreated God, the sensible and the intelligible, earth and heaven, the world and Paradise, masculine and feminine. Instead of diversity in unity as willed by God, the cosmic reality of death that so graphically separates man's soul from his body reigns over the universe, separating and dividing what was meant to be united (*cf.* Appendix, No. 64).

How is the cosmos to regain its diversity in unity? Man who stands between heaven and earth, possessing both spirit and matter, must first find self-unity and then perform his God-given task of mediation between the rest of the created cosmos and its Creator. The Divine Logos-made-man provides Maximus with the means to effect this unity, first in individual men, then through christified men, in the cosmos (*cf.* Appendix, No. 65).

The Logos and the Logoi

Although his predecessors, John the Evangelist, Justin, Irenaeus, Clement of Alexandria, Origen, Athanasius, and Gregory of Nyssa, had used the Logos doctrine to explain the incarnational activity of Jesus Christ in the cosmos, no Greek Father has developed it as deeply and systematically as Maximus. Lars Thunberg maintains that in Maximus the Logos concept

> . . . is deeply integrated into a personal, general vision of the mysterious and deifying presence of Christ the Logos in the world. The *logos* denotes the created existence of a thing as founded in God's will that it should be; it is the principle of its coming to be and implies a participation in God as being.[31]

The logos of each creature is its principle of harmony that shows us the relationship of a given creature to God's total providence or to the total order of salvation. The whole world is interlocked and interrelated, but thinking man alone is capable of seeing the harmonious relationship between the logoi and the Logos (*cf.* Appendix, No. 66).

The Logos is Jesus Christ, as an "all-powerful center, precontaining thc sources of its rays and gathering them all together."[32] All things are created through him, the Logos and the Alpha, and all things are to be eventually reunited in him, the Omega. Maximus conceives the Logos on different levels of incarnational activity. He first sees him as the preexistent Second Person of the Trinity, the Word that speaks eternally the Mind of the Father and hence is the model according to which all creatures have their fullness. Next, Maximus understands the Logos more precisely as a parallel to the historical Incarnation. The Logos, God-Man, gloriously resurrected, is inserted into the material world and is actively working to bring both man and the sub-human cosmos to the likeness of the divine ideas possessed by the preexistent Logos.

The harmony and unity between the logoi and Logos is effected by man who by contemplation learns to see the intelligibility "within" the created order, and in love lives according to God's purpose. But to see the logoi in all creatures, man must submit to the illuminating activity of the Logos. Maximus writes in his *Four Centuries on Charity:*

> Just as the sun when it rises and lights up the world manifests both itself and the things lit up by it, so the Sun of Justice, rising upon a pure mind, manifests itself and the essences of all the things that have been and will be brought to pass by it.[33]

Only he who has this gift from the Logos to see beyond the appearances can unlock the world and see the harmony existing among all creatures. He is able to enter somewhat into God's very purpose, into God's very mind, to see the *raison d'être* of each created being.

Three Phases of the Spiritual Life

In describing the various stages of progress in knowledge and love of God, Maximus builds upon the doctrine earlier enunciated by Evagrius of Pontus. The first stage is called *praxis.*

This touches the area of man's own activity in his attempt to discipline his disoriented nature. It is fundamentally the removal of impediments to God's graces brought about by self-love and the positive acquisition of virtues. "Vices are mistaken judgments of our ideas upon which follows the misuse of a thing," writes Maximus.[34] And again he says, "It is with misuse of the soul's powers that the vices come upon us—the vices of the concupiscible, irascible and rational elements."[35]

True to the traditional Eastern Christian asceticism, especially as taught by the Hesychastic Fathers,[36] Maximus insists on the suppression of impassioned, disordered thoughts. There can be no purification from disordered acts unless there be *nepsis,* or vigilance, over thoughts that disorient man away from his final end. It is in the struggle to order one's thoughts and actions according to the perfect model, Jesus Christ, that the Christ-like virtues are developed.

As man develops virtues in imitation of Christ, a similar *perichoresis,* or interpenetration, between human nature and divine nature takes place in a union that parallels, however distantly, the hypostatic union in Christ. Man, made to God's image, is brought into a living relationship with Christ inasmuch as Christ lives in man through man's virtuous life (*cf.* Appendix, Nos. 67 and 68).

The second stage in the recapitulation of all things in the Logos (Christ) is called *theoria physica.* After purification, man moves to a contemplation of the world about him. This world brings him to the inner world beyond the sensible, the phenomena. It is here that he encounters the mind of God. At this point he passes from self-activity to become the subject of divine infusion.

By infusion, God gives us the gift to see the logoi in all

his creatures. Seeing the inner relationship of a given creature with its Creator, man will use that creature properly, according to the Creator's intention. The contemplation of the logos in each creature, therefore, is a wisdom given men by God so that man can put on the mind of God. Thus for Maximus, as well as for the Eastern Fathers who preceded him, to live according to nature meant to live according to the logos within each given nature.

Maximus divides all created beings into three classes: things, Sacred Scripture, and man himself. In all of these three groups we find the *superficies,* the *epiphaneia,* that which presents itself to our senses. Then there is, as shown above, the inner knowledge of the logos, the principle of harmony, revealing the relationship of a created being to God's providence. The logos is the reason of the creature's existence in the mind of God which corresponds to the wisdom of God in things. Persons without this infused gift of *theoria physica,* or contemplation, judge things, Sacred Scripture, and man himself by sense knowledge. But the person possessing this inner knowledge penetrates beyond sense knowledge, beyond the letter of Scripture, to the spirit or *pneuma.* Here he sees the mind of God behind the written letter or person encountered, the inner mind (*nous*) that reveals the author's or person's real personality, his logos.

The ordinary person reads Holy Scripture and sees nothing but the letter. He does not penetrate behind the type to the antitype (model). Symbols in the Old Testament fail to reveal God's mind to him. But the person with the gift of contemplation sees the deeper meanings. Every word, every picture tells him something about God.

The same applies to man in relation to other men. Most men view other men only as they present themselves externally. The man of interior vision can see beyond to the inner logos. He can pierce through the phenomenal, the physical appearance of the sensible order, as unimportant and enter into an interior vision that allows him to see others in God's light.

The third degree of the spiritual life is that of *theoria theologica.* This is not meant in the sense of our "theology," but rather it is a mystical contemplation of the Holy Trinity. In the highest type of contemplation, man progresses farther and farther from earthly thoughts as he becomes gradually assimilated to God. The gnoseological principle that guides all theory of contemplation and deification in the Christian East is that like can be known only by like. True knowledge of the Trinity can be given to man only in the proportion that man is assimilated to the likeness of God.

We see once more the importance of the image and likeness doctrine in Oriental spirituality. Assimilation consists in becoming just and holy as God is. This is salvation in the fullest sense. It is restoration of man to the integrity in which God created him and which he wished him to possess. This is only perfect in the beatific vision, but to those who have attained *theologia* in this life, God reveals himself no longer through creatures or the logoi in creatures, but in his own Trinitarian life of active love dwelling within the individual soul. Man attains this end perfectly only in the life to come, but by these three degrees of progressive growth he begins now to be assimilated to God's own life. It is through *praxis* that the obstacles to a more intimate knowledge of God are removed. It is through *theoria physica* that the mind of God is discovered in his effects upon the created world. It is through *theoria theologica,* God speaking about himself, that a direct knowledge of God is given the individual.

One might think that for Maximus knowledge is salvation.

On the contrary, perhaps no other Father so stressed the importance of the affective element of charity in bringing about a cosmic synthesis. His *Four Centuries on Charity* shows the importance he attached to love as the motivating force or cosmic energy that alone is capable of recapitulating all things in Christ. Without charity, *praxis,* and *apatheia* (detachment), the state of harmony and tranquility in all of man's passions would become mere stoicism. Without charity, contemplation becomes mere philosophical speculation. For Maximus, charity proceeds in steps. The first is the virtue that insures the presence of all other virtues in the attainment of harmony within man. This then feeds contemplation to discover the mind of God in all things. The final goal of every man, which is charity towards God, is attained only at the end of man's life when he meets his Maker, no longer in the darkness of faith and hope, but face to face in an eternal act of intense love. Thus for Maximus, charity is, in its most dynamic aspect, like an embryo that grows through man's activity and the activity of God in his being.

We saw earlier the antithetical divisions into which sin, through self-love, sundered a world that was meant by God to be a harmonious unity. We can now see in summarizing Maximus' synthesis how the three stages of growth in knowledge and love of God and of his creation effect this unity. The division of the sexes into male and female is a symbol of what is in each man. The male aggressive element, typified by anger, and the female receptive, possessive element, typified by inordinate concupiscence, are transformed from unregulated passions into virtues that make man Christlike. Man achieves unity without destroying the complexity of his senses and passions. He becomes like Christ in whom there is "neither male nor female" (*cf.* Mt. 22:30).

The division between Paradise and earth is overcome by

virtues also, as man obeys the divine commands and mirrors forth the perfect human life of Christ who came on earth to do the will of his heavenly Father. The state of paradisiacal harmony of man with other men and with the animal, plant, and inanimate worlds is restored to the degree that man overcomes his overweening self-love by opening himself to the commands of God.

The division between heaven and earth is removed by the contemplation of the logoi in nature. Man sees God's purpose in creating the world. Christ in the Incarnation has come down to earth in order to bring us back to his heavenly Father's mind. The fourth division, between the intelligible and the sensible worlds, is overcome also by the infused gift of contemplating the logoi, the purpose of each creature in relation to God's creational finality. The last separation, between infinite God and finite creation, is removed by the highest form of contemplation wherein the Trinitarian energies are seen mirrored forth in each existing creature.

The Church

Christ's transforming activities through the power of the Holy Spirit continue in the cosmos through the Church. In the Church the living Logos is preached, and through the sacraments Christ is encountered in his resurrectional life by the Christian faithful. As has been pointed out, the supreme work of God living in men is to effect a unity among disjointed creatures, separated from their Creator and from one another by ignorance and sin. It is the work of the Church to achieve this unity and it does this first by unity of faith in the teachings of revelation. If man is to be sanctified and approach to the likeness of God in holiness, hence be united with his Maker in thought and affection, it must be through an exact profession of the faith. Subjectivism and self-delusion are overcome by obedient submission to the teaching hierarchy that Christ established over his Church (*cf.* Appendix, No.69).

It is the Church that exposes to us the Incarnate Christ, living in his glorious resurrected life to be encountered by us through the sacraments. Baptism administered by the Church opens to us the fruits of the Incarnation. But it is especially in the reception of the Divine Logos and High Priest in the Holy Eucharist that man is deified and is able to fulfill his priestly function of making all things holy. Man conforms himself to the Logos present by grace within him. Then he is able, through the enlightenment of the Logos, to perceive the logoi in other creatures and to perform the sacred role of priest by offering a sacrifice of praise and glory to God through man's proper use of creatures. Christ sacrifices himself totally in the Eucharist to give himself to man in order that man, through the use of his illumined reason, might be raised to the perfection of Christ (*cf.* Appendix, No. 70).

The Church herself is the unifier of all that divides men from one another. It achieves an ecclesial unity which is not only a type of the future cosmic unity but is the basis for it. It is the human race already united in the fullness of Christ, but not yet fully in all the cosmos (*cf.* Appendix, No. 71).

Man stands at the center of the cosmos. Deified man, in whom God lives and through whom he acts to fulfill the world, is the mediator between the disparate and disjointed world and the unity that has been achieved perfectly in the God-Man's humanity through the Incarnation. Maximus insists over and over on the intimate connection between man's deification and the transfiguration of the material cosmos. Man, permeated by grace, achieves a unity within himself which allows him to effect a cosmic unity in the material world around him.

Vladimir Lossky gives us a fitting close to this section on Maximus the Confessor: "In his way to union with God man in no way leaves creatures aside, but gathers together in his love the whole cosmos disordered by sin, that it may at last be transfigured by grace."[37]

CONCLUSION

We have cursorily studied some of the ideas of the leading early Greek Fathers in an attempt to see how they envisioned the presence and activity of Christ in the cosmos. In fact, the Fathers wrote theology mainly as a living answer drawn from the Church life in which they participated, and used to pluck out certain heretical tares that had begun to grow in the field planted by the Lord.

Irenaeus, Clement, and Origen worked out their theology in combating the heresy of Gnosticism. Athanasius defended the faith against Arianism. Gregory of Nazianzus and Gregory of Nyssa fought against Apollonarianism; Cyril against Nestorianism and Maximus the Confessor against Monothelitism. Many of the Fathers used the philosophical concepts popular among their readers, a fact which often only obscures rather than clarifies their theology for us. Another point to bear in mind in appraising the value of the Greek Fathers is the place they occupied in the evolutive process of human knowledge. With their level of scientific knowledge, the Fathers were in no position to see the interrelationships of all material creatures and their mutual dependence.

It is the total, unified vision of these early Fathers that is most enriching for us in the twentieth century. By viewing man in his relation to God, to fellow men, and to the rest of the created world from the fourth dimension of God's finality, they were able to avoid the dichotomy that in the West was mainly responsible in theological thought for the diminishment of the cosmic dimension of Christ's activity in our present world. Rather than an antithesis between *nature* and *supernature,* they opposed *natural* and *unnatural. Nature* was not only the embryonic seed but the fulfillment in all the creature's final fruition. Man's nature was always destined, not only by God's finality in creating man, but also in God's loving activity to accomplish his plan, to make man a divinized son of God. Man's total entity, body, soul, and spirit (God's Divine Life dwelling in man), was to move in a continuous process of loving activities in the cosmos to a more conscious relationship to God.

Sin, however, disrupted the harmony within man's diverse powers of intellect, will, memory, emotions and external senses. The only true evil was the unnatural. It consisted in thwarting, through self-love, man's nature in its destiny to be united with God and with all things in and through God. As long as man and the other creatures of the world lived according to God's plan, they lived according to *nature*. The moment man willfully violated nature, evil was introduced into nature. The unnatural was now man's lot.

But man could not restore by himself the condition of friendship and sonship with God that God had willed as a part of his fulfilled nature. There was need of a perfect man, a Second Adam, who could undo the work of Adam, of Everyman, in his unnatural aborting of God's plan. This Second Adam would be human nature in all its perfection, the image of God that through human actions of loving submission to God progressed to the likeness of God. The Only-begotten of God the Father by nature becomes the First-born of the human race in his humanity by participation in the divine nature. By his death and resurrection he is "glorified" in his humanity and thus passes into a new modality of existence. He remains inserted into our cosmos; by his glorified humanity he is radically related to every human being. Through his activities within saved humanity, the Church, especially through the sacraments and the preaching of his living word, other humans pass into an ontological living relationship as brothers of Jesus Christ and sons of God by participation.

The Greek Fathers were never preoccupied with how much man had to do in the process of restoration. A harmonious *synergism* of mutual cooperation preserved the full gratuity of salvation and yet required that man was to overcome self-centeredness by virtuous living, especially by charity, the bond of unity and harmony among men that did most to restore man's dominance over the rest of creation.

We have seen how the Fathers, while strongly emphasizing Christ as head of humanity and the recapitulator of all things in God, deemphasized the material cosmos as an entity in itself. It was conceived, when thought of by any Father, as a mere instrument to help man grow in his divine filiation. Except for a rare Clement of Alexandria, most of the Fathers conceived the material side of the universe either as a source of sinful temptation or an area worked on by man's virtuous efforts through the sacramental system of the Church to be a pliant instrument in man's future sanctification.

In following the giant footsteps of Paul and John, the Greek Fathers had secured the transcendence of God the Creator and the centrality of man in the created world as the co-creator with God by stressing that he possessed in his intellect and will the seeds of a likeness to God in grace. They stressed that Jesus Christ was not only the perfect model, the Image of the Father according to whom man and the whole cosmos were created, but that through his Incarnation he was also in the midst of the material world exerting his power to bring the whole created order into its fullness through the instrumentality of other human beings, motivated by reciprocal love towards him.

The Church was the sign wherein the created cosmos entered into a transfiguration, and through its instrumentality the resurrectional life of Jesus Christ was extended to the cosmos. Retaining its own individuality each creature was able to be assumed into a new transcendent relation with God as its end. The material world, through the Church, meets the spirit. Retaining its materiality, it still participates in a new existence of spirituality. The *eschaton,* through the Church, has been realized in the *now,* but *not yet* fully. The resurrection of Christ is applied to the transformation of the world into "God in all" to the degree that the baptized in Christ rise from a self-centered life to put on a new life in him. The rest of the world waits for man to stretch out in a yearning (*epectasis*) that will be climaxed only in the *parousia* when Jesus Christ shall come to render explicit what was always implicit, to reveal what was hidden, to fructify the powers in creation which were lying there in potency.

The work of the Greek Fathers of the first seven centuries of Christian existence was well done. The Church has need of thinkers of the twentieth century who can complete the teaching of the Fathers in terms that are intelligible to us today. We turn to one such modern teacher, Teilhard de Chardin, as representative of a modern school of Fathers eager to explore the cosmic dimensions of the christology formulated by the Greek Fathers, in ways, at times, so strikingly presaging Teilhardian thought, as when Maximus speaks, across twelve centuries, of "Christ . . . as a center upon which all lines converge."

VI

THE COSMIC CHRISTOLOGY OF TEILHARD DE CHARDIN

In one of his assemblage sculpture pieces entitled, "The Crucifix," Albert Ceen, an American artist now residing in Rome, has made the body of Christ on the cross out of cast-off junk. The face of Christ is a bicycle chain; monkey wrenches inserted into one another form the stark outline of Christ's arms and hands. A stove-grate forms his halo; parts of an automobile transmission form his chest, legs, and feet, while a gnarled-up chain forms the groin cloth.

The artist found Christ's body in the junk. The initial reaction of most viewers is one of shock, not only at the almost macabre effect of neo-realism that the artist captured in the sufferings of Christ suggested by the bare bone structure, but at the mere fact that he should have taken such "unspiritual" objects as bicycle chains, stove pieces, monkey wrenches, and car transmissions to fashion the sacred, suffering body of Christ.

But "after a while," and this little phrase says everything, "after a while" the spectator's consciousness enters into the sculptor's vision, and one begins to see what he saw. This message is fundamentally what Teilhard de Chardin was trying to give to others of the twentieth century. The Jesuit scientist-philosopher asks, "Will the material world remain ever closed to modern man in his attempt to find God? Will man yield himself to the material world, whose many mysteries he does not understand, as though it were uncontrollable, and hence incomprehensible to the human mind? Or will he merely abandon the material world and the possibility of ever rising through it to find God in the very heart of the matter?" We must see with another vision, the artist and Teilhard both are telling us, and we must not stop with the material world. We must not judge the mere sense, phenomenal world as it presents itself to our gaze. A monkey wrench is a monkey wrench for all that; a bicycle chain is just that and no more. But we must find within these scraps the assemblage, the unity in the apparent disunity of the material multiplicity.

Modern man's religious problem concerns the fundamental questions of faith, God, Christ. For the modern generation, does the historical Christ have any real relevance? Can the Christ of the Gospels be found in our universe that is ever expanding, breaking upon our consciousness with greater and greater complexity, beauty and harmony? Teilhard sensed this growing restlessness as early as 1927 when he wrote the most complete synthesis of his spiritual vision, *The Divine Milieu,* for those who were asking, "Is the Christ of the Gospels, imagined and loved within the dimensions of a Mediterranean world, capable of still embracing and still forming the center of our prodigiously expanded universe? Is the world not in the process of becoming more vast, more close, more dazzling than Jehovah? Will it not burst our religion asunder? Eclipse our God?"[1]

Jesus Christ, in a theology of "up there," seems too remote for the modern man thirsting for a personal encounter with the God he so ardently wants to love, not merely on Sundays, but every moment of his day and night. The devotion to Christ as King, so popularized by St. Bernard of Clairvaux and St. Ignatius of Loyola in an age of feudal chivalry, contemplated Christ as the perfect model, the divine example of human goodness. A Christian was to reconstruct in his mind the life of our Lord, mull over his example and words, then strive to imitate the divine model by thinking and acting in a Christ-like manner.

Today's psychology of personal encounter stresses that the knowledge of another person leading to a person-to-person relationship in love is not merely a question of conceptual knowledge. The question is not an essential one of "what he is" but an existential one, rather, of "who he is" who is being encountered. The individuality, that which makes this person uniquely *this* person, can never be captured completely in a mental concept.

The inner core of a person remains sealed off to others unless a mutual love engenders a deeper insight into *who* this person is. In our encounter with Christ today it is not enough to contemplate him as the historical person revealed in the Gospels. Nor is it enough to contemplate him in the encounter of faith through grace by which we become united with him and the other members of his Mystical Body as branches to the vine. We must also be able to meet Christ in the divine, continual act of creation, redemption, and sanctification of the total universe. His loving activity for us individually is discovered in an intuition of faith that reveals Christ as the keystone to the multiple mystery of created being. In him we discover the *Absolute,* the beginning and end of all unity in the cosmos. Faith gives us the eyes to see, not *what* God is but, in his personal, loving activity over the millennia for us, destined children of God, *who* he is.

But to foster a steady growth of faith, an environment, a divine milieu, must be created in which Christ can be personally contacted. He is to be found at the root, the ground of our very existence. Teilhard insists that for the Christian of sensitive vision, God, as Creator and more specifically as Redeemer, penetrates the world.[2] It is not an appearance of God in the world, but a shining of God through his creation. Not an epiphany but a "diaphany" of God shining through the transparent world.

This Christ, diaphanously shining through every creature of the universe, is encountered in a loving act of surrender in which he becomes the *Thou,* complementing our *I.* Each Christian, now awakened to a new consciousness of Christ's universal presence, will discover his own self-realization and full maturity in "being-with-Christ." Teilhard summarizes the key to the mystery of life very simply: "That which gives true value and happiness to existence is to lose oneself in another greater than oneself."[3]

To appreciate in greater detail the role of Christ in Teilhard's vision we must first see the broad outline of his spiritual vision as proposed in his writings, but especially in *The Divine Milieu.*

Creating a Divine Milieu

Teilhard himself tells us the purpose that he had in mind in writing *The Divine Milieu.* It was to be a book of piety presenting an ascetical or mystical doctrine that would be meaningful for the modern world.[4]

Teilhard was thinking of the scientific minds of his day torn between the seemingly convincing facts of evolution, on the one hand, and on the other, the divine revelation of God about man's supernatural destiny. He felt drawn, even as was St. Francis Xavier, to bring the saving doctrine of Christ to the modern generation that was unable to see the reality behind sensory phenomena. The whole universe was exploding into ever greater multiplicity. But was there any unity beneath this increasing complexity? The immensity of space and time, the richness of the world that is ever unfolding in a continuous creation, have caused a fear in the heart of modern man. A universe growing to such cosmic heights has dwarfed man into insignificance, sundered the narrow containers into which man had forced his throbbing world. A whole new concept of space-time is at the root of the disquiet in the hearts and minds of modern man. ". . . the 'malady of space-time' manifests itself as a rule by a feeling of futility, of being crushed by the enormities of the cosmos . . . Sickness of the dead end, the anguish of feeling shut in. . . ."[5] To light the way out of this maze of enclosing mechanistic fatalism, and from a mind and heart that knew each turn with intimate expertise, there suddenly flashed forth the astonishing vision of Teilhard de Chardin.

Behind the seemingly rigid determinism of matter, Teilhard discovers the delicate hand of the Holy Spirit giving order to the universe. For one who has faith to pierce beyond appearances, chance and hazard dissolve into an illusion.[6] In the foreword to *The Phenomenon of Man,* Teilhard states his purpose, that men might *see* more and more beyond appearance to the inner order and finality of the physical cosmos. The human mind through reflection on the cosmic past and present can trace, he insists, the gradual unity in multiplicity in an ever progressive ascent that irreversibly produces a cosmogenesis, biogenesis and, finally, anthropogenesis. But only faith discovers a personal God permeating the universe with his conscious activity to bring the totality to a final point of convergence. *The Divine Milieu* is Teilhard's vision of faith that seeks not only to present God as the beginning and end of all order and perfection found in the universe but also to outline in a practical way a plan whereby man can find God, loving and acting to bring him to his completion in Christ. Through a free act of love man can insert himself within this process and not only realize his own potentialities, thus achieving happiness, but precisely through his active cooperation with his Maker, help the whole universe move to its completion.

Mystique of Action

The modern Christian lives in two worlds: the world of matter and the world of spirit. He is drawn by the beauties of this world and the challenge to make it an ever more beautiful place in which to live. His Christian *credo* tells him on the other hand that these ephemeral material beings will soon pass away and that the Christian must lift his heart and his eyes heavenward. One cannot love God and mammon at the same time. Thus he feels a dual pull: one drawing him to full citizenship of this earthly city, the other recalling his future citizenship in the City of Heaven.

Christians have faced this dilemma and answered it in one of three ways. One could ignore and repress the desires for the things of the created world and live for "the things above" through a philosophy of flight from the present world. Another possibility would be to turn away from the evangelical summons (other-worldly values) and live completely in and for this world. The third possibility would be a compromise resulting in a split-personality which would now live for God, now for the world, never really resolving the dilemma.

Teilhard, in working out a mystique of action, insists that there is still a fourth way. The fourth way consists in reconciling the tension between a deep love of God and a passionate love of the world, between the desire for greater self-development and the striving for greater detachment from the things of this world.[7]

Spiritual writers all too often in the past presented work as a penance, a result of Original Sin. "Thou shalt earn thy bread by the sweat of thy brow" (Gen. 3:19).[8] Or again it was presented as conflicting with love of God. By a pure intention of pleasing God, regardless of what one did, one could give his work a supernatural orientation. This spirituality conveyed the impression of a static world and a transcendent God somehow outside of the material universe. Human activities had eternal value only as symbols of our submission to God. Man was on trial before the eternal Eye, and man's purpose on this earth and his growth in true education consisted in learning how to obey and love God by doing all his human actions from the pure intention of pleasing God.

Teilhard recognizes much truth in this traditional spirituality of work but seeks to complement it by seeing the whole material universe, with man at its center, from the viewpoint of God's finality. He strives to see man and his circumscribed work of everyday as an important part of a total design, of God's plan wherein the past, present, and future are vitally joined together by dynamic interrelationships of all things, the whole process moving under God's personal activity to final completion. In *The Divine Milieu,* he insists that through the Incarnation nothing in the universe is "profane" for those who can see the inner presence of the resurrected Christ bringing the world to its consummation.[9] It is a gift of God that will allow us to see how all of our labors can be directed towards the building of the Kingdom of Heaven.

Teilhard insists that to have a pure intention to use creatures properly is not sufficient for sanctity in today's expanding universe. The glorious power of Christ's resurrection touches not only the soul of man but his body and the whole subhuman cosmos to "confer the hope of resurrection upon their bodies."[10] Since the appearance of rational man, carrying in his intellect and will the image of his Maker, God evolves the universe and brings it to its completion through the instrumentality of human beings. Man is called to be a "co-creator," a "cooperator" with God in the transformation of the universe from seed to fruit, potency to act, imperfection to perfection. Therefore, it *does* matter what man does, for only through his action can he encounter God. Through his grace-infused soul man can touch the chaos of the material world and apply the Incarnation to it. This world can be spiritualized by man developing it and using it according to the eternal mind of its Creator.[11]

St. Paul had pointed out how the incarnational activity of Christ was still going on in the universe. "For it pleased God the Father that in him all fullness should dwell, and that through him God should reconcile to himself every being, and make peace both on earth and in heaven through the blood shed on the cross" (Col. 1:19–20).

Teilhard never forgot Paul's clear teaching that man was not by the mere fact of his natural existence called to be a "new creature" but that this renovation in man was completely due to God's gratuitous gift through Christ. He also never forgot Paul's clear injunction that God has entrusted to us the sacred priesthood of reconciling the cosmos in Christ.

If, then, any man is in Christ, he is a new creation; the old state of things has gone; wonderful to tell, it has been made over, absolutely new! All this comes from the action of God, who has reconciled us to himself through Christ, and has entrusted us with this ministry of reconciliation. We know that God was truly reconciling the world to himself in Christ, not reckoning against men their sins, and entrusting to us the message of reconciliation (II Col. 5:17–19).

Detachment

But human activities tend to flatter man's sense of independence. How keep the delicate balance between being a fully dependent creature, yet a full "cooperator" with the divine Creator? Here Teilhard gives us his presentation of detachment and mortification which is in total harmony with the best in the Christian ascetical tradition. "Passionate indifference" is Teilhard's description of a Christian who has put on God's view of reality and has forgotten self as a point of reference and "in-centration." Man's passivities, where he is an active recipient of God's gifts in all their manifestations, are the absolutely necessary means to keep his activities centered on God and free from any self-love. God acts in us through the passivities of growth whereby we have a built-in thirst for higher forms of life, greater complexity within a greater integrated unity of experience. St. Irenaeus in the second century described it well by saying: "The glory of God is man living fully." A desire to participate more fully in life, in true being, is the urge that keeps man striving daily with ever-renewed energy.

The "joie de vivre" becomes such only when it is recognized as a haunting expression of God's loving invitation rooted deeply in the marrow of our being to "be perfect as your heavenly Father is perfect" and is capable of fulfillment through our cooperation with God's activities in our lives. These activities and the "passivities of diminishment" are the two hands of God, the Son and the Holy Spirit, touching us in the external and internal events of each moment to bring us from the death of self-love to a new emerging life in the Trinity. As the death of Christ on the cross had meaning only as a step to the restoration of his Divine Life to humanity through his glorified body, so too the little crosses that come from either outside forces or from our own being have full meaning only as a purging from us of any un-Christly element in order that the image according to which we have been created, Christ himself, may shine more brilliantly in us.

A universal law found in nature can be stated as a summary of Teilhard's vision of the cross in a Christian's life: nothing lives but something dies; nothing dies but something lives. But all of nature, the sub-human cosmos and man himself, does not merely shed imperfection for perfection, less life for more life, *alone*. Each advance to new forms of being has a repercussion on the total perfection of the universe. No man with God's grace ever perfects himself without at the same time touching the world around him and raising it to a higher life. In fact, it is precisely through the activities and passivities of man's daily life that he becomes always a "new creation" along with the created world he now touches and changes "in Christo Jesu."

Transfigured Universe

Thus, development and renunciation are not opposed as antinomies. Attachment and detachment are necessary complements. The cross and resurrection are two phases of the seed maturing into the fruit. Matter and spirit, body and soul, evil and good, are all interrelated phases of a continuous progression in true, ontological life, the life that Christ came to give us in greater abundance. The unifying element is precisely that God in his immanence is in all his creatures, acting to fulfill them. Teilhard uses the example of Jacob who was awakened to perceive in a new way that the world around him was truly a holy place. The divine presence through the physical, created world "assails us, penetrates us and moulds us."

God is revealing himself everywhere, through our groping efforts as a universal milieu, an environment, the air that we breathe. All beings have full reality in the proportion that they converge upon this Ultimate Point. God is the source of all perfections and the goal towards which created beings are moving in an *élan vital* to their completion.

This vision of worshipful communion between creature and Creator whereby man loses himself in God as in an "Other" is grounded in the Word Incarnate, Jesus Christ. In him, as St. Paul taught with such insistence, all things are reunited and are consummated. By the resurrectional presence of Christ who fills all things, the whole of creation has a meaningful consistency.[12]

By our actions, no matter how insignificant, we are building up the Body of Christ until it shall reach its consummation-Omega-Point in the pleroma, when Christ shall appear in his fullness of glory in the parousia and recapitulate under himself as Head the whole created order.

All created beings are tied together in their thrust toward fulfillment. "Natures" of created beings, as conceived by Teilhard, are no longer the tight compartments of Aristotelian metaphysics, static, formed, and self-contained. All matter is rushing in a "forward" and at the same time in an "upward" movement towards the Spirit. Natures are not only apt for receiving a "supernatural" ingrafting, but they present themselves as "supernaturalizable" in the divine decree and activity creating and bringing them to their completion. Divinity shoots through all of creation if only men would *see*.

In his work, *Super-Humanité, Super-Christ, Super-Charité,* Teilhard attempts to describe the interpenetration of the divine presence throughout all of reality. The mystics see all of reality surcharged with God; hence all of creation becomes lovable in God and "reciprocally God becomes knowable and lovable in all that surrounds us." No longer does the swirling, maddening multiplicity of creation take us away from the God of creation, but the very created world becomes a "milieu" and a point of encounter for a universal communion between man and God.[13]

With this spiritual vision of Teilhard as background, we can now examine the role Christ plays in his vision. The Christian, living in this Divine Milieu, sees beyond the phenomena of sense experience. Faith gives him the inner vision. "After a while" he can penetrate through surface impressions to perceive the inner logos, the meaning of each creature or event. He can see all creatures as events in the fulfillment of God's salvific designs.

But the greatest "event" for every Christian is always the encounter with the Logos, the Lord Jesus Christ himself, in and through these same material creatures. He it is who gives reality to each being. He it is who evolves the whole universe into the "new creation" foretold by St. Paul (II Cor. 5:17–19).

The Christology of Teilhard de Chardin

The last entry that Teilhard made in his Journal (April 7, 1955) could serve as an introduction to his christology as well as an adequate, although quite succinct, summary.[14]

Maundy Thursday. What I believe.

1. St. Paul—the three verses: *En pasi panta Theos.*
2. Cosmos-Cosmogenesis-Biogenesis-Noogenesis-Christogenesis.
3. The Universe is centrated-Evolutively Upward
Forward

The two articles of my Credo — Christ is its center — The Christian Phenomenon

Noogenesis = Christogenesis
(= Paul)

Cosmogenesis through Evolution

The above scheme serves as a synopsis of how Teilhard views Christ in the universe. It shows how intimately his christology was connected with and derived from his evolutionary cosmology.

In his *Phenomenon of Man* he painstakingly traced his cosmogenesis from the first created proton to atoms, molecules, mineral, plant, and finally human life: the *noosphere.* The path included the pre-human, pithecanthropus and sinanthropus, on up to homo sapiens by way of the neanderthaloids: man, at last, standing above all the other creatures of the universe, cries out, "I alone know and I know that I know." No other animal has man's unquenchable longing for eternal life. He alone can turn within himself and reflect on the purpose of his being and his relation to all other beings. He can penetrate the mystery of life, discover the purpose behind this movement of evolving multiplicity, and even foster or hinder the process.

From the law of cephalization that showed nervous systems increasing in volume and arrangement with a simultaneous concentration in the anterior cephalic region of the body, there was derived the law of complexity. Matter was moving always to higher forms of greater complexity in molecular structure with a proportionate development in consciousness.[15] In his unedited work, *Comment Je Crois,* Teilhard confesses that he is aware of an interior movement that animates the whole universe as well as each individual part of the universe. That movement is "towards Spirit."

Teilhard loved matter because he saw it always in its movement towards the spiritual. When, through collective cerebralization, man appeared with the power of reflection, a living being became the center of personalization. Even this personalization evolves from a self-centered being intent on self-preservation, to a being going out through communication and a conscious act of love for "another self." The whole process of hominization of men unites humanity into a unity of multiple complexity and differentiation.

What is this point of union, this point of convergence towards which all matter, all men are moving? The process of moving together through space and time is likened by Teilhard to a cone. The tip or point of the cone Teilhard calls Omega. This is the goal towards which evolution is moving, the point of convergence of all inferior lines which meet in it.

Before Teilhard identifies this Omega Point with Christ, he

describes it in greater detail. The ultimate point drawing not only all men but all the universe through reflecting men (as instruments of the universe's fulfillment) shows three characteristics: (1) It must be of an objective nature; it cannot be a mere figment of man's imagination. As real as the process of evolution and the laws of its development, so too must be the end towards which it is moving. (2) It must have the power in itself to draw, by its own activity, all creatures into a unity to their full consummation. In order to draw intellectual beings, this point of attraction must also be an intellectual being, a person. But if this person draws other persons he must do this through his own power, goodness and, ultimately, through the act of love by which a person draws another into the highest union of self-communication. (3) It must be able to move the whole universe to its united perfection without any fear of regression, destruction, or total frustration.[16]

Jesus Christ Is the Omega Point

What follows in Teilhard's thinking has received much criticism from scientists who have followed his argumentation up to this point. When he seeks to clarify and "incarnate" the Omega Point he is accused of having left science. Through an extrapolation he finds himself in the realm of mysticism. His reasoning can be stated thus: Man has evolved, and his highest perfection in the individual consciousness is his power of self-reflection. The total progress of humanity can likewise be measured by conjoined reflection of united human beings. Thus, in the process of evolution through a progressive, irreversible movement of heterogeneous elements in divergence, convergence must be a real, existing point of unity. It must be a person, existing, yet transcending all other finite, inferior forms. This person is not caused by the resulting convergence of humanity but is the moving force that converges, draws the diversity of human persons into a real unity around this center of attraction. This person is spiritual, since he attracts other spiritual beings as their fulfillment. He must be eternal and transcendent, the fullness of being, never adding to his being but possessing all perfections desired by mankind in its ever-growing thirst for more being, for a richer and more intense life. This person, finally, must be immanent. Only because this person transcends *all* finite being is he capable of being immanent to *each* being. But there is only one person who has been inserted into the human race and is capable of drawing other human beings by a human act of love, yet who remains completely transcendent to all men. This person must be infinite in order to command the aspirations of all men for all times. But the only infinite person drawn from among men is Jesus Christ, the God-Man.

In his work, *Super-Humanité, Super-Christ, Super-Charité,* Teilhard identifies this Omega Point with Christ. By taking upon himself a human nature, Christ becomes the perfect human being—*apparuit humanitas,* "humanity appeared." But as Christ also actively consummates the totality and fullness of humanity he is the appearance of this super-humanity—*apparuit Super-humanitas,* "super-humanity appeared." Christ is the Omega Point, capable of attracting other human beings to their fulfillment.[17] Teilhard does not wish to speak of another Christ, a second Christ, different from the first who lived historically in space and time, who "dwelt among us." He intends to speak of the same Christ, the eternal Christ who discloses himself to us under a new form and a new dimension.

In his work, *The Phenomenon of Man,* Teilhard, using technical language, unmistakably describes the historical

Christ and the converging point of all evolution as the same Person. He is drawing to himself the total "psychism" of the earth until that time when all will be transformed into God, to use St. Paul's words.[18] But in that final consummation of all things in God there will be no annihilation of our own individuality through a swallowing up into divinity as pantheism teaches. Each element, retaining its own proper identity, will reach its full perfection by being united with the Omega Point.[19]

Teilhard's starting point, as we have seen, is the evolutionary process which he considers proven fact. He projects this process into the future with his theory of the ever-converging universe, moving with greater affinity to Spirit. Into this scientific hypothesis he injects his Christian faith based on revelation, especially as given to us in the inspired writings of St. John and St. Paul. Science and religious faith comprise two different sources of knowledge, but do not contradict each other, as the Positivists maintained. They are facets of truth leading to the same Center. But it might be legitimately asked: If the cosmic Christ coincides with the development of the cosmogenesis, does not the historical Christ disappear? Is the cosmic Christ, the Omega Point, merely a poetic description of the gradual unfolding of the law of cosmic evolution? Teilhard's expressions at times would lead us dangerously close to such a conclusion. In his essay, *Comment Je Crois,* he insists that mankind is consummated with and attains to the total Christ only at the end of evolution. In such expressions, do not the historical acts of Christ's Incarnation, Redemption, Resurrection, and Ascension seem to be unimportant, even unnecessary?

Teilhard repeatedly insists that his cosmic Christ is the Christ of the Gospels. In *The Divine Milieu* he equates St.

Paul's recapitulating, universal Christ with the same flesh-and-blood Christ who was born of Mary and who died on the cross. Without this identity with the historical person of Jesus Christ, he realizes that he would be in the company of the wildest-eyed visionaries and illuminati.[20]

The danger for superficial readers of Teilhard is to confuse his two sources of knowledge, the laws of scientific evolution and those of divine revelation, and thus erroneously conclude that Teilhard was destroying the gratuity of the supernatural order by making the fulfillment of each creature in the final pleroma a matter of mere cosmogenesis. In an early work, his *Milieu Mystique* (1917), Teilhard clearly distinguishes between what is due to nature and what is a purely gratuitous gift of God. Yet he points out how Christ builds, by transformation, this supernatural structure that remains always a gratuitous gift of God, resting upon natural perfection.

Henri de Lubac, in his much discussed book *Surnaturel* (1946), seeks to show that the early Fathers, with their dynamic approach based on concrete, historical human nature, the only one that ever existed, had never admitted a nature that was not at the same time by its very ontological makeup, as it came from the hand of God, radically oriented towards its supernatural end. It would be wrong to assert that the Fathers denied the *possibility* of "pure" nature, a human nature not having the vision of God as its final end. The Greek Fathers, as we have already pointed out in the preceding chapter, simply never thought of the problem, absorbed as they were with the historical order of the present economy of salvation, and this shows us their sense of "realism." Never faced with the Pelagian heresy and therefore the need for the important and subtle distinctions in Western theology to highlight the gratuity of God's gift, his freedom and independence in his bestowal of graces on man, the early Fathers viewed the interrelationship of nature and grace in terms of one continuous unfolding process of two different but not contradictory entities: man's ontological nature as God made him with potencies that would be actuated with God's help only when the end was attained that God had destined for man; and God's gratuitous bestowal of the gift of Divine Life that drew out of the image according to which God created man a more perfect similitude to the perfect Image of God, the Divine Logos, the Omega Point.

In a very similar way, Teilhard, in his essay *Mon Univers,* looked at the universe as having only one Center which operated on both levels with distinction, the natural and the supernatural. This Center was moving creation to greater consciousness while at the same time drawing creation to the highest degree of sanctity. This Center, he insists again, as he had done in many other writings, is Jesus Christ, both in his historical person as well as in his projected glorified person in the cosmos.[21]

In one of his brief interchanges of letters with the Christian existential philosopher, Maurice Blondel, Teilhard more explicitly tells us how he views the interrelationship of the natural and supernatural levels of being. The supernatural fullness of Christ is being formed by the re-creation of the natural. Christ gives himself to us to the degree that the world is more fully and more naturally developed.[22]

He stresses that through the Incarnation, the Divine Word has inserted himself within our material "natural" universe and has become the cosmic Center drawing all beings, now elevated by the gratuitous loving activity of God, to a united destiny around the supernatural Center, Christ, the Omega Point.

Cosmic or Christic "Nature"

Teilhard was equally convinced that the total material universe is in movement toward a greater unified convergence in consciousness, a hyper-personalized organism, as he was of the truths of the Christian revelation concerning the building up of the Mystical Body and the recapitulation of all things *in Christo Jesu.* He complains in *Le Christique,* another of his unedited works (1955), that up to the present, despite the dominant place that St. Paul gives it in his vision of Christ's presence in the world, the third aspect or third "nature" of Christ has not been given sufficient consideration by theologians. He does not wish to establish a new third nature in the strict sense of the word as opposing the human and divine, but he refers to the "cosmic" function of Christ in the universe. With the convergence of human experiences allowing us to see a unity within so much multiplicity, Teilhard insists that it is time for Christianity to awaken to a distinct consciousness of this third dimension or function of Christ.

In times past Christ's relationship to the material universe (often conceived as a static cosmos) was understood in a juridical way. He was King over all creation because he was declared to be such. There was little reflection on any organic relation of dependence of creation upon him.[23]

Earlier in the written summary of his personal views, entitled *Comment Je Vois,* published in 1948, Teilhard used the term "Christic nature" but with somewhat more caution. He distinguishes between the preexisting Word on the one hand and the historical, incarnate Man-Jesus on the other. Between these two aspects, Teilhard distinguishes, as he did in *Le Christique,* a sort of "third nature," one that is Christic (he adds the words: "if I dare to say so! . . ."), that emerges.

This is the aspect of Christ that St. Paul constantly writes about, the full, total Christ whose activity consists precisely in "recapitulation" or in bringing the universe to its ultimate center through the transforming energies of his resurrection.[24]

We have already pointed out that in the mind of Teilhard there was not a third nature distinct and different from the two natures, divine and human, that made up the total, historical person, Jesus Christ. In his use of the term cosmic or christic "nature," Teilhard did not intend to give a metaphysical definition of a new and distinct nature, existing outside of the gloriously resurrected Jesus Christ. In his preoccupation to stress Christ's new and ever-growing relation with the created cosmos, not only through a juridical declaration of Christ's kingship over all created beings but in a phenomenological and mystical way through a real, "physical" relationship, Teilhard strongly emphasizes the building up of the Mystical Body of Christ, as a physical third "nature." With seeming impatience against the juridical conceptualizing of christology in the past, Teilhard complains in his *La Vie Cosmique* that the strong analogy used by St. Paul of the Body of Christ has theologically been interpreted more often as a social agglomeration and not as Paul had envisioned it, as a natural organism. He claims that the Body of Christ, in the doctrine not only of Paul but also of St. John and the Church Fathers, meant a living and moving organism wherein we as members were united in a physical and biological sense.[25]

It has been pointed out in reference to the above quotation that Teilhard uses the words "nature," "physically" and "biologically" quite loosely. It is precisely his christology that most of his critics have attacked. But he has told his readers that his thoughts were not always complete nor expressed in precise language. The great confusion comes from his eagerness to bring together, after centuries of theological conceptualization had kept them distinct and separate, the evolution of all created natures climaxing gradually in their fulfillment in Christ as the One who fulfills all creatures and, thus, really the One who completes himself in completing them.[26]

There is, of course, a vital relation between the natural, evolutive perfection of the universe as a community of human persons dominating the non-human cosmos by conscious interpersonalism and the growth of the Mystical Body of Christ to its fullness. But readers of Teilhard must keep distinct that which he did not always take pains to distinguish in his writings.

> Christian salvation makes use of natural instruments which dispose men to accept God's gifts in a more fitting manner, and thus enable these gifts to bear more fruit. The one essential is not to confuse the disposition to receive, with the gift that has been received.[26a]

Physical Center

Teilhard thought that the modern mind did not take St. John's words literally, that "all things came into being through him [Christ, the Logos] and without him there came to be not one thing that has come to be" (Jn. 1:3). St. Paul's recapitulation by Christ whereby "God shall be all in all" (I Cor. 15:28); "All things have been created through him [Christ] and for him . . . and in him they are all preserved in being" (Col. 1:16–17); "He it is who fills all things" (Col. 2:19)—these and other Pauline texts (such as Eph. 4:9 and Col. 3:11) were sufficient doctrinal basis, Teilhard thought, to take Christ, the Omega Point of the universe personalized, as the literally physical center of the cosmos. He boldly asserts in his essay, *Super-Humanité, Super-Christ, Super-Charité,* that if we were to take the daring statements of St. Paul literally, then Christ would appear to us as the Omega Point of convergence and there would follow a whole series of marvelous properties as qualities of his risen humanity.[27]

These properties are: (1) Christ physically and literally is the one who fulfills the universe. Every element in the universe, every event in the history of the world, is moving itself or is being moved somehow under his guiding influence. He is immersed in space and the unfolding time of our human existence, but he is also actively working to bring to completion this "groaning creation" described by St. Paul. (2) Christ is physically and literally the one who is consummating the universe, both as its intrinsic form, the organic principle of growth in unity and harmony (as the soul is the principle of organization and unity in the human person), and as the Head of all creation which will be completed only when the whole universe will have been culminated in him.

What does Teilhard mean when he says that Christ is literally the physical Center of this expanding universe? Was this hyperbole, or did Teilhard really mean that Christ forms some sort of a "physical" bond with other human beings in this world? Certainly the frequency of his use of the word "physical" would imply that he meant it literally. Most modern men think of "physical" as synonymous with "material," hence in opposition to "spiritual," but Teilhard's "physical" must be seen in the context of his own thought and system.

Physical as used by Teilhard has some of the nuance and breadth of the term as used by the early Greek Fathers. *Phusis* means nature, but not in the strictly metaphysical sense. Perhaps "reality" or "ontological reality" would be a better way to translate Teilhard's sense of *physical,* for it signifies not only a given being in its present existence and metaphysical constitutive parts, but above all it includes the total being in its dynamic progression towards fulfillment. Its perfect fulfillment coincides with God's finality which is the purpose for God's immanent activity in creatures. What makes up an essential part contributing to the full "reality" of a given human being is the continuity that joins the Head and members, Christ and us, and effects the individual divinization which is our fullness, flowing out into the collective divinization.

Thus, not only body and soul, matter and spirit, make up the physical human person, but the real, ontological being would find its physical fullness only in a divinization of his whole being by the indwelling of the Holy Trinity. Union with Christ through grace leading to an immanent union with the Blessed Trinity, for Teilhard as for the early Greek Fathers, was a "physical" union, meaning both ontologically real and according to the fullness of man's created potencies. Man's God-given nature (*phusis*) had always been destined by God to be a christified nature through sanctifying grace. Thus the "real" man was the full man with his human potentialities fulfilled only in and through Christ who alone could actuate man's true being to become, finally, filiated to the Father as a divinized son of God, not by his own nature but, as St. Peter writes, as a "participator in the divine nature."

Christopher Mooney has observed that, for Teilhard, "whatever meaning 'physical' is to have . . . it will have to be situated in the realm of the human and the personal."[28] Christ must be human to make direct contact with humans. Through his gloriously resurrected humanity, he is able to transcend all space and time, to be omnipresent and immanent in all beings. He must be a person able to be present to us and draw us by his love towards him. Yet this presence of Christ in the universe is physical (ontologically real) and personal, the person identical with the historical Son of the Virgin Mary. In *The Divine Milieu* Teilhard unites the physical body of Christ, the physical Center, the personal present, the christic Center, into the one Body of Christ. This becomes the true Center of the cosmos that actively radiates its divine energies to all men in an activity of transformation and deification, "an omnipresence which acts upon us by assimilating us to it, *in unitate corporis Christi*"[29] (in union with the Body of Christ).

In lines written on the battlefront in 1917 (*Le Milieu Mystique*), Teilhard confesses that he found two forces or movements pulling him. One drew him forward in a movement of human development (l'En-Avant). Another pulled him upward (l'En-Haut). Christ becomes for him the synthesis between the God "ahead" and the God "on high." The meeting of these two movements, an expanding cosmogenesis and a divinization through grace of God's creation, he called the "christogenesis" or "christification" of the universe. Christ is the source of energy which is at the center of this process, a "christic energy."

But still there seems to be an element missing, the bond of union. How does man make contact with Christ, the Center of the universe? How can a human person encounter the person Christ? The sacrament of the Eucharist is for Teilhard the chief bond of contact, of union between the Incarnate Word, Christ, and an individual human person. The Eucharist is shorn, however, of the false overtones of self-centered, individualistic pietism and is presented in the context of an evolving, expanding universe that is moving always under the guiding hand of the cosmic Christ towards an ever greater consciousness and convergence or centricity through amorization. In *Le Milieu Mystique,* Teilhard writes, "I discovered that everything was again centered upon a Point, upon a Person, and this Person was You, Jesus! . . . From the moment that you said 'This is My Body,' not only the bread on the altar, but to a certain extent everything in the universe that nourishes in our souls the life of grace and the spirit became Yours."[29a]

From the consecrated species of bread and wine wherein is contained, in space and time, the physical Body-Person of Jesus Christ, a "universal transubstantiation" was taking place. Christ's transforming activity moved from the church's altar to the altar of the material universe. In *Le Christique* Teilhard develops this insight by describing through the eyes of faith that the transubstantiation of bread and wine into the eucharistic Body and Blood of Jesus Christ is extended into the converging world to include the totality of all the joys and pains that result from the convergence process. The words of consecration fall over these and thus render possible a universal communion.

In still more powerful words Teilhard, in *The Divine Milieu,* expresses how Christ's cosmic activity emanates from the Eucharist to touch each of our material activities. The eucharistic transformation, begun on the altar through the spiritual transformation of the material gifts of bread and wine and ourselves into a living relation to Christ, is extended into the universe. Thus the sacramental species of the Body and Blood of Christ are in a way being formed not only through the instrumentality of the bread and wine but by the total, created, material world. The whole time of the creation, he insists, is the time required for its consecration.[30]

Christ makes contact with us in his Body-Person under the accidents of material species of bread and wine in the Holy

Eucharist. He also makes contact with us as individual human beings in the proportion that we offer him that limited part of the universe entrusted to us in the work of "reconciliation," as St. Paul says, bringing it under his christifying influence. Thus the universe gradually is subjected to the transforming activities of Christ living in us through the life he brings us in the Blessed Eucharist. Through our loving submission to him, his life is extended even to the sub-human cosmos, his sacred humanity touches this or that area of the brute world to transfigure it into a united eucharistic hymn of praise to the Eternal Father.

The Church, a Phylum of Love

To every believer in God, the statement that all human progress is in the final analysis a work of God seems self-evident. But to imagine an indefinite human progress that God would allow for no purpose would be a shocking effrontery to his transcendent dominion over all creatures and his infinite loving goodness towards those whom he created to his own image. God bestows his divine filiation on men always gratuitously but does so in the ambit of man's human development. Pope Pius XII highlighted this relation of a developed sense of human collectivization and the increased growth of the Mystical Body in an allocution in 1958 to Italian Catholic Youth. "For the first time, men are becoming conscious, not only of their interdependence, but even of their marvelous unity. This means that humanity will become always more and more disposed for becoming the Mystical Body of Christ."[31]

This does not mean that the building up of the supernaturalized Mystical Body of Christ flows necessarily from the high degree of human collectivization achieved in the world. Nor does it mean that the Mystical Body of Christ did not exist in periods of more simple, individualistic societies that had not attained a high degree of social consciousness and technical progress. Teilhard clearly distinguished between the human development and the supernatural insertion into that human structure of the purely gratuitous kingdom of God. In one of his earliest writings, "Mon Univers" (1918), he clearly distinguishes between the "natural term of human and cosmic advances" and "Omega, the supernatural term of the Kingdom of God," of the "Plenitude of Christ."[32]

It has always been a teaching of the Church, notably in its condemnation of any type of Manichaeism, that God sanctifies the whole man, including his material body. St. Thomas taught that grace is proportioned to nature as the perfection to that which is perfectible. Nature was not to be conceived as a static entity cut off completely from a supernatural destiny but, viewed from God's finality, it contained the seeds of a supernatural end which, through man's loving cooperation, would be actuated by God's gratuitous gift of grace.

The more developed the universe becomes, the more God is working to bring about the apt conditions for the fuller realization of a divinely amorized universe. Both the evolution of the human race and the growth of the Mystical Body imply a loving God working constantly. Here are two distinct levels of activity, yet not separated from each other (as a seed is not separated from its fruit, as an adult continues the same substratum as the child from which he evolved). As has been pointed out by Teilhardian scholars, with greater evolutive unity actually attained among men, with more conscious, personal freedom enjoyed by individual human beings, conditions are more favorable for a more universal growth in true supernatural charity.

Yet there also exist greater possibilities of yielding to the basic temptation at the root of all sin—to use these wonderful inventions and social developments for our own egoistic ends. Does it not bring us back to our Lord's parable of God's distribution of diverse talents? If God gave to St. Paul more graces than he gave to the pagans of Paul's times, God also awaited greater loving submission and greater development of those gifts by Paul in his service to other humans for love of God. If our modern generation through development of technical discoveries can enjoy greater abundance, more variety of material and intellectual goods, than our ancestors, it means we have more opportunities of responding to God's manifest love with greater, more universal charity shown to other human beings.

Man can abort the progress of his evolution. He contains within himself freedom to submit this cosmogenesis to the influence of Christ in his dynamic élan to draw all creatures upward to their fullness in him in the process of christogenesis, or to withdraw it from his influence. As has been pointed out, these two movements should be complements to each other, not by necessity but through man's free cooperation, in loving submission to the influence of Christ. Without this cooperation, all human achievements and progress are to be reckoned meaningless. In a letter written in 1919, Teilhard emphasizes his strong belief that human accomplishments achieve their ultimate value only in relation to Christ. "I do not attribute any definitive or absolute value to the varied constructions of nature. What I like about them is not their particular form, but their function, which is to build up mysteriously first what can be divinized, and then, through the grace of Christ coming down upon our endeavor, what is divine."[33]

This is the crux of his christology, that Teilhard conceived the whole of natural evolution as coming under the influence of Christ, the physical Center of the universe, through the free cooperation of human beings. We will treat shortly his vision of the parousia when these two movements will have reached their mutual fulfillment in convergence at the Omega Point. What interests us now is Teilhard's conception of the building up of what he calls the "phylum of Salvation," the Church of Christ.

Teilhard usually does not envision the Church as a community founded by Jesus Christ with a given hierarchical structure and a collective unity in faith, sacraments, and teaching magisterium, but, allowing for the institutional elements, he focuses on its dynamic aspect—the "core" concept of the members transformed by the incarnational activity of Christ in their lives. Through the intensity of lives lived "in Christ Jesus" by purity, faith, and fidelity, they converge to "form Christ." This he expresses in strong terms in *The Divine Milieu.*[34] Whatever we do by deed or suffer by diminishment with faith and love makes us a more integral part of Christ's Mystical Body. All such actions not only are turned to good but they are turned into Christ.

Through this body of christified persons, Christ reaches the rest of mankind and the material universe. Teilhard develops his concept of the growing Body-Person Christ in terms of his cosmic vision. The christified, the new Israel's People of God, is a "phylum of salvation" that spreads its inner life and hyper-personalism (engendered by the life of the physical Body-Person of Christ) in a movement of greater consciousness, always ascending until the completion of the Body in the parousia. Teilhard summarizes his whole view of the human phenomenon on its way to a more perfect cosmogenesis in closing his work, *The Phenomenon of Man.* He compares the Christian "leaven" to a *phylum* that, through greater consciousness, moves towards a unity effected by love. This consciousness reaches its fullness in the spiritual relationship of love to the transcendent pole of the whole universal process of convergence, and that is Jesus Christ.[35]

The Church as a growing phenomenon is like a biological phylum, with its special set of characteristics common to all its members and distinguishing them from members of other phyla. This *body* of members grows in an ascent of greater consciousness, freedom, reflection, synthesized by the Christian act of fraternal love.

The source and object of this common *agape* is the Omega Point, the cosmic Christ. The christic energy of grace deepens the reflective consciousness of the individual members and draws the highly individuated persons into a convergence by a hyper-personal love of each towards Christ Omega and towards one another. Love, Teilhard points out, is the "within" of things, the immanent force unifying all conscious beings, "personalizing" by totalizing.

We are witnessing material unions of human beings today that all too frequently lower and enslave the consciousness of the members. No truly personalized union between rational beings is possible without love. Love alone can bring about a unity of human beings, the greatest fulfillment of themselves. He urges a question in *The Phenomenon of Man:* If in our love relationship with another we find our truest "person," why should it not be true also on a world-wide dimension?[36]

In spite of the evident increase in the twentieth century of the collectivization of people without any love beyond an egocentric environment, Teilhard's optimism and deep Christian faith drove him on to assert that this phylum of love, the Church, would continue to expand, unleashing men's ability to be more personalized by becoming more reflectively conscious in their love-motivated activities.

In the summary of his personal views, *Comment Je Vois,* he shows the three levels of cosmic evolution: cosmogenesis, biogenesis, noogenesis. A fourth level, christogenesis, the formation of the "Church" through the christification of the members of this phylum of "salvation," is now formed. And this not by any necessitating force in nature, but solely because the Omega Point draws the universe to a unity in love in which man freely responds to his loving attraction.[37]

The Church is thus a living organism inserted into the greater phylum of material creation. Teilhard returns to this biological concept of the Church often in comparing it to a plant, a stalk, a shoot inserted inside of humanity to effect the gradual transformation of the human race. "Only in the Roman 'trunk', taken in its entirety, do I see the biological support sufficiently vast and differentiated to carry out the transformation of humanity which we await."[38]

Christianity is for him "a phylum of love in nature," and this phylum is none other than the one Church founded by Jesus Christ. He describes it as "the living Church which needs only to be left to grow."[39] "I was born right into the Catholic phylum,"[40] he explains, "the seed of supervitalization implanted in the Noosphere by the appearance of Christ Jesus."[41]

He recalls an insight that he received while praying in the Basilica of St. Peter in the Vatican which throws further light on his conception of the Church as a Christian phenomenon growing up within the human phenomenon:

In St. Peter's, I really felt the tremendous character of the "Christian phenomenon": What I mean is the clear and unshakable assurance, unique in this world, of being in direct contact with a personal Center of the universe. From the "planetary" and "biological" point of view that, I repeat, is a phenomenon of the first order; it is unique.[42]

Again while in Rome he writes in 1948:

. . . I seem to feel an awareness of the extraordinary focus of spiritual radiation concentrated by the two thousand years of history these places have witnessed. In these days it is here in Rome that we find the Christic pole of the earth; through Rome, I mean, runs the ascending axis of hominisation.[43]

The Parousia

This Church, like a true leaven, will go out to christify new areas of existence heretofore not consciously living under the influence of Christ. Through the amorization process of Christ affecting individuals, the law of complexity consciousness becomes the law of growing amorization, which means that only love-energy can draw us eventually toward unity. Christianity is the only religion that engenders a progressive relationship in our consciousness between the cosmic demands of the Incarnate Word and the spiritual potencies of a convergent universe. The Church of Christ was founded with a power of activation and attraction, capable of stimulating its members to the maximum activity of self-development and, at the same time, able to draw that activity into a unity around the Center, Christ. In *Le Christique,* Teilhard writes that

this power the Church alone possesses, of "energizing" completely through the act of "amorization." It alone contains the full powers of growth and life along with the powers of diminution and death that lead to greater development.

Christ is the evolver of this super-humanity. He amorizes his members by making their love or charity (the only ultimate criterion of the degree of covergence of cosmic evolution with its ultimate end) "universalized," "energized," and "synthesized."[44] The charity is universalized because christified individuals find God is lovable in all creatures and events. The diaphany of God shines through the material universe; the world becomes charged with God's loving presence. Teilhard has beautifully expressed in his essay, *Super-Humanité, Super-Christ, Super-Charité,* the interpenetration of the Divine Presence throughout the material world. The cosmos no longer is an obstacle to the vision of God, but rather it becomes the mirror in which we see God; it becomes the "milieu" in which we can enjoy a constant and universal communion with him.[45]

Our charity towards our neighbors becomes energized into a love proved by deeds. No longer content with a glance of commiseration or a vague desire to reduce the evil in the world, we are now activated to bring the whole of humanity to a greater consciousness. We approach Christ and grasp him in our efforts to perfect and unify all in him. To help form Christ in others is the greatest act of charity that we can do.

And, finally, our charity becomes unified or synthesized. A great part of our life lacks true charity as its impelling motive for action. Our contact with material creatures or with our fellow men is motivated by self-interest or utility. But when, through conscious reflection, we center ourselves and all our activities on the central reality of Christ, the evolver of the universe towards whom and in whom the whole universe is converging, then the mass of our activities becomes synthesized. Teilhard insists that only when we give to all of our disparate actions a "psychic" character, a person-to-person, center-to-center, relationship to Christ, will our lives be meaningful. Our innermost energies are transformed and sublimated within "the field of the Omega."[46]

The Church, the phylum of salvation, and the material cosmos are moving to a completion that will be realized only in their convergence at the Omega Point in the parousia. Teilhard views these two complementary growths as being directed totally by Christ, as has been pointed out, and climaxing in him as in their final end. He is the "summit" towards which both the Church and the cosmos are evolving. As a human embryo gestates in the womb, is nurtured by the mother, and passes through different stages of painful growth, undergoing constant changes yet continuous with the beginning embryo and the mature adult, so the Church and the cosmos move through steady growth and diminishments into their transfigured fullness.

Teilhard rejects any cosmic catastrophe or cataclysm bringing an end to our universe by total destruction. The renovation of St. Paul's "new creation" will take place after a point of maturation has been reached when man, completely reflective, not only individually but collectively will reach the limit of this world.[47] In his *Le Coeur du Probleme,* he pleads for a new view of the parousia along more cosmic, evolutive lines.

But why should we assume, in accordance with the latest scientific view of mankind in a state of anthropogenesis, that the parousia-spark of physical and organic necessity can be kindled only between heaven and a mankind which has biologically reached a certain critical evolutionary point of collective maturity?[48]

Full neurological maturation is a condition, necessary as Teilhard conceives it, but not, however, a determining cause for the emergence of rational man. The Son of Man will return on his own initiative, yet there is a relationship because the activity of Christ in the universe bringing it to maturation is precisely devised so that he may appear at the end of the process, when the divine plan will have been brought to its full completion. When or how this will take place constituted idle speculation for Teilhard. But the important point of emphasis placed by Teilhard is the continuity between the state of nature's gestation and its full maturation into a creation ever new, yet ever old.

In *The Divine Milieu,* Teilhard gives some signposts that can be noted as the universe moves closer to the Omega Point in the parousia. There will be an increase of attraction exercised by Christ on his members. Then there will be an increase of interest in the preparation and consummation of the parousia. This interest will spring from a clearer perception of the relationship between Christ's recapitulation action and our work that is adding to the "construction" of the world in its fullness in Christ.[49]

The progress of the universe, he points out, is not in competition with God. The last pages of Teilhard's *The Divine Milieu* summarize what we have tried to formulate earlier in this chapter. The parousia, as the same goal of the material, evolutive universe and the Church, gives meaning to our human lives and their relations with the material created world by giving us a glimpse into the finality of God, that which is last to be achieved in execution but is the raison d'être, creating, developing, and consummating all creatures. The world cannot have two goals, two ends, two summits, two centers. Christ alone is the center and the goal of our universe. The more man becomes conscious of Christ's presence at the very heart of the earth, the more beautiful creation becomes, thus preparing a mystical body worthy to be resurrected into a full participation of the life that is already his at the center of our created world.[50]

Teilhard's Christological Contribution

Teilhard would have been the last to claim originality in the content of his christology. His frequent appeals to the doctrine of St. Paul, St. John, and the early Fathers indicate his conviction that he was careful of the traditional mind of the Church. Yet his approach to christology cannot be called the traditional approach as presented by the majority of dogmatic theologians. Because he was a scientist deeply immersed in the scientific problems of the modern age, he brought to his treatment of christology not only profound respect for empirical methodology but a new perspective in which to view the traditional christology of the Christian faith.

He felt deeply the schism between science and faith, the dichotomy between modern life, with its immersion in material tasks, and the spiritual life. By approaching christology through the perspective of cosmic evolution, he has essayed, at least, a synthesis of scientific, theological, and philosophical knowledge.

Daniélou has pointed out how Teilhard sought to correct the static concept of man by returning to the dynamic Biblical view of his three-dimensional unity:[51] (1) Man becomes master of the cosmos and actuates the divine image within himself by his work, his actual daily labors. (2) He moves through his work and social relationships into a community of interpersonalism based on love, and through love of neighbor he ascends to love of God. (3) Thus, both as individual and as member of a community, man opens his whole being to adoration of God, his Maker and final end.

Teilhard's optimism finds a way to unite these three stages, so that the technical world of man's daily activities is shown as the "stuff" out of which the community in Christ is formed to give adoration through the whole universe to God. The Incarnation is, of course, the heart of his cosmic christology. At the decisive moment in the evolutive process of the universe and, more specifically, of man in the noosphere, God becomes man. Christ is the Speech of God telling us of God's plans. He is the key to the mysterious ways of God that unfold in the perspective of cosmic evolution. He is the climax, perfect man, everything men are groaning to become, the fulfillment of the human race.

In a real way Jesus Christ is humanity fulfilled. He is the image according to which all human beings have been created. But he is also the means or axis along which man moves to the higher and last step of evolution, to christogenesis. St. Paul has told the Ephesians: "And this good pleasure he decreed to put into effect in Christ when the designated period of time had elapsed, namely, to gather all creation both in heaven and on earth under one Head, Christ" (Eph. 1:9-10). Teilhard is telling the modern world that Christ, immersed in the evolving cosmos, is actively guiding this world to himself as the Omega Point of reconciliation with his heavenly Father.

Science and faith blend as complementary reports of the presence of God actively working to fulfill his universe. Science sees in this divine activity an unfathomable object of intricately ordered matter and energy. Faith reveals that this activity proceeds from a love both divine and intensely personal towards the persons that human beings are. Faith discovers the Divine Milieu that is this unfolding Love in the smile of a child, in the steady rhythm of the subway, in the water drop that mirrors his wondrous, turbulent world thrusting toward completion.

Man is to hear the Speech of God, Christ, in every creature as it groans its way to greater perfection. But, sadly, he can close his ears and refuse to hear the Speech of God. But when he does turn away, he locks himself within himself in the deaf egoism which produces self-destruction. Thus the process of the evolving universe goes forward and upward at the same time. And inserted within this total process guided always by Christ to the fullness which will presage his parousia is that phylum of salvation, the Church, those members of Christ who, through detachment, excentration, the cross, have rendered themselves "passionately indifferent" to everything but Christ.

Christ is being formed in them in a very real, ontological way as they yield themselves more perfectly to his direction. Charged with the living presence of Christ within them, these christified human beings, living within an expanding universe, extend the process of christification to hasten the day when the lines of the evolving universe and the evolving Christ in his members will converge in the Omega Point. Then he will truly be "all things in all." "For it pleased God the Father that in him all fullness should dwell, and that through him God should reconcile to himself every being, and make peace both on earth and in heaven through the blood shed on the cross" (Col. 1:19–20).

VII

THE LOGOS AND THE SECULAR CITY

The power of St. Paul, St. John, the early Eastern Fathers, and Teilhard de Chardin lies precisely in their ability to pierce through spatial and temporal concepts in order to view the history of salvation, of man's relationship to God, not from man's myopic point of view, but from the all-encompassing view of God himself. This *fourth-dimensional* perspective regarded God's extra-Trinitarian activity as a unity, unfolding, it is true, in time and space, but organically reflecting the unity of its Source and the constancy of its originating Love. It was God's infinite love that initiated the first act of creation, and it is the same dynamic divine love which evolves this initial creation into the fullness of his plan when the whole universe will be finally *amorized* into the "new creation" foretold by St. Paul.

The greatest reality that Jesus Christ came to reveal to the world, in the eyes of the early Christians, newly converted Jews and pagans, was that God so loved the world that he gave us his only-begotten Son. And this living Word came that we might have God's own life and have it more abundantly. The whole universe had its meaning, its *logos,* only in and through the Divine Logos. The fullness of human nature would be found only in a man in whom the Logos lived through divine grace. Thus man's fullest meaning, his fruition, does not reside in himself, but in Another. All of the early Greek Fathers agree with St. Paul and St. John that man has been made "according to Christ," "in whom," says St. Paul, "we have our redemption, the remission of our sins. He is the image of the invisible God, the first-born of every creature, because in him were created all creatures in the heavens and on the earth, both visible and invisible . . . All have been created through him and for him. He exists prior to all creatures, and in him they are all preserved in being" (Col. 1:4–7).

Jesus Christ, the Logos of the Eternal Father, is not only the model according to which all things are created, but he becomes the point of reference, the goal, the Omega Point (Teilhard's phrase) of all created beings. To describe the ultimate meaning that gave reality to any given creature, the Eastern Fathers developed their doctrine of the participated *logoi*, which they found, at least implicitly, in the writings of St. Paul and St. John. Each creature possessed a *logos* as its principle of harmony relating it to the Creator. But its "intelligibility" (logos) lay hidden beneath its exterior appearances. To penetrate beneath the surface of the phenomena that are perceived by our five senses and to get at this inner *logos* of a given creature would mean, to the early Fathers, to know its place and its role in the whole drama of the history of salvation. It would be to see each creature's meaning in the light of Christ's redemption of the entire cosmos. Christ is the greatest reality and gives meaning to the whole created world.

Man is God's masterpiece. He has been created by God "according to the image" (Gen. 1:26), and that perfect image is Jesus Christ. But uniquely among all creatures, man is privileged by God's gratuitous grace to be a temple in which the perfect image of the Father, the Divine Logos, dwells. With his intellect and will, man is to respond to this living Logos within, and thus God will change this image into the likeness of himself.

Such thinking about man's intimate relationship to Christ remained, for the Eastern Fathers, on the level of a dynamic unfolding of the created *logos* within us, actuated and realized by the love of Jesus Christ and by our personal response to his living presence. Modern man has increasingly rejected a Christianity that is overly abstract, categorical, rational, divorced from any total, living experience of God. Although theology requires definitions and concepts, these are not its total, nor indeed its primary, business. Its niceties and careful precisions must illuminate, not lose the Reality.

Divine Communication through Matter

Early Christian writers are characterized by their dynamic search to find the "really real" behind the fading, the temporal, the phenomenal. But they also stress the intimate, ontological relation of the material, phenomenal world to the "really real." Matter, in St. Paul, St. John, the Eastern Fathers, and Teilhard de Chardin, is not evil, nor a principle of evil. Matter is the starting point of a moving process that climaxes in spirit. It is in this sense that Teilhard often insists: "all matter is spirit." All matter is made for spirit; it receives its reality insofar as it is a medium between the Ultimate Reality, God, and man, made to God's image and likeness.

In this history of salvation, of God's communication and self-giving to mankind, he has always worked through his creatures. Man encountered God not in sleep nor by passive attitudes but in and through his own activities, in the very mundane circumstances in which he found himself.

To nomadic Jewish race of shepherds, God proved himself a provident Father by caring for them in both their material and spiritual needs. Moses and his followers carried the presence of God with them in the transportable Ark of the Covenant. God moved, lived, and acted with his people.

In the New Testament God reveals himself by his actions in the Person of Jesus Christ. Christ works, travels about, uses the material world, to reveal himself and give himself to us, through the sacrament of his humanity. Through bread, water, wine, a look, a touch, a word, he brings to individual persons a living experience, a deep consciousness of his divinity, above all through the Holy Eucharist.

Even outside of the sacramental system, Christ is using the material world to reveal himself and to give himself to us. And this puts theology today at a crossroads. It is not that Christian believers doubt the presence and action of Christ in the sacraments and in the material world of today, but they search for a new expression, a *new way* of conceiving and expressing Christ's presence and activity both in and outside the ecclesial, sacramental system. Christian theology is in crisis, not because of its unchangeable doctrines, but mainly because the *modes of representing* the essentials of Christianity do not have meaning any longer for urban man. Confrontation of theology with modern science, Jean Daniélou affirms, is a good thing for the simple reason that it detaches theology from its dead parts and makes its unchangeable substance shine more brightly.

Contact with non-Western cultures and non-Christian religions has expanded our perspectives of the working presence of Christ in our world. Our habitual mode of thinking—culturally, philosophically, and theologically—had become restricted, insular, and eventually irrelevant. Wider contacts with other philosophical, theological, and cultural expressions can refine and enrich the timeless elements in Christianity, freeing them from excessively Western, Aristotelian-Scholastic accretions. Currents of modern thought, inspired by the writings of Hegel, Bergson, Heidegger, are, in some aspects, unacceptable to Christian thought; for example, a phenomenology that denies the existence of a metaphysical absolute. Yet many positive advances in human thought have been made by these modern phenomenological philosophies.

But the danger is precisely what we have been warning about in describing Christian secularity. The tendency too often is not to search these systems for their intrinsic goodness and values, but to reinterpret them according to a fixed sacral ideology, and thus fail to discover God in the "secular." We impose the sacral upon the secular, thus destroying the possibility of finding God in the "secular," his own creation, and the ordinary medium whereby he first reveals himself to the majority of men.

Anonymous Christianity

How safeguard the autonomy of a world which is somehow both "secular" *and* "sacral"? What is the true meaning of "consecrating" these sources of so much human beauty and creativity to the cause of Christianity? Need a truly humanistic work of art *change* to become truly "Christian"?

Karl Rahner[1] incorporates these humanistic, cultural expressions of art, including also the religious yearnings of non-Christian peoples, into what he calls an "anonymous" Christianity. He distinguishes the first aspect of the Church as the incarnate presence of Christ and his grace within the human race, a unity brought about by Christ's incarnation and universal redemption of all men. Then he presents the social, juridical, sacramental Church. Rahner shows there is, indeed, no salvation outside of the Church if "Church" is understood in the first sense.[2] Thus men can be saved *ex voto Ecclesiae,* by an *implicit* desire for the Church, contained in their explicit desire to believe and to do all God wills for their salvation. Their "non-sacral" activities and institutions can sanctify those who have been inculpably deprived of the knowledge of the full, concrete expression of the divine will as manifested in Christ's Church. Rahner shows that the whole human race is united by a concrete unity, not only in the natural order but also in its orientation towards salvation as shown by the fact of original sin and the radical redemption wrought by Christ for all men. The insertion of man into this unity is a reality accomplished independently of any personalized, free act on man's part. Endowed with a human nature and the possibility of free, self-determining acts, man already possesses this oneness with all men, an orientation as a person in the unity of the "people of God" towards God. By taking upon himself the same human nature, Christ effects in mankind God's intention of sharing with them his Trinitarian life. But this is a vocation, a call, already present in the world, radicated in man's nature:

If then man as a spiritual person realizes his "nature" by a total decision concerning himself, this personal decision is always concretely and inevitably a choice either to accept or reject the supernatural calling of man to the participation in the Trinitarian life of God Himself.[3]

Rahner distinguishes clearly the sacral, juridical, socially structured Church from the presence and activity of Christ and his Church as non-sacral, yet orientated towards the sacral Church. Man's secular pursuits, though not sacral as such, do not contradict but complement the activities of Christ in his established Church-Community. E. Schillebeeckx sums up the relationship between the two distinct but complementary orders:

This means that in the plan of salvation the concrete world, by definition, is an implicit Christianity; it is an objective, non-sacral but saintly and sanctified expression of mankind's communion with the living God; whereas the Church *qua* institution of salvation, with her explicit creed, her worship and sacraments, is the direct and sacral expression of that identical communion—she is the *separata a mundo* [unworldly]. To speak of the relationships between the Church and the world does not mean therefore that a dialogue is to be launched between the strictly Christian dimension of our human life and its distinctly non-Christian dimension; nor is it a question of conducting a dialogue between the religious and the profane, between the supernatural and the natural or intra-worldly—it is rather a dialogue between two complementary authentically Christian expressions of one and the same God-related life concealed in the mystery of Christ, namely, the ecclesial expression (in the strict sense of the word) and the worldly expression of that identically same life, internalized within human life through man's free acceptance of grace. In other words, the implicitly Christian and the explicitly Christian dimension of the same God-related life, that is, of human life hidden in God's absolute and gratuitous presence.[4]

What then is implicit Christianity? It is the whole human, earthly, profane, "secular" reality assumed into the God-related life which the secular expresses objectively, even though the relationship to the God-life is not recognized explicitly. A delicate balance must be maintained to prevent a true Christian secularity from falling into a mere instrumentalization for Christian evangelization or from falling into a sacralized ideology by confusing the sacred and the secular. Not only is the Church the visible sacral institution established by God to prolong the explicit activity of Christ's redemptive acts in mankind, but there are also sacral vocations, professional religious who by the profession of the three vows of poverty, chastity, and obedience, are a constant living witness to the sacral element that must comprise a portion of every man's interior life. But there must always be kept clearly in mind the distinction between the two, sacral and secular, orders.

The opposite danger to a true Christian secularity would be to push it so far from any God-orientation that it would be, in fact, secularism. C. A. van Peursen, cited by Harvey Cox, calls secularization (or secularity) "the deliverance of man first from religious and then from metaphysical control over his reason and his language."[5] Cox goes on to describe secularization:

It is the loosing of the world from religious and quasi-religious understandings of itself, the dispelling of all closed world-views, the breaking of all supernatural myths and sacred symbols . . . the discovery by man that he has been left with the world on his hands, that he can no longer blame fortune or the furies for what he does with it. Secularization is man turning his attention away from worlds beyond and toward this world and this time . . . Secularization simply bypasses and undercuts religion and goes on to other things. It has relativized religious world-views and thus rendered them innocuous. Religion has been privatized. It has been accepted as the peculiar prerogative and point of view of a particular person or group. It has convinced the believer that he could be wrong, and persuaded the devotee that there are more important things than dying for the faith.[6]

The element that Cox fails to inject into his Christian "secularization" is the relationship of the secular order to the supreme and universal dominion of God—and of his Christ.

Demythology of the Gospels

The basis of a Christian secularization that refuses to place the secular city under the dominion and direction of Christ is Bultmann's position that we can be sure of nothing or very little about the historical Jesus. His person becomes a reality when we encounter him through the "myths" of the Gospel and, in a way, "create" him as we allow him to enter into our lives. For Christ is dead, but we are alive!

How different is the view of Paul and John and the early Christian writers! For them the Gospel narration was truly the living word, the point of contact with Jesus Christ, the gloriously resurrected Lord of all creation, who stood outside of time, even while time coursed in and through his presence and activities. The Gospel is not merely an account of certain historical events like similar events recorded in history books. It is the account of events that occurred in time, yet are of universal application.

For example, when Jesus Christ forgave the sins of the paralytic, he did this *action* with *this* intention. But because he was (and is) the God-Man, his action, intention, and words are capable of being duplicated beyond any stricture of Palestinian geography or ancient time. As man with a human body capable of direct communication with other human beings, he communicated with concrete human beings in history. But because that human body died on the cross and was raised up on the third day by God to live gloriously in a new spiritualized manner, because that human body still was the body of the Divine Word, God himself, that divinized human body, that Body-Man, Jesus Christ, is able to make contact with men of all ages and in all places. Prayer uncovers for us the sensible sign in the Gospel and applies to us in our concrete circumstances of this or that given day the living presence and activity of the cosmic Christ.

Through the insertion of his divine Son into this material world by means of the Incarnation and his continued presence and activity through his resurrected, glorified humanity in that world, God has not only oriented his world towards the "explicit Christ" but is actually bringing such a goal to completion with man's cooperation. It is not entirely "man's world" to do with as he pleases. And it is not "sacralization" to recognize God as both the ground of our being and the goal, at least implicit, of all our human actions. The full man is both sacral and secular, as God intended him to be. Man is at once both profane, a part of the amorphous mass of indeterminate reality of the cosmos, and also sacred, a being fixed upon God as upon the ground of his being. Man is contingent, material, imperfect; yet he is also capable of stretching towards the wholly Other because of his basic impulse towards transcendence. Man desires communication with the Supreme Reality and it is in this personal encounter that man achieves a sacred transcendence.

Man, the Cooperator of God

Man, to be truly man, must become transcendent. The more he can act with full consciousness and reflection, the more he "humanizes" himself, unleashing the spiritual powers that enable him to transcend the material, the limited, the particular, and pass over to the realm of enduring and limitless spirit. Only by a conscious realization that his work has lasting value can man truly give himself wholly to the "secular" tasks. Unreflective persons, doing their work but not knowing why, also contribute to the fulfillment of God's universe. But only the reflective person opens himself fully to the communication of God. Teilhard de Chardin gives this practical advice on how to unite the secular and the sacral:

Try, with God's help, to perceive the connection—even physical and natural—which binds your labor with the building of the Kingdom of Heaven. . . . Never, at any time, "whether eating or drinking," consent to do anything without first of all realizing its significance and constructive value *in Christo Jesu,* and pursuing it with all your might. This is not simply a commonplace precept for salvation: it is the very path to sanctity for each man according to his state and calling. For what is sanctity in a creature if not to cleave to God with the maximum of his strength? And, what does that maximum cleaving to God mean if not the fulfillment—in the world organized around Christ—of the exact function, be it lowly or eminent, to which that creature is destined both by nature and supernature?[7]

The late Martin Buber introduced the world to the intimate personalism of the *I-Thou* encounter between man and God. It has been suggested that this kind of relationship better suits today's urbanized man in his encounter with God, since it stresses the intimacy between two persons. Although it implies love, the love may or may not be proved by actions. It could easily deteriorate into spiritual sensuality—loving God merely for what he can do for us. But an I-Thou relationship with God stresses a partnership not between equals, but a *synergism,* the harmonious relationship of God and man, grace and nature, as it was called by the early Greek Fathers. I encounter God as a cooperator through the work I am given to do. Moved by the basic conviction that every action performed by a human being is capable of contributing to the completion of God's plan of creation, I become more and more consciously aware that my actions are important, not only for self-realization, but also in aiding the whole created world, human and sub-human, to which I am tied by inextricable bonds.

The modern man must have his sacral moments of retirement when he can return within himself and find the immanent life of the Trinity not only present but exercising the mutual love of the Father for the Son and the Holy Spirit. Through the sacramental life of the Church, especially in the celebration of the Divine Liturgy, man in union with fellow men performs religious acts that have God as their explicit object of adoration. Still the major portion of modern man's time is spent in action, not necessarily physical labor, but in absorbing immersion in material things of the world. And never before has man had access to a larger array of creatures. He cannot choose *all* of them; he must choose some, to the exclusion of others. And in a way, man *becomes* his choice. If he chooses only the gross pleasures of life, he freely cuts himself off from more elevating, transcending values. He cuts himself off from greater human growth, to the degree that these pleasures dominate him. On the contrary, the more often he chooses before God as before a "Thou," and seeks to act in order to find God, the more he liberates himself and is truly free.

And the *You* of today, as was always true but not so evident, wants us to work in union with him on behalf of our fellow men. The almighty perfect God has no need of our actions, not even of our prayerful submission in adoring and glorifying him. He has gratuitously offered by our creation and redemption to give himself by giving us his own Trinitarian life, not only in the *eschaton,* or final life to come, but even now, in this present life. But the conditions of our receiving the communication and gift of himself to us depend on relinquishing our self-love to submit to him through a loving relationship of creature to Creator, adopted son to a heavenly Father.

This submission is symbolized precisely by our work. The first man, Adam, even before the Fall, was obligated to work and cultivate the earth. His actions concretized his interiority. After sin, original and personal, human work has become more difficult; the earth yields itself to man less easily. Yet work becomes man's asceticism whereby he overcomes his self-centeredness, egotism and self-love. But it is more than an instrument for self-perfection. It is more than the mere basket-weaving of some of the early Fathers of the desert, unweaving in the evening what they had woven during the day. What each individual man does is important and has repercussions on the whole of the universe. Man is charged as co-creator with God. He has been given the awesome responsibility in cooperation with God to bring this universe from chaos to the order willed by God. Each man's work contributes to the greater realized perfection of the universe.

God does not create for death or annihilation but gives us life and a universe teeming with millions of fellow creatures in order to achieve his one, united plan. God is not like a jealous Zeus, punishing Prometheus for having given the gift of fire to man. All created beings are God's gifts to be used and developed by thinking man so that eventually "creation itself would be delivered from its slavery to corruption, to enjoy the freedom that comes with the glory of the children of God. For we know that all creation groans and travails in pain until now" (Rom. 8:21–22).

The Church, Sacral and Anonymous

At the center of this created universe our Christian faith presents to us Jesus Christ. The preceding chapters have traced the revealed teaching of Christ's presence and activities in the universe through St. Paul, St. John, the early Eastern Fathers, and Teilhard de Chardin. We merely recapitulate here what we said earlier in a more detailed treatment of Christ's presence and activities in the soul of the individual Christian, in the Church-Community, and in the cosmos.

Our eschatological hope through Christ's revelation is that, not only our soul, but our body, our total *person,* will be joined to the resurrectional life of the living Savior. But if our material being will reach its completion by a transformation and "ascension" from this earthly existence to an "incorruptible" one, the Christian faith expresses the hope that the whole cosmos will be transfigured into a "new creation." It is the glorified Christ that associates himself as mediator in bringing the universe to its appointed completion. St. Paul pictures Christ bringing all under subjection to him so that he can bring it back to his heavenly Father "in order that God may be everything to everyone and everything" (I Cor. 15:28). In Jesus Christ, God the Father has destined that the fullness of the whole universe should dwell. He is reconciling, recapitulating, leading back to his heavenly Father the created universe, but one fulfilled and actuated in its fullness by being one with Christ (Col. 1:15–20).

God's will is "to gather all creation both in heaven and on earth under one head, Christ" (Eph. 1:10). Christ has complete primacy and dominion over the cosmic universe through his death and resurrection. "He [God] has subjected every single thing to his authority and has appointed him sovereign head of the Church which is truly his body, the complement of him who fills all members with all graces" (Eph. 1:21–23). The Body of Christ is his Church (Eph. 5:23–30). He is united to his followers as the head is united with all the members of the body.

But the Body of Christ must grow until it reaches its fullness (*pleroma*). The Vatican II Constitution, *De Ecclesia,* says:

> The Church, or, in other words, the kingdom of Christ now present in mystery, grows visibly through the power of God in the world.[8]

Further on it recalls the universal will of God:

> All men are called to belong to the new people of God. . . . It fosters and takes to itself, insofar as they are good, the ability, the riches, and customs in which the genius of each people expresses itself. Taking them to itself, it purifies, strengthens, elevates and ennobles them.[9]

The Church is not opposed to the world but it guarantees its only completion. In a very real sense, the whole "secular" world, to use St. Paul's strong metaphor, is groaning and travailing in pain (Rom. 8:22) until it reaches its full growth united to Christ. It is *in via* toward becoming the actualized, explicit Body of Christ. The ecclesial function of giving God's life (grace) to individuals extends beyond the limitations of the visible hierarchical Church. And the world in its hominisation process of growing to a greater consciousness of the unity among fellowmen is not altogether separate, yet it is distinct, from the visible Church.

Christ's life in its full expression is found only in his established Church. In regard to the "anonymous" Church, the secular world, we may avail ourselves of E. Schillebeeckx' example. A stone tossed into a placid lake produces ripples that spread out into continuous concentric circles, moving from the center until the circles touch the landed shore. The Church is the center from which grace goes out to touch all parts of the world. At this center, generating the outward movement, are the sacraments, chiefly the Eucharist, which gives us the Body-Person of Jesus Christ as physically present and acting among us. The circles spread out, becoming larger until they almost merge, but even here the impact of Christ, the *Pantocrator,* continues to be felt.[10] Thus we have the sacraments and Christ's living Word through the Church's preaching, added to the Christian human activities informed by grace, spreading out beyond the physical limitations of the visible Church to make Christ's grace manifest to the world in a visible form.

And we see that the life of Christ in the individual Christian and that same life shared by members of the *koinonia* (Church-Community) through Christian charity flows outwardly and becomes the means of contact whereby Christ offers himself through a communication and self-giving in grace to the world. The world is basically religious and oriented towards the explicit, full life of Christ found only in the Church. This orientation is from within the world of creatures by the very fact that God created all beings. Christ lives in his Church through the Holy Spirit, guiding the members and the hierarchy to persevere in knowing and "in doing the truth" (Jn. 3:21). But the same Holy Spirit is actively building up the Church, the Body of Christ, among those persons who are not *formally* members of Christ's Church.

Here we see how the "secular" occupations are potentially, at least, oriented towards the full Church. In the human conscience, also, where the Holy Spirit breathes and moves men towards unity in Christ, the Church is increasing. This growth cannot be measured, but its reality is as undeniable as the fact of conscience itself. It is this "invisible Christianity" that Karl Rahner refers to in the following quotation:

> Today we know that there exists an invisible Christianity where, under the effect of God's action, the justification of sanctifying grace is really found. Even though a man belonging to this hidden Christianity may deny it, claim that he does not know if he is a Christian or that he cannot state with certainty that Christ is the Son of God, he may all the same have been through grace the object of divine election.[11]

All men are made by God in potency to be other sons of God through Christ the Logos come alive by God's pure gratuitous gift of his own life. But this life of the Trinity, though it infuses our total being, body and soul, is radicated in our intellect and will as the source of continued, progressive growth in Christ. Though always remaining distinctly ourselves, we approach a greater likeness to Christ by our generous response to the Logos speaking within us. The activity of the Holy Spirit that leads us to the Logos, the Speech of God within us, operates also in a man immersed in his secular, monotonous activities of each day. It can be an activity that remains hidden, appears completely "secular" and far removed from the sacral or a religious ideology. Above all, it may not be recognized at all by the individual as anything extraordinary. Yet the Holy Spirit builds up Christ's Church, his Body, particularly in those purely profane actions where man forgets himself as the center of all his thoughts, to project himself outside toward his fellow men, in response to his conscience.

Transcending Action

When man does respond to his "inner self," his true person expands and becomes more open to further communications from God, leading him always to the fullness of life as dispensed in Christ's Church. In all religions, especially in the fullness of God's revelation in the Christian mysteries, after the initial encounter with a God "outside," the believer turns within to encounter his Maker at the core that made him a free, loving being. This is precisely what makes a man different from animals and plants, what makes him an image of the one Image of God, the Logos. Man's progression from an imperfect being to a more perfect one, from a lesser man to a more fully realized human being, consists in a gradual progression from the phenomenal world of choices, rooted in senses and passions, guided always by the determining motive of his choice. He moves to *eros* (what do I, as a god with a small *g,* get out of it?) and gradually advances through unselfish love of himself to *agape,* where the determining motive of his choice is love of God, heedless of any reward. God becomes the object of an "excentration" in which man finds and expands the core of his real being.

People at different levels of personality development express this inner core of being where their outflowing energy approximates closely the divine act of creation. A man and a woman, deeply in love, experience this divine creativity in their conjugal union when they leave selfish *eros* to find their own beings and to expand by giving without reserve to the other, to bring forth in that outflowing energy of life a new life, made to the image and likeness of God himself. This is creativity at its highest, union through *agape,* finding God in a sharing of his loving creation.

A mother working patiently to form her child, a Peace Corps worker in the heart of Africa, a religious or lay person teaching a class, all have experienced what it means to transcend the empirical, external *eros*-determinations in order to penetrate deep within themselves, and, at the core of their being, to find the spark of divine creativity which enables them to give themselves in unselfish love for others.

This is true liberation, a true expansion, a resurrection to a new and higher level of life. It may be consciously achieved through faith in ontological union with God living within us, or unconsciously in the performance of our "secular" actions. Yet the law of God holds always true in regard to our self-development. To "ascend" to a higher form of existence, a greater liberation, we must undergo a "descending" process, a dying to the elements in our total make-up that act as obstacles to a higher mode of existence. The more man, on a purely secular level with no reflective reference to God, gives up his selfish aggrandizement by thinking of and helping others, the more he prepares himself for a fuller living according to his total nature as God destined him.

In order to move outside of ourselves we must work through our sense experience. We do not love our neighbor or God except by approaching them transcendently through vivid, consciously lived sense experiences. One of the great dangers of modern life is that we have been allowing our senses to atrophy through our thermostated, controlled life. We find it difficult to hear the music in a child's voice, the rhythm of the traffic, the steady beat of our own heart. The touch of cool, cleansing water on a sweaty face has lost its restorative meaning for us. The taste of clean, freshly baked bread on hungry lips, the smell of the ozone in the air after a clearing rain, are lost experiences. In a word, because we do not live intensely sensory experiences, we are no longer "open" to move from the material world to values of a more transcendental nature. Thus we close ourselves off from the possibility of God communicating to us through his material world.

We have a great need today to re-educate our senses in order that they bring to consciousness sharp, vital, full sense experiences, the only way in which the material world can make contact with our interior selves, in which eventually the transcendent God can become truly the core of our immanent true selves. Perhaps abstract and pop art can help to awaken our eyes to "see" deeply in color and dimension. Can we not learn how to make contact with the transcendent God present in all of his created, material world as we walk, step by step, down the hard concrete streets of big cities? We could learn to see the beauty of the cross and the possible resurrection through grace in the drop of water lying in the dirty, urban street. In that drop of water we could after a while come to see the different colors of God's world, in which he is vitally immersed and dynamically working, reflected mirror-like. The symbol of a drop of water in a Harlem gutter, able to mirror the whole world around it, God's world, but still more deeply able to symbolize as water, can lead us to the promise and hope of a newly cleansed life in God. We have no other way to meet God but by beginning with his created world. In the activities of our commonplace life, in the sense experiences overly familiar to us from a lifetime of routine, in every human being that we encounter through our senses, we have a contact point with God.

End of Man—Divinization

Henri Bergson has strikingly said: "The universe is a machine to make gods."[12] In a sense different from Bergson's, who thought men could raise themselves to the life of God, we can say that the universe can make us gods. God has created the universe as a united whole for one purpose—to build up the Body of Christ. It is only by an intimate union with Christ and a sharing of his own Divine Life that man, even in this life, finds his peace, happiness, and fullness. Christ "descended" from within the Trinitarian life to take upon himself a new modality of existence in the Incarnation. The Trinitarian life, through the hypostatic union between the Second Person of the Trinity and his humanity, inserts itself within the human race.

Yet the determinate physical presence of Christ, limited in space and time by his physical body, hinders his self-giving to all men for all times and in all places. In the Ascension, Christ lost this determinate presence but only in order that through the Holy Spirit he could come into his disciples' existence in a new and more effective way. Their beings were deprived of one modality of Christ's existence in order that a new world be opened to them. They and we also are deprived of Christ's historical, physical, material presence only to participate in a far richer presence on a spiritual and sacramental level. So that his followers might be one, that he might remain in them and in us and we in him, he no longer lives among us in the same material modality. To unite us into a oneness of life with his Father, he had in a certain way to cease to be among us. Only when this absence took place could the presence of the Holy Trinity be felt in us. Through Christ's resurrectional life bestowed on us by Baptism, we ascend to a new life where God inhabits our being. Christ truly lives in the "new man" among whom St. Paul could count himself. "It is now no longer I that live, but Christ lives in me" (Gal. 2:20).

As the three Persons are inseparable, so we are united most intimately through Christ to the Father in the Holy Spirit. This is the embryonic life of the Trinity that grows through our response to God until it climaxes in eternal life. Not only in man is the Trinity present and working to fulfill him, but the whole universe bears the stamp of the Trinity. All created beings make contact with the Trinity through man who is directed by the Trinitarian life within himself. The Trinity, without losing its transcendence, is made present and active in the cosmos by the historic and continued cosmic mediation of the Body-Person Jesus Christ in whom live also the Father and the Holy Spirit.

The whole theory of Irenaeus, Origen, Athanasius, Gregory of Nyssa, and Cyril of Alexandria concerning Christ the Recapitulator of the whole universe, fulfilling it and bringing it back to God in eternal glory at the parousia, flows from this central New Testament doctrine of the cosmic mediation of Christ.

> This is why the Word of God became man . . . that man . . . might become the son of God.[13]

Through Christ and the life that he brings us, we reach the Person of the Father in a union that is mysterious but nonetheless real. In this union we become, to use St. Augustine's term, *filii in Filio,* "sons in the Son," sons of God in and through the only-begotten Son of the Father. Our human nature does not change, but it reaches, at least in a seminal way, a state of higher existence, becoming in St. Peter's words "partakers of the divine nature" (II Pet. 1:4). Our destiny is to grow into the likeness of the first-born Son of God. Even now we possess this eternal life. The eschatological life is already ours. We are already living in eternity but at an imperfect level of fulfillment.

But we progress towards fullness by our life lived "in Christ," especially by our love for God incarnate in our love for our neighbor. In loving his children, we love them in whom he dwells actually or in potency.

Eschatology

Our rebirth, as Christ told Nicodemus, was to be a total transformation of our whole person, not according to the "flesh" (meaning the limited self-centered way of judging), but according to the "spirit." The Holy Spirit infuses not merely our intellects but all of our faculties, becoming the principle of a new life whereby we live according to the values of God. This totality of the Holy Spirit's influence extends, as we have already said, to all areas of human activity, impervious to the Cartesian dichotomy of sacred versus profane, Christian versus human, supernatural versus natural. "I will pour my Spirit over all flesh" (Joel 2:28). All things were made through Christ (Jn. 1:2). All things have been created for him and he preserves all creatures in being (Col. 1:17–18). He is now reconciling every being by bringing it to its fullness, to its goal as intended by God (Col. 1:20).

A true Christian eschatology, as we have seen in the eschatology of Paul, John, and the Eastern Fathers, shows forth this universal character of renewal in Christ through his Holy Spirit. One must note well the dual emphasis in these writings, especially in the New Testament, upon an eschatology that views the material world with scorn and pessimism and an eschatology of optimism towards the whole created cosmos. Modern man, especially, finds the pessimistic view difficult to digest as he sees himself on the verge of mastering not only the earth on which he lives but even the planets that lie millions of miles away. It seems to him that he is becoming the creator of his own destiny and that of the whole universe as well. St. Thomas' *omne ens est bonum* (all being is good) is to be preferred, so modern man reasons, to St. John of the Cross' *nada* (nothing, i.e., renunciation, etc.).

But to make *nada* an ontological principle and the *omne ens est bonum* a principle of spirituality is a grave error. The two are complementary aspects; their relationship must be maintained. Louis Bouyer expresses this in terms of the cross and redemption:

> The redemption has meaning only as restoring and perfecting the creation, in line with God's original and immutable plan for it. The Cross, therefore, with its culmination in the Resurrection, is not just something for which a place must, of course, be found in human life, but which is not to be allowed to permeate it through and through, for fear of the work of creation being retarded; quite the contrary, it has become a necessity for the creation. Apart from the Cross, the creation is doomed to failure, and only by the Cross can it be saved, recovered, and brought to its true end.[14]

When the material world and its "corruptible" aspect is presented in relationship to the end of this fleeting world, the materiality is presented in pessimistic tones. We find this negative eschatology in regard to current history strong among the prophets Isaias and Daniel. It is a running away and hiding, an other-worldliness that finds its way into the preaching of Christ himself in regard to this present "world." But they do not mean to announce any ontological principle here; they are simply reminding us that the material, corruptible world will eventually yield to a spiritualized, transformed world. In this light, their severe eschatological warnings can well be understood.

Ontologically the world as viewed both by the Old and New Testament writers is good as it comes from the hands of God and goes forward to its victorious completion at the end of time. The material creation is viewed as a homogeneously knitted whole, continuously moving forward to be gradually transfigured from its material, corruptible modality of existence into an incorruptible, spiritualized "Heavenly Jerusalem." Because the emphasis is placed on the divine life through grace that will be ours eschatologically in the life to come, the eschatology is conceived as already begun. The same divine life is living in us. We already possess the principle of incorruptibility. Irenaeus says:

> Our bodies in receiving the Eucharist are even now no longer corruptible.[15]

Thus, due to the presence of God's life in us even now, Christian eschatology is viewed in two phases: the first coming of Christ in his Incarnation until the end of the world, and his second coming in the parousia. Irenaeus gives as the main difference between the second coming and Christ's present coming to us in grace, that in the second coming there will be a *multitude*, on a universal scale, enjoying the fullness of life;

however, he implies that the inner principle of this life will be the same.

Gustave Thils gives an example from the life of our Lord to illustrate the change that will take place in us. Christ was really God as he preached in Nazareth, Capharnaum, and Jerusalem. Yet his divinity was not fully manifested in his humanity except on Mt. Thabor in the Transfiguration. There was no change in Christ, yet a radical change took place in the belief of Peter, James, and John. The same life of God lives within us, but its glory is withheld from our conscious experience. In the final coming we will be transfigured so that the same Trinitarian life which we now enjoy will be manifested to us in the glory of seeing God "face to face."

Death—Encounter with the Cosmic Christ

Much has been written recently by leading Catholic theologians like Roger Troisfontaines, Karl Rahner, Ladislaus Boros, Robert Gleason, P. Glorieux, and A. Winklhofer on the theology of death.[16] Stimulated by a deep sense of human dignity due to the great personal love that Jesus Christ has for each individual redeemed by his blood, these authors have richly illumined the traditional teaching of Catholic eschatology in the light of studies of human freedom, consciousness, and personalistic values.

In death, man will attain his full consciousness as a total person. In this life we are "torn" individuals, torn by our disordered passions and interior faculties of knowing and judging. We are torn by the many separated and disconnected acts of the past, present, and future. This hinders our inner integration and unity. In the very moment of death we will encounter Christ not only as the object of our acceptance or rejection, but we will see him in his full cosmic dimensions. This cosmos that revelation tells us is now christocentric, is now under the guiding power of the resurrected Christ, will be revealed in its complete relationship to Christ "in whom we breath and move and have our being" (Acts 17:28). Our Christian faith tells us that through Christ's Incarnation, Resurrection and Ascension, he is intimately associated with the created, material world through his glorified humanity. God has decreed, as we see in Paul's capitivity letters, that all things are under Christ's rule and dominion and through him are to be brought to their completion unto the full glory of God. But in the moment of death our souls will become cosmic in their relation to Christ and to all created beings. Each man will be presented, even if in this life he did not know Christ fully through faith, with the choice of Christ as the source of his full self-realization, as the goal for which the individual person was created, even though this direction may not have been consciously and formally sought. In full consciousness, before the soul departs from the body, man will choose Christ or choose self as the center of his being.

Many of us will have already chosen Christ through a lifetime of progressively intensive acts of submission to him as manifested by our interior "conversion" towards him in faith and by our service on behalf of the other members of the Mystical Body of Christ. The final choice will be a climax in full freedom, following the many acts that prepared us during our lifetime with a gradual progression in freedom to choose in accordance with our *total* person. If one rejects Christ, he will reject him totally and consciously. In doing so, the individual, made ontologically by God to find his completion only in Christ, will eternally desire with full, conscious disposition to cut himself off from a personal relationship to Christ. Retaining his human nature, although incomplete and unfulfilled, he removes himself from the stream of humanity, from intimate relationship with the rest of the cosmos which is destined for completion in Christ.

God creates no "evil place," a Hell, to which he consigns such damned souls. But Hell is one of the greatest realities, as revealed to us by Jesus Christ. It is the eternal punishment brought about freely by an individual's choice to reject Christ. It is the condition in which the damned will exist for an eternity of intense, interior conflict of the senses, passions, interior faculties of knowledge and love. The total being, made with a desire for union with the full Perfection of Being, can no longer change its choice. It has directed itself away from God, yet all its parts are warring within with a burning desire to stretch out in the opposite direction towards God. Such a being will be in total estrangement and enmity with the cosmos. The whole cosmos, transfigured and harmoniously ordered completely to glorifying God in its relationship to Christ as the Center of the cosmos, will be a source of pain to the damned who know that the cosmos is to be transfigured in God and that they cannot enjoy its purified beauty and plentitude.

Parousia

Christian doctrine teaches us that Christ will come at the end of time to transform this universe by bringing it to its completion in and through himself. Then Christ's work, which began after his death and resurrection, continued through his glorious risen life in mankind and in the whole of the subhuman cosmos, will be completed. In a real sense, the parousia, the appearance of Christ, is already present in our universe. He is now achieving *in via* the victory over cosmic evil, a victory that will be full and perfect only at the end of time. In those in whom Christ is now living, there flows the same eschatological life he will live in them in the parousia or second coming. He is overcoming the forces of death, sin, and disorder to bring about a gradual transformation in the final parousia. *How*, in this last stage, this transformation will be brought about, God did not deem it necessary for us to know. We know Peter's dramatic description which largely follows the Old Testament apocalyptic literature that used images favoring a total cataclysm:

Then the heavens will pass away in a roaring flame and its elements will burn up and be dissolved. . . . By that coming the heavens will be set afire and dissolved, and the elements will be burned up and melted (II Pet. 3:10–13).

But for Paul who first met Christ on the road to Damascus as an immanent force, actively working, suffering, rejoicing, growing in the cosmos of God's creation, Christ is here and now being formed in his Body. This Body is, for Paul, a living entity of diverse members in whom Christ truly lives as the source of their new divine filiation. And his living members are to cooperate with him in reconciling the universe back to God.

If, then, any man is in Christ, he is a new creation; the old state of things has gone; wonderful to tell, it has been made over absolutely anew! All this comes from the action of God, who has reconciled us to himself through Christ, and has entrusted us with this ministry of reconciliation. We know that God was truly reconciling the world to himself in Christ (II Cor. 5:17–19).

Each individual member has a role to play in the reconciliation of the cosmos to Christ's power and rule. It is not only through the duty received in Baptism to announce the Gospel of salvation to the whole world, but above all through a daily life of constant response to the living Word within us, that we cooperate in filling up the Body of Christ.

In order that we can find Christ reconciling his cosmos and can actually cooperate to some small degree in his cosmic redemption, we must turn within ourselves daily and hear the Spirit of Christ guiding us. A constant purification of selfish motivation, a metanoia or change of heart, is needed whereby we turn away from inordinate self-love to a loving service of Christ. This is the proper attitude of a true Christian. Our conversion is not to be an event that occurs once, but it should be an abiding mental attitude of saying "yes" to Christ, the living Speech of God within us.

From the teaching of Christ and the way in which he worked in the lives of his early followers, we can be assured that there is no true Christianity without love of neighbor. This is the basic commandment that Christ gave us—to love one another with the love that he had for us. But love, as St. John and St. James continually tell us in their epistles, must be proved by deeds. By our continuous conversion to Christ as cooperators in effecting his reconciliation of all things according to the plan of his heavenly Father, the Holy Spirit works gradually more and more in us, giving us new gifts to be put at the service (*diakonia,* a favorite term of the early Church) of the whole Church-Body of Christ. This service will not entail merely ministering to the social or physical needs of God's creatures, but will embrace the range of the Holy Spirit's *charismata,* his gifts that are given for the "building up" of the Body of Christ, the Church.

Thus Christ is actually, even now, absolute Head of the material created cosmos, but his primacy will not be completely recognized until his second coming when he will return in a mysterious way to lead the created world ("all things were made by him," Jn. 1:2) back to the Father.

No longer will there be chaos, distension, aversion of the created, sub-human world from God. The whole brute world will have reached its completion in being transfigured from its deformity, its "vanity" as Paul calls it, into a "renovated creation." Our world will not be annihilated, but transfigured. Through the Incarnation, Jesus not only dwelled upon this material earth but he began the process of recapitulating all things according to his Father's plan.

Today we greatly need to recapture the vision of St. Paul, St. John, and the early Christians, especially as typified by the early Greek Fathers. They saw in Jesus Christ the *Alpha,* the beginning, the image according to which not only man but the whole material world was created. He was for them also the *Omega,* the goal, the end towards which every finite creature was moving as toward a magnet that drew by an active force of personal love all human beings, who alone, incorporated in Christ Jesus, were *fully* human. Unwilling humans, who would refuse to accept their fulfillment in Christ, would eject themselves from the stream of humanity moving towards Christ. But the stream, as God intended, would flow on to its goal.

Thus, early Christianity was filled with an optimism that knew the material world was moving from death and corruption, the wages of sin, up to incorruptible life in Christ. In the person of Jesus Christ, vibrantly alive and inserted into the material world and working actively with our imperfect cooperation, is to be found the key to progress and the full meaning of this created cosmos. The whole created cosmos, including man, is to be brought into the glorification of God. Jesus Christ is *now* accomplishing *in* the created universe the completion and fulfillment which his first coming began, and which his second coming will tell us is finished.

Once everything has been brought into subjection to him, then the Son himself, in order that God may be everything to everyone, will be brought into subjection to the Father who subjected everything to him, in order that God may be everything to everyone and everything (I Cor. 15:28).

APPENDIX
SELECTED QUOTATIONS FROM THE GREEK FATHERS

IRENAEUS

1. With God there are simultaneously exhibited power, wisdom and goodness. His power and goodness appear in this, that of His own will He called into being and fashioned things having no previous existence; His wisdom is shown in His having made created things parts of one harmonious and consistent whole; and those things which, through His supereminent kindness receive growth and a long period of existence, do reflect the glory of the uncreated One, of that God who bestows what is good ungrudgingly. . . . and thus in all things God has the preeminence, who alone is uncreated, the first of all things and the primary cause of the existence of all, while all other things remain under God's subjection. But being in subjection to God is continuance in immortality and immortality is the glory of the Uncreated One. By this arrangement, therefore, and these harmonies and a sequence of this nature, man, a created and organized being, is rendered *according to the image and likeness of the uncreated God*—the Father planning everything well and giving His commands, the Son carrying these into execution and performing the work of

creating and the Spirit nourishing and increasing what is made, but man making progress day by day and ascending towards the perfect, that is, approximating to the Uncreated One (*AH,* IV, 38, 3–4, pp. 521–523).[1]

2. For by the hands of the Father, that is, by the Son and the Holy Spirit, man, and not merely a part of man, was made in the likeness of God. Now the soul and the spirit are certainly a part of the man but certainly not the man; for the perfect man consists in the commingling and the union of the soul receiving the spirit of the Father and the admixture of that fleshly nature, which was moulded after the image of God . . . But when the spirit here blended with the soul is united to God's handiwork (*plasma*), the man is rendered spiritual and perfect because of the outpouring of the Spirit and this is he who was made in the image and likeness of God. But if the Spirit be wanting to the soul, he who is such is indeed of an animal nature, and being left carnal, shall be an imperfect being, possessing indeed the image of God in his formation (*in plasmate*), but not receiving the similitude through the Spirit, and thus is this being imperfect . . . Neither is the soul itself, considered apart by itself, the man; but it is the soul of a man and part of a man. Neither is the spirit a man, for it is called the spirit, and not a man; but the commingling and union of all these constitutes the perfect man . . . For this cause he (Paul) declares that those are "the perfect" who present unto the Lord the three component parts without offence. Those then are the perfect who have had the Spirit of God remaining in them, and have preserved their souls and bodies blameless, holding fast the faith of God, that is, that faith which is directed towards God and maintaining righteous dealings with respect to their neighbors (*AH,* V, 6, pp. 531–532).

3. How then shall he be a God who has not as yet been made a man? Or how can he be perfect who was but lately created?

How again can he be immortal who in his mortal nature did not obey his Maker? . . . . If, however, thou wilt not believe in Him and wilt flee from His hands, the cause of imperfection shall be in thee who didst not obey, but not in Him who called thee . . . The skill of God therefore is not defective, for He has power over the stones to raise up children for Abraham; but the man, who does not obtain it, is the cause to himself of his own imperfection. The light does not fail because some persons have become blind. The light remains ever the same. It is those who are blinded that are involved in darkness through their own fault. The light does not enslave anyone by necessity; nor does God exercise compulsion upon anyone unwilling to accept the exercise of His skill. Those persons, therefore, who have apostatized from the light given by the Father and transgressed the law of liberty have done so through their own fault since they have been created free agents and possessed of power over themselves (*cf. AH,* IV, 39, 2–3, pp. 522–523).

4. And thus also it was that the knot of Eve's disobedience was loosed by the obedience of Mary. For what the virgin Eve had bound fast through unbelief, this did the Virgin Mary set free through faith . . . an inversion of the process by which these bonds of union had arisen (*AH,* III, 22, 4, p. 455).

5. . . . in doing away with that disobedience of man which had taken place at the beginning by the occasion of a tree, "He became obedient unto death, even the death of the cross"; rectifying that disobedience which had occurred by reason of a tree, through that obedience which was brought out upon the tree (*AH,* V, 16, 3, p. 544).

6. For this is why the Word of God is man, and this is why the Son of God became the Son of Man, that man might possess the

Word, receive adoption and become the son of God. In no other way could we receive incorruptibility and immortality. But how could we be united with incorruptibility and immortality, unless incorruptibility and immortality had first become what we are, in order that what is corruptible might be absorbed by incorruptibility and what is mortal by immortality, that so we might receive the adoption of sons? (*AH,* III, 19, 1, pp. 448–449).

7. For as God is always the same, so also man, when found in God, shall always go on towards God. For neither does God at any time cease to confer benefits upon, or to enrich man; nor does man ever cease from receiving the benefits, and being enriched by God. For the receptacle of His goodness, and the instrument of His glorification, is the man who is grateful to Him that made Him (*AH,* IV, 11, 2, p. 474).

8. But as the engrafted wild olive does not certainly lose the substance of its wood, but changes the quality of its fruit and receives another name, being now not a wild olive, but a fruit bearing olive and is called so, so also when man is grafted in by faith and receives the Spirit of God, he certainly does not lose the substance of flesh, but changes the quality of the fruit of his works and receives another name, showing that he has become changed for the better, being now not mere flesh and blood but a spiritual man and is called such (*AH,* V, 11, 1–2, p. 536).

9. And therefore throughout all time, man, having been moulded at the beginning by the hands of God, that is, of the Son and of the Spirit, is made after the image and likeness of God: the chaff, indeed which is the apostasy, being cast away; but the wheat, that is, those who bring forth fruit to God in faith, being gathered into the barn. And for this cause tribulation is necessary for those who are saved, that having been after a manner broken up, and ren-

dered fine, and sprinkled over by the patience of the Word of God, and set on fire (for purification), they may be fitted for the royal banquet. As a certain man of ours said, when he was condemned to the wild beasts because of his testimony with respect to God: "I am the wheat of Christ and am ground by the teeth of the wild beasts, that I may be found the pure bread of God" (*AH*, V, 28, 4, p. 557).

CLEMENT OF ALEXANDRIA

10. Knowledge, to speak generally, is a perfecting of man as man and is consummated by acquaintance with divine things, in character, life and word . . . conformable to the Divine Word. By it faith is perfected, inasmuch as it is solely by it that the believer becomes perfect (*Strom.,* VII, 10, p. 538).[2]

11. For the image of God is His Word, the Genuine Son of Mind, the Divine Word, the archetypal light of light; and the image of the Word is the true man, the mind which is in man, who is therefore said to have been made "in the image and likeness of God," assimilated to the Divine Word in the affections of the soul and therefore rational (*Protrep.,* 10, p. 199).

12. For the image of God is the divine and royal Word, the impassible man; and the image of the image is the human mind. And if you wish to apprehend the likeness of another name, you will find it named in Moses, a divine correspondence (*Strom.,* V, 14, p. 466).

13. For conformity with the image and likeness is not meant of the body (for it were wrong for what is mortal to be made like what is immortal), but in mind and reason, on which fitly the

Lord impresses the seal of likeness, both in respect of doing good and of exercising rule (*Strom.,* II, 19, p. 370).

14. He is the gnostic, who is after the image and likeness of God, who imitates God as far as possible, deficient in none of the things which contribute to the likeness as far as compatible, practising self-restraint and endurance, living righteously, reigning over the passions, bestowing of what he has as far as possible and doing good both by word and deed (*Strom.,* II, 19, p. 369).

15. . . . a divine power of goodness clinging to the righteous soul in contemplation and prophecy and in the exercise of the function of governing, impresses on it something, as it were, of intellectual radiance, like the solar ray, as a visible sign of righteousness, uniting the soul with light, through unbroken love, which is God-bearing and God-borne. Thence assimilation to God the Savior comes to the Gnostic as far as permitted to human nature, he being made perfect "as the Father who is in heaven" (*Strom.,* VI, 12, p. 504).

ORIGEN

16. Wherefore we recognize that God was always the Father of His only-begotten Son, who was born indeed of Him and draws His being from Him, but is yet without any beginning . . . Wisdom, therefore, must be believed to have been begotten beyond the limits of any beginning that we can speak of or understand. And because in this very subsistence of wisdom there was implicit every capacity and form of the creation that was to be, both of those things that exist in a primary sense and of those which happen in consequence of them, the whole being fashioned and arranged before hand by the power of foreknowledge, wisdom,

speaking through Solomon in regard to these very created things that had been, as it were, outlined and prefigured in herself, says that she was created as a "beginning of the ways" of God, which means that she contains within herself both the beginnings and causes and species of the whole creation (*OFP,* I, 2, 2, p. 160).[3]

17. It is probably in this way that, so far as our weakness allows, we shall maintain a reverent belief about God, neither asserting that His creatures were unbegotten and co-eternal with Him, nor on the other hand that He turned to the work of creation to do good when He had done nothing good before . . . And certainly if all things have been made in Wisdom, then since Wisdom has always existed, there have always existed in Wisdom by a prefiguration and a pre-formation, those things which afterwards have received substantial existence . . . All genera and species have forever existed, and some would say even individual things; but either way it is clear that God did not begin to create after spending a period of idleness (*OFP,* I, 4, 5, p. 43).

18. . . . we understand it in such a way as to say that the first creation of rational creatures was also an incorporeal one, which was not meant to be in bondage to corruption for the reason that it was not clothed with bodies; for wherever bodies are, corruption follows immediately (*OFP,* III, 6, 1, pp. 246–247).

19. Now when God is said to become "all in all," just as we cannot include evil, when God becomes all in all, nor irrational animals, lest God should come to be in evil and in irrational animals; nor lifeless things, lest God, when He becomes all, should even come to be in them, so neither can we include bodies, which in their own nature are lifeless (*OFP,* III, 6, 2, p. 247).

20. One must therefore portray the meaning of the sacred writings in a threefold way upon one's own soul, so that the simple man may be edified by what we may call the flesh of the scripture, this name being given to the obvious interpretation; while the man who has made some progress may be edified by its soul, as it were; and the man who is perfect and like those mentioned by the apostle (I Cor. II, 6, 7)—this man may be edified by the spiritual law, which has a "shadow of the good things to come." For just as man consists of body, soul and spirit, so in the same way does the scripture, which has been prepared by God to be given for man's salvation (*OFP,* IV, 2, 4, pp. 275–276).

21. . . . when it is said that God is "all in all," it means that He is also all things in each individual person. And He will be all things in each person in such a way that everything which the rational mind, when purified from all dregs of its vices and utterly cleared from every cloud of wickedness, can feel or understand or think will be all God and that the mind will no longer be conscious of anything besides God and God will be the mode and measure of its every movement; and in this way God will be all to it. For there will no longer be any contrast of good and evil, since evil nowhere exists; for God, whom evil never approaches, is then all things to it; nor will one who is always in the good and to whom God is all things desire any longer to eat of the tree of the knowledge of good and evil (*OFP,* III, 6, 3, p. 248).

22. For now He will show to them, as to sons, the causes of things and the perfection of His creation . . . And when they have gone through everything connected with the reason of the stars and with those ways of life that exist in heaven they will come to "the things which are not seen," or to those whose names alone we have as yet heard, and to the things "invisible." . . . And so the

rational being, growing at each successive stage, not as it grew when in this life in the flesh or body and in the soul, but increasing in mind and intelligence, advances as a mind already perfect to perfect knowledge no longer hindered by its former carnal senses, but developing in intellectual power, even approaching the pure and gazing "face to face," if I may so speak, on the causes of things. And it attains perfection, first that perfection by which it rises to this condition, and secondly that by which it remains therein, while it has for the food on which it feeds the problems of the meaning of things and the nature of their causes. . . . I think that the mind, when it has come to perfection, still feeds on appropriate and suitable food in a measure which can neither admit of want nor of superfluity. But in all respects this food must be understood to be the contemplation and understanding of God, and its measures to be those that are appropriate and suitable to this nature which has been made and created. These measures will rightly be observed by everyone of those who are beginning to "see God," that is, to understand Him through "purity of heart" (*OFP,* II, 11, 7, pp. 153–154).

ATHANASIUS

23. Like a musician who has attuned his lyre, and by the artistic blending of low and high and medium tones produces a single melody, so the Wisdom of God, holding the universe like a lyre, adapting things heavenly to things earthly, and earthly things to heavenly, harmonizes them all, and, leading them by His will, makes one world and one world-order in beauty and harmony (*Contra Gentes,* 41, p. 26).[4]

24. . . . but, because He is good, He guides and settles the whole Creation by His own Word, who is Himself also God, that by governance and providence and the ordering action of the Word,

Creation may have light, and be enabled to abide always securely. For it partakes of the Word who derives true existence from the Father, and is helped by Him so as to exist, lest that should come to it which would have come, but for the maintenance of it by the Word, namely, dissolution,—"for He is the Image of the invisible God, the first-born of all Creation, for through Him and in Him all things consist, things visible and things invisible, and He is the Head of the Church" (Col. 1, 15–18), as the ministers of truth teach in their holy writings (*Contra Gentes,* 41, p. 26).

25. If there be an Image of the invisible God, it is an invisible Image; nay, I will be bold to add, that, as being the likeness of the Father, never was it not. For when was that God, who according to John, is called Light (for "God is Light"), without a radiance of His proper glory, that a man should presume to assert the Son's origin of existence, as if before He was not? But when was not that Image of the Father's Ineffable and Nameless and Unutterable Subsistence, that Expression and Word, and He that knows the Father? For let him understand well who dares to say, "Once the Son was not," that he is saying, "Once Wisdom was not," and "Word was not," and "Life was not" (*De Decretis,* 27, p. 168).

26. . . . being God, God gives them (men) a share in His own Image, our Lord Jesus Christ, and makes them after His own Image and after His likeness; so that by such grace perceiving the Image, that is, the Word of the Father, they may be able through Him to get an idea of the Father, and knowing their Maker, live the happy and truly blessed life (*De Incarnatione,* 11, p. 42).

27. For God, Maker of all and King of all, that has His Being beyond all substance and human discovery, inasmuch as He is

good and exceedingly noble, made, through His own Word, our Savior Jesus Christ, the human race after His own image (*kat'-eikona*) and constituted man able to see and know realities by means of this assimilation to Himself, giving him also a conception and knowledge even of His own eternity, in order that, preserving his nature intact, he might not ever either depart from his idea (*logikos*) of God, nor recoil from the communion of the holy ones; but having the grace (*charis*) of Him that gave it, having also God's power from the Word of the Father, he might rejoice and have fellowship with the Deity, living the life of immortality unharmed and truly blessed (*Contra Gentes,* 2, p. 5).

28. He gave them a further gift, and He did not barely create men, as He did all the irrational creatures on the earth, but made them after His own image, giving them a portion even of the power of His own Word; so that, as it were, having a kind of reflection of the Word, and being made rational, they might be able to abide ever in blessedness. . . . (*De Incarnatione,* 3, p. 37).

29. Just then, as though a man had plunged into the deep, and no longer saw the light, nor what appears by light, because his eyes are turned downwards, and the water is all above him; and perceiving only the things in the deep, thinks that nothing exists beside them, but that the things he sees are the only true realities, so the men of former times, having lost their reason, and plunged into the lusts and imaginations of carnal things and forgotten the knowledge and glory of God, their reasoning dull, or rather following unreason (*alogos*), made gods for themselves of things seen, glorifying the creature rather than the Creator, and deifying the works rather than the Master, God, their cause and Artificer (*Contra Gentes,* 8, p. 8).

30. The Son of God became the Son of man in order that the sons of men, the sons of Adam, might be made sons of God. The Word, who was begotten of the Father in Heaven in an ineffable, inexplicable, incomprehensible and eternal manner, came to this earth to be born in time of the Virgin Mary, Mother of God, in order that they who were born of earth might be born again of God, in Heaven. . . . He has bestowed upon us the first-fruits of the Holy Spirit, so that we may all become sons of God in imitation of the Son of God. Thus He, the true and natural Son of God, bears us all in Himself, so that we may all bear in ourselves the only God (*De Incarnatione et Contra Arianos,* PG XXVI, 5, 992).

31. But now the Word having become man and having appropriated what pertains to the flesh, no longer do these things touch the body, because of the Word who had come into it, but they are destroyed by Him, and henceforth men no longer remain sinners and dead according to their proper affections, but having risen according to the Word's power, they abide ever immortal and incorruptible. Whence also, whereas the flesh is born of Mary, Bearer of God, He Himself is said to have been born, who furnishes to others an origin of being; in order that He may transfer our origin into Himself, and we may no longer, as mere earth, return to earth, but as being knit into the Word from Heaven, may be carried to Heaven by Him. Therefore, in like manner not without reason has He transferred to Himself the other affections of the body also; that we, no longer as being men, but as proper to the Word, may have a share in eternal life. For no longer according to our former origin in Adam do we die; but henceforward our origin and all infirmity of the flesh being transferred to the Word, we rise from the earth; the curse from sin being removed, because of Him who is in us, and who has become a curse for us. And with reason; for as we are all from earth and die in Adam, so being regenerated from above of water and Spirit, in the Christ we are all quickened; the flesh being no longer earthly, but being

henceforth made Word by reason of God's Word who for our sake "became flesh" (*Contra Arianos,* III, 33, p. 411).

32. But we by imitation become virtuous and sons; therefore not that we might become such as He, did He say "that they may be one as We are," but that as He, being the Word, is in His own Father, so that we too, taking an exemplar and looking at Him, might become one towards each other in concord and oneness of spirit, nor be at variance as the Corinthians, but mind the same thing as those five thousand in the Acts, who were as one (*Contra Arianos,* III, 19, p. 404).

33. When the Logos descended into the Holy Virgin Mary, the Spirit came at the same time into her and in the Spirit it is that the Logos was formed and His body was adapted, wishing through Him to unite and offer the Creation to the Father (*Ad Serapionem,* I, 31, PG XXVI, 604 C-605A).

34. It is then in the Spirit that the Logos glorifies Creation and deifies it and adopts and conducts it to the Father. But He who unites Creation to the Logos would not make a part of the created world just as He who confers filiation upon creatures would not be a stranger to being a Son. If such would be the case, one must search for another Spirit because in the first Spirit man is united to the Logos. This, however, is absurd. The Spirit does not make part of created things, but is proper to the divinity of the Father and it is in Him that the Logos deifies the creatures (*Ad Serapionem,* I, 25, PG XXVI, 589B).

35. For all things that are of the Father are of the Son also; therefore those things which are given from the Son in the Spirit are gifts of the Father. And when the Spirit is in us, the Word

also, who gives the Spirit, is in us, and in the Word is the Father (*Ad Serapionem,* I, 30, PG XXVI, 600B).

GREGORY NAZIANZEN

36. The Father is the begetter and emitter; without passion of course, and without reference to time and not in a corporeal manner. The Son is the begotten, and the Holy Spirit the emission; for I know not how this could be expressed in terms altogether excluding visible things (*Oratio,* 29, 2, p. 301).[5]

37. Now the Creator-Word, determining . . . to produce a single living being out of both the visible and invisible creations, fashions man; and taking a body from already existing matter and placing in it a Breath taken from Himself (Gen. 2, 7), which the Word knew to be an intelligent soul and the Image of God, as a sort of second world. He placed him, great in littleness (a microcosm), on the earth a new Angel, a mingled worshipper, fully initiated into the visible creation, but only partially into the intellectual; King of all upon earth, but subject to the King above; earthly and heavenly; temporal and yet immortal; visible and yet intellectual; halfway between greatness and lowliness; in one person combining spirit and flesh; spirit, because of the favor bestowed on him; flesh, because of the height to which he had been raised; the one that he might continue to live and praise his Benefactor, the other that he might suffer, and by suffering, be put in remembrance and corrected if he became proud of his greatness (*Oratio,* 38, 12, p. 348).

38. —for the tree was, according to my theory, Contemplation, upon which it is only safe for those who have reached maturity of habit to enter; but which is not good for those who are still some-

what simple and greedy in their habit . . . but when man . . . forgot the commandment . . . he put on the coats of skins . . . that is, perhaps, the coarse flesh, both mortal and contradictory. . . . Yet here too he makes a gain, namely death and the cutting off of sin, in order that evil may not be immortal. Thus his punishment is changed into a mercy; for it is in mercy, I am persuaded, that God inflicts punishment (*Oratio,* 38, 12, p. 348).

39. As these required a greater aid, so also they obtained a greater. And that was that the Word of God Himself . . . Who is before all worlds, the Invisible, the Incomprehensible, the Bodiless, the Beginning of being, light of light, source of life and immortality, the image of the archetypal beauty, the immovable seal, the unchangeable image, the Father's definition and Word . . . came to His own image, and took on Him flesh for the sake of our flesh, and mingled Himself with an intelligent soul for my soul's sake, purifying like by like; and in all points except sin was made man. O new commingling! [O strange conjunction! the self-existent comes into being; the uncreated is created, that which cannot be contained is contained, by the intervention of an intellectual soul, mediating between the Deity and the corporeity of the flesh.] And He who gives riches becomes poor, for He assumes the poverty of my flesh, that I may assume the richness of His Godhead. He that is full empties Himself, for He empties Himself of His glory for a short while, that I have a share in His fullness. What are the riches of His goodness? What is this mystery that is around me? I had a share in the image; I did not keep it. He partakes of my flesh that He may save the image and make the flesh immortal. He communicates a second communion far more marvelous than the first, inasmuch as then He imparted the better nature, whereas now Himself partakes of the worse. This is more godlike than the former action, this is loftier in the eyes of all men of understanding (*Oratio,* 8, 17, p. 294).

40. This is the purpose for us of God, who for us was made man and became poor to raise our flesh and recover His image and remodel man that we might all be made one in Christ who was perfectly made in all of us . . . that we may bear in ourselves only the stamp of God, by whom and for whom we were made and have so far received our form and model from Him that we are recognized by it alone (*Oratio,* 7, 23, p. 237).

41. For He is the Maker of all these, filling all with His essence, containing all things, filling the world in His essence, yet incapable of being comprehended in His power by the world; good, upright, princely, by nature not by adoption; sanctifying, not sanctified; measuring, not measured; shared, not sharing; filling, not filled; containing, not contained; inherited, glorified, reckoned with the Father and the Son; held out as a threat; the finger of God; fire like God; to manifest, as I take it, His consubstantiality; the Creator-Spirit who by Baptism and by resurrection creates anew; the Spirit that knows all things, that teaches, that blows where and to what extent He wishes; that guides talks, sends forth, separates, is angry or tempted; that reveals, illumines, quickens or rather is the very Light and Life; that makes temples, that deifies; that perfects so as even to anticipate Baptism, yet after Baptism to be sought as a separate gift; that does all things that God does . . . and making all things clear and plain; of independent power, unchangeable, almighty, all-seeing, penetrating all spirits that are intelligent, pure, most subtle . . . (*Oratio,* 31, p. 327).

42. . . . just as He gave existence to that which did not exist, so He gave new creation to that which did exist, a diviner creation and a loftier than the first, which is to those who are beginning life a seal, and to those who are more mature in age both a gift and a restoration of the image which had fallen through sin, that we may not, by becoming worse through despair, and ever being borne downward to that which is more evil, fall altogether from

good and from virtue, through despondency; and having fallen into a depth of evil (as it is said) despise Him; but that like those who in the course of a long journey make a brief rest from labor at an inn, we should be enabled to accomplish the rest of the road fresh and full of courage. Such is the grace and power of Baptism; not an overwhelming of the world as of old, but a purification of the sins of each individual, and a complete cleansing from all the bruises and stains of sin (*Oratio,* 40, 7, p. 361).

GREGORY OF NYSSA

43. In saying that "God created man" the text indicates by the indefinite character of the term all mankind; for was not Adam here named together with the creation as the history tells us in what follows? For here the name given is not the particular but the general one. Hence by the universal nature of the term, we are led to some such view as this; that in the Divine foreknowledge and power, all mankind was included in the first constitution. . . . I think that the entire plenitude of humanity was included by the God of all, by His power of foreknowledge, as it were in one body, and that this is what the text teaches us which says, "God created man, in the image of God created He him." For the image is not in part of our nature, nor is the grace in any one of the things found in that nature, but this power extends equally to all the race; and a sign of this is that mind is implanted alike in all. For all have the power of understanding and deliberating and of all else whereby the Divine nature finds its image in that which was made according to it. The man that was manifested at the first creation of the world and he that shall be after the consummation of all, are alike; they equally bear in themselves the Divine image (*De Opif. Hom.,* 16, 16, p. 406.)[6]

44. I take up once more in my argument our first text. God says, "Let us make man in our image, after our likeness, and God

created man, in the image of God created He him." Accordingly, the image of God which we behold in all human nature had its consummation then, but Adam as yet was not (*De Opif. Hom.*, 22, 3, p. 411).

45. For by "in summing up" it is shown that all things were made together, and "in the beginning" indicates the instant and simultaneous . . . The commencement of this cosmogony teaches that the sources, causes and powers of all things were collectively sent forth in an instant and in this first impulse of the Divine Will the essences of all things assembled together, heaven, ether, star, fire, air, sea, earth, animal, plant, all beheld by the eye of God and manifest by the word of Power, as the prophecy says, "He sees all things before their genesis." But through the Power and Wisdom together sent forth for the perfecting of each of the parts of the world, there followed a certain necessary series according to a certain order . . . appearing not by a kind of automatic chance according to an unordered and fortuitous movement but just as the necessary arrangement of nature required succession in the things coming into being, so each one is said to have come about . . . (*In Hexameron,* PG, XLIV, 72–73).

46. "God created man," it [Genesis] says, "in the image of God created He him." There is an end of the creation of that which was made "in the image"; then it resumes the account of creation and says, "male and female created He them". . . . Thus the creation of our nature is in a sense twofold: one made like to God; one divided according to this distinction (*De Opif. Hom.*, 16, 7, 8, p. 405).

47. For the grace we look for is a certain return to the first life, bringing back again to Paradise him who was cast out from it. If

then the life of those restored is closely related to that of the angels, it is clear that the life before the transgression was a kind of angelic life, and hence also our return to the ancient condition of our life is compared to the angels (*De Opif. Hom.*, 17, 2, p. 407).

48. One who regards only the dissolution of the body is greatly disturbed and makes it a hardship that this life of ours should be dissolved by death; it is, he says, the extremity of evil that our being should be quenched by this condition of mortality. Let him, then, observe through this gloomy prospect the excess of the divine benevolence . . . Now since by a motion of our self-will we contracted a fellowship with evil . . . falling away from that blessedness which is involved in the thought of passionlessness, we have been viciously transformed—for this reason, man, like some earthen potsherd, is resolved again into the dust of the ground, in order to secure that he may part with the soul which he has now contracted, and that he may, through the resurrection, be reformed anew after the original pattern; at least if in this life he has preserved what belongs to that image (*De Oratione Catech. Magna,* 7, p. 482).

49. Now the removal of what is foreign is a return to what is connatural and fitting; and this we can only achieve by becoming what we once were in the beginning when we were created. Yet to achieve this likeness to God is not within our power nor within any human capacity. It is a gift of God's bounty, for He directly bestowed this divine likeness on our human nature at its creation (*De Virginitate,* PG XLVI, 370B).

50. By whom was man to be recalled to the grace of his original state? To whom belonged the restoration of the fallen one, the

recovery of the lost, the leading back the wandered by the hand? To whom else than entirely to Him who is the Lord of his nature? For Him only who at the first had given the life was it possible, or fitting, to recover it when lost. This is what we are taught and learn from the Revelation of the truth, that God in the beginning made man and saved him when he had fallen (*De Oratione Catech. Magna,* 9, pp. 484–485).

51. For as the principle of death took its rise in one person and passed on in succession through the whole of mankind, in like manner the principle of the resurrection-life extends from one person to the whole of humanity (*De Oratione Catech. Magna,* 26, p. 489).

52. Since He is in all, He takes into Himself all who are united with Him by the participation of His body; He makes them all members of His body, in such wise that the many members are but one body. Having thus united us with Himself and Himself with us, and having become one with us in all things, He makes His own all that is ours. But the greatest of all our goods is submission to God, which brings all creation into harmony. . . . Thus all creation becomes one body, all are grafted one upon the other, and Christ speaks of the submission of His body to the Father as His own submission (*In Illud: Tunc ipse filius subjicietur,* PG XL, 1317).

53. But the descent into the water and the triune immersion of the person in it involved another mystery. For since the method of our salvation was made effectual not so much by His precepts in the way of teaching as by the deeds of Him who has realized an actual fellowship with man and has effected life as a living fact,

so that by means of the flesh which He has assumed and at the same time deified, everything kindred and related may be saved along with it, it was necessary that some means should be devised by which there might be, in the baptismal process, a kind of affinity and likeness between him who follows and Him who leads the way (*De Oratione Catech. Magna,* 35, p. 502).

54. . . . since God infused Himself into perishable humanity for this purpose, namely, that by this communion with Deity mankind might at the same time be deified, for this end it is that, by dispensation of His grace, He disseminates Himself in every believer through that flesh whose substance comes from bread and wine, blending Himself with the bodies of believers, to secure that, by this union with the immortal, man, too, may be a sharer in incorruption (*cf. De Oratione Catech. Magna,* 37, p. 506).

CYRIL OF ALEXANDRIA

55. Through one body, His own, He blesses, by a mysterious communion, those who believe in Him, and He makes them concorporal with Himself and with one another. Who can now separate them or deprive them of their "physical" union? They have been bound together into unity with Christ by means of His one holy body. For if we all eat of the one bread we all become one body, since there can be no division in Christ. . . . Since we are all united with the one Christ through His sacred body, and since we all receive Him who is one and indivisible into our own bodies, we ought to look upon our members as belonging to Him rather than to ourselves (*In Ioann.,* PG LXXIV, 11, 560).[7]

56. Though He is the Only-begotten with respect to His divinity, having become our brother now He is also called the First-born,

so that just as He has been made the first-fruits of the adoption of men, He might make us also sons of God. Consider that He is called the First-born in regard to the mystery of the economy, for in His divinity He is the Only-begotten. Again, as the word of the Father He is Only-begotten having no natural brothers nor any others numbered with Him, for the consubstantial Son of God the Father is one and alone. But He is the First-born because of His condescension toward creatures (*Comm. in Lucam,* PG LXXII, 485D and 488B).

57. Therefore He is both the Only-begotten and the First-born; Only begotten as God, but indeed First-born among us and among many brothers because He has become man by a mysterious union . . . Just as it has come to pass that the humanity of Christ, because it has been united to the Word through the exchange of the Incarnation, is and is rightly called "Only-begotten," so it has become proper to the Word, which was united to flesh, to be and to be called "First-born" as among many brothers. . . . By this we also in Him and through Him according to nature and grace have been made sons of God. According to nature insofar as we are one in Him (through the same human nature); by participation and according to grace through Himself in the Spirit (*De Recta Fide ad Theodosium,* PG LXXVI, 1177A).

58. Christ, then, is clearly the bond of our unity with God the Father—as Man, He has bound us to Himself, but also to God, inasmuch as He is God inherently. For in no other way could that nature which is subject to corruption be uplifted to incorruption, except by the descent of that Nature which is above all corruption and change, raising to its highest good that which is sunk low, and by communion and commingling of Itself with the condition of created things, transforming unto Itself the nature which is in itself completely other (*In Ioann,* 17:26, PG LXXIV, 564C).

59. Taking the chalice the Lord gave thanks, that is, He prayed to the Father as if declaring Him Associate and Collaborator in giving us the life-giving mystery—as well as giving us a pattern of first giving thanks and then breaking and distributing the bread . . . Most clearly moreover, He said: "This is my body . . . this is my blood." Lest you think that these things are a figure, rather than that they are truly offered to be transformed by the mysterious power of Almighty God into the body and blood of Christ, having been made partakers of which, we take on the vivifying and sanctifying power of Christ (*In Matt.,* 26:27, PG LXXII, 452C).

60. If mere contact with the sacred flesh of Jesus gives life to a dead body, should we not experience effects still more wonderful when we receive the sacred Eucharist? Surely it must completely transform those who receive it into its own perfection, i.e. into immortality . . . Corruptible as we are in the flesh, we lose our weakness by this "mingling" and we are transformed into what is proper to the Eucharist, that is, into life (*In Ioann.,* PG LXXIII, 4, 2, 577).

61. Our transformation will not be a transfer into some other nature . . . for we shall be what we are, that is, men—but we shall be incomparably better. The point is this, we shall be incorruptible and imperishable, and besides this we shall have been glorified (*In Ioann.,* PG LXXIV, 316).

62. The Creator devised as it were a second root of our race, to bring us back to our former incorruptibility, in order that, just as the image of the first man, the man from the earth, engraved on us the necessity of dying and involved us in the meshes of corruption, so, conversely, the second beginning, the one after Him,

that is, Christ, and the likeness to Him through the Spirit, would stamp us with indestructibility, and just as disobedience subjected us to punishment in the former, so in the latter compliance and complete obedience might make us partakers of the blessings from heaven and the Father . . . The Only-begotten Word of God came down among us of His own accord, not to have death rule over Him as well as over us, as though Adam transmitted death to Him as well; for He it is who gives life to all. His purpose was to show our form held fast by corruption and transform it into life . . . For it would be absurd to think that Adam, who was earth-born and a man, could send hurtling into the whole race, like some inheritance, the power of the curse that was leveled at him, while Emmanuel, who is from above, from heaven, God by nature, did not give on His part a rich participation in His own life to those who might elect to share His kinship through faith (*Glaphyra in Gen.,* PG LXIX, 28).

MAXIMUS THE CONFESSOR

63. The mystery of the Incarnation of the Word contains in itself the meaning of all the symbols and all the enigmas of Scripture, as well as the hidden meaning of all sensible and intelligible creation. But he, who knows the mystery of the Cross and the Tomb, knows also the essential principle of all things. Finally, he who penetrates yet further and finds himself initiated into the mystery of the Resurrection, apprehends the end for which God created all things from the beginning (*Capita Theologica et Oeconomica,* PG XC, 1108A–B).[8]

64. Those who have been followers and ministers of the Logos have been directly initiated into a knowledge of created things. They have received the continuous tradition from the ancient and holy writers who have found all beings divided into five different categories. The first they say is the distinction between the un-

created nature and the completely created one which receives by generation its existence . . . The other distinction among those creatures which receive their own existence from God is that between intelligible (known by an intellect: *noeta*) and sensible (perceived by the senses: *aistheta*) creatures. The third category is the distinction, among objects perceived by the senses, into heaven and earth. The fourth is the category which distinguishes earth into paradise and the inhabited earth. The fifth distinction divides the human being into male and female (*Ambigua,* PG XCI, 1304D–1305C).

65. Therefore man comes at the end of all creatures as a certain natural link joining through his own members himself with the other creatures and joining in himself those things which naturally are very distinct from one another. By union with God Who is the universal cause Who made creatures distinct from one another in the beginning, man can then gradually and orderly progress through means to the end in a sublime ascension. This union of all things is found in God in Whom there is no distinction, as we said above, such as that which exists in man according to male and female. In God this category does not exist but man is represented in his true essence, not distinguished by being male or female and not insofar as he is divided into parts, but rather man exists in God in his perfection that makes him truly man, namely, his reason (logos) from which comes knowledge.

Then man makes one earth by uniting paradise with his inhabited world through chaste conversation. His united world then becomes no longer distinct by reason of the diversity of so many parts, but rather it is brought together into a synthesis so that man no longer suffers proliferation into separated parts. Then heaven and earth are united through a virtuous life similar to that of angels. Man no longer is bound down by his bodily condition but rises through an elevation of his soul to the invisible presence of God. He thus is able to make his own way by discerning what is prior and then go back to the material creation, to the things that are secondary.

Then man unites the things known to his intellect and those known to his senses through a knowledge similar to that of the angels who see all of creation, not as separated into known and unknown, but man, become like to angels, is able to know by a knowledge that is the greatest infusion of true wisdom and given only to the worthy to know the difficult and the ineffable. Thus uniting created nature with the Uncreated through charity (O new and wonderful thing wrought in us through divine condescension [*philanthropia*]) man shows all as one and the same through the power of grace (*charis*). He sees all things in God, first as flowing from God into existence and secondly through them, rising to God as to the end of all moved creatures and the fixed and stable ground of their being, Who is the end of every rule and law, the end of every word and mind and of every nature, the infinite and unbound goal of all beings (*Ambigua,* PG XCI, 1305C–1308C).

66. Of all things that exist or will substantially exist . . . the logoi, firmly fixed, preexist in God, in accord with which all things are, having become, and abide, ever drawing nearer through natural motion to their purposed logoi (*The Earlier Ambigua*).[9]

67. For the substance of all the virtues is Our Lord Jesus Christ Himself . . . All men therefore who, by constant fidelity acquire such virtue, participate without doubt in God—the substance of all the virtues (*Ambigua,* PG XCI, 1081D).

68. They say that God and man are exemplars one of another and that God makes Himself man for man's sake out of love, so far as man, enabled by God through charity, deifies himself; and that man is rapt up by God in mind to the unknowable, so far as

man has manifested through the virtues the God by nature invisible (*Ambigua,* PG XCI, 1113B–C).

69. I cannot grieve God by keeping silent what He ordered to be spoken and confessed. For if, according to the divine Apostle, it is He Himself who has set in the Church, first apostles, secondly prophets, thirdly doctors, it is clear that he has spoken through them. By all of Holy Scripture, by the Old and the New Testament, by the holy doctors and synods we are taught. (*Relatio Motionis,* PG XC, 124A).

70. However, Christ now becomes high priest of the good things to come, He sacrifices Himself an ineffable sacrifice and in addition to His flesh gives His blood to those who have the senses of their soul exercised by perfection, for distinguishing good and evil (*Quaest. ad Thal.,* PG XC, 381B).

71. Men, women and children, profoundly divided as to race, nation, language, manner of life, work, knowledge, honor, fortune . . . the Church recreates all of them in the Spirit. To all equally she communicates a divine aspect. All receive from her a unique nature which cannot be broken asunder, a nature which no longer permits one to take into consideration the many and profound differences which are their lot. In that way all are raised up and united in a manner which is truly catholic. In her none is in the least degree separated from the community, all are grounded, so to speak, in one another by the simple and indivisible power of faith . . . Christ, too, is all in all, He who contains all in Himself according to the unique, infinite and all-wise power of His goodness—as a center upon which all lines converge—that the creatures of the one God may not live as strangers or enemies one with another, having no place in common, where they may display their love and their peace (*Mystagogia,* PG XCI, 665–668).

BIBLIOGRAPHY

CHAPTERS I AND II

Barrett, C. K., *From First Adam to Last, A Study in Pauline Theology*. New York, Scribner, 1962.

Cerfaux, Lucien, *Christ in the Theology of St. Paul,* 2nd ed. New York, Herder and Herder, 1959.

———, *The Church in the Theology of St. Paul.* New York, Herder and Herder, 1959.

Deissmann, A., *Die neutestamentliche Formel "In Christo Jesu."* Marburg, 1892.

———, *The Religion of Jesus and the Faith of Paul.* New York, Doran, 1923.

———, *Paulus, Eine kultur-und religionsgeschichtliche Skizze.* Tubingen, 1925.

Galloway, A. D., *The Cosmic Christ.* London, Nisbet, 1951.

Huby, J., *Les Épitres de la Captivité.* Paris, Beauchesne, 1947.

Knox, W. L., *St. Paul and the Church of the Gentiles.* New York, Cambridge University Press, 1939.

Montague, G., *Growth in Christ.* Kirkwood, Mo., Maryhurst Press, 1961.

Robinson, John A. T., *The Body, A Study in Pauline Theology.* Naperville, Ill., Allenson, 1952.

Scott, Charles A. A., *Christianity according to St. Paul.* Cambridge, Cambridge University Press, 1961.

Spicq, C., *Agape in the New Testament, II.* St. Louis, Herder, 1965.

Taylor, L. H., *The New Creation.* New York, Pageant Press, 1958.

Whiteley, D., *The Theology of St. Paul.* Philadelphia, Fortress, 1964.

Wikenhauser, A., *New Testament Introduction.* New York, Herder and Herder, 1958.

———, *Pauline Mysticism.* Freiburg, Herder, 1956.

Benoit, P., "L'Horizon paulinien de l'Épitre aux Éphesiens." *Exégèse et Theologie* (Paris, 1961).

———, "Corps, tête et plérome dans les Épitres de la Captivité." *Exégèse et Théologie* (Paris, 1961).

———, "La reconciliation universelle selon Michaelis." *Revue Biblique* (1952).

Keinkneck, H., "eikon," in G. Kittel, ed., *Theologisches Worterbuch,* II (Stuttgart: Kohlhammer, 1935).

Lyonnet, S., "La redemption de l'univers." *Lumière et Vie* (July–August, 1962).

Stanley, D. M., "Christ's Resurrection in Pauline Soteriology." *Analecta Biblica,* 13 (1961).

Viard, A., "Expectatio creaturae (Rom. VIII, 19–22)." *Revue Biblique* (1952).

CHAPTER III

Albright, W. F., *Recent Discoveries in Palestine and the Gospel of St. John: The Background of the New Testament and its Escha-*

tology, ed. by W. D. Davies and D. Daube. Cambridge, Cambridge University Press, 1956.

Bernard, J. H., *The Gospel according to St. John,* 2 Vols. Edinburgh, Clark, 1928.

Bréhier, E., *Les idées philosophiques et religieuses de Philon d'Alexandrie.* Paris, J. Vrin, 1908.

Bultmann, R., *Das Evangelium des Johannes.* Gottingen, Vandenhoeck and Ruprecht, 1956.

Dodd, C. H., *The Interpretation of the Fourth Gospel.* New York, Cambridge University Press, 1953.

du Pont, J., *Essais sur la christologie de saint Jean.* Bruges, l'Abbaye de Saint-André, 1951.

Howard, W. F., *The Fourth Gospel in Recent Criticism,* 4th ed., rev. by C. K. Barrett. London, Epworth Press, 1955.

Lebreton, J., *History of the Dogma of the Trinity from its Origins to the Council of Nicaea.* London, Burns, Oates and Washbourne, 1939.

Lightfoot, R. H., *St. John's Gospel: A Commentary.* Oxford, Oxford University Press, 1956.

Mersch, Emile, *The Whole Christ.* Milwaukee, Bruce, 1938.

Sanders, J. N., *The Fourth Gospel in the Early Church.* Cambridge, Cambridge University Press, 1943.

Sidebottom, E. M., *The Christ of the Fourth Gospel in the Light of First Century Thought.* Naperville, Ill., Allenson, 1961.

Strachan, R. H., *The Fourth Gospel,* 3rd ed. London, S. C. M. Press, 1941.

von Schrenck, E., *Die johanneische Anschauung vom Leben.* Leipzig, 1898.

Westcott, B. F., *The Gospel according to St. John.* Grand Rapids, Mich., Eerdmans, 1954.

Wood, C. T., *The Life, Letters and Religion of St. Paul.* Edinburgh, Clark, 1925.

Zeller, E., *Die Philosophie der Griechen in ihrer geschictlichen Entwicklung,* IV, I. Hildesheim, G. Olms, 1963.

Charue, A., "Vie, lumière et glorie chez saint Jean." *Collationes Namurcenses* (1935).

Frey, J. B., "Le concept de 'vie' dans l'Evangile de St. Jean." *Biblica* (1920).

CHAPTER IV

Aulen, Gustav, *Christus Victor*. New York, Macmillan, 1954.

Bardy, K., *Origène* in *Collection: Les moralistes chrétiens*. Paris, Lecoffre and Gabalda, 1931.

———, *Saint Athanase*. Paris, Gabalda, 1925.

Bernard, Régis, *L'Image de Dieu d'après saint Athanase*. Paris, Aubier, 1952.

Bertrand, F., *Mystique de Jésus chez Origène* in *Collection Théologie*. Paris, Aubier, 1951.

Beuzart, Paul, *Essais sur la theologie d'Irénée*. Le Puy-en-Velais, Juillet, 1908.

Bonwetsch, G. Nathaniel, *Die Theologie des Irenaeus*. Gutersloh, Bertelsmann, 1925.

Bouyer, L., *L'Incarnation et l'Église-Corps du Christ dans la théologie de saint Athanase*. Paris, Éditions du Cerf, 1943.

Butterworth, C., *Origen: On First Principles*. New York, Harper Torchbooks, 1966.

Cadiou, R., *Introduction au system d'Origène*. Paris, Les Belles Lettres, 1932.

———, *La jeunesse d'Origène*. Paris, Beauchesne, 1935.

Camelot, P. T., *Foi et gnose: Introduction a l'étude de la connaissance mystique chez Clement d'Alexandrie*. Paris, 1945.

Crouzel, H., *Origène et la "connaissance mystique."* Paris, Aubier, 1962.

———, *Origène et la philosophie*. Paris, Aubier, 1962.

———, *Théologie de l'image de Dieu chez Origène*. Paris, Aubier, 1956.

Daniélou, J., *Origen*. New York, Sheed and Ward, 1955.

de Faye, E. E., *Esquisse de la pensée d'Origène,* in *Bibliotheque historique des Religions.* Paris, Leroux, 1925.

———, *Origen and His Work,* 3 Vols. New York, Allen and Unwin, 1926.

Fairweather, W., *Origen and Greek Patristic Theology.* New York, Scribner, 1901.

Gross, Jules, *La divinisation du chrétien d'après les pères grecs.* Paris, Gabalda, 1938.

Ladner, G. B., *The Idea of Reform.* Cambridge, Mass., Harvard University Press, 1959.

Lawson, John, *The Biblical Theology of Saint Irenaeus.* London, Epworth Press, 1948.

Mondesert, C., *Clement d'Alexandrie: Introduction a l'étude de sa pensée religieuse a partir de l'Écriture.* Paris, 1944.

Osborn, E. F., *The Philosophy of Clement of Alexandria.* Cambridge, Cambridge University Press, 1957.

Quatember, F., *Die christliche Lebenshaltung des Klemens von Alexandrien nach seinem Paedogogus.* Vienna, 1945.

Sagnard, F., *La gnose valentinienne et le témoignage de saint Irénée.* Paris, J. Vrin, 1947.

Sträter, H., *Die Erlosungslehre des hl. Athanasius.* Fribourg-en-Breisgau, 1894.

Tollinton, R. B., *Clement of Alexandria,* 2 Vols., London, Williams and Norgate, 1914.

Völker, W., *Der wahre Gnostiker nach Clemens Alexandrinus, Texte und Untersuchungen.* Leipzig, 1952.

von Balthasar, H. Urs, *Parole et Mystère chez Origène.* Paris, Editions du Cerf, 1957.

———, *Origène: Esprit en Feu.* Paris, Editions du Cerf, 1959.

Werner, Johannes, *Der Paulinismus des Irenaeus,* in Beghart and Harnack, eds., *Texte und Untersuchungen,* VI Leipzig, 1889.

Wingren, Gustaf, *Man and the Incarnation. A Study in the Biblical Theology of Irenaeus.* Philadelphia, Muhlenberg, 1959.

Berchem, J. B., "Le rôle du Verbe dans l'oeuvre de la creation et de la sanctification d'après saint Athanase." *Angelicum* (Rome, 1938).

D'Ales, P., "La doctrine de la recapitulation en saint Irénée." *Recherches de Science Religieuse,* 6 (1916).

———, "La doctrine de l'Esprit en saint Irénée." *Recherches de Science Religieuse,* 14 (1924).

Gaudel, A., "La théologie du logos chez saint Athanase." *Revue des Sciences Religieuses* (Strasbourg, 1929 and 1931).

LeBachelet, X., "Athanase," in *Dictionnaire Théologie Catholique,* I (Paris, 1923).

Reynders, B., "La polemique de saint Irénée: Methode et principes." *Recherches de Théologie Ancienne et Medievale,* 7 (1935).

———, "Optimisme et théocentrisme chez saint Irénée." *Recherches de Théologie Ancienne et Medievale,* 8 (1936).

Vernet, F., "Saint Irénée," in *Dictionnaire de Théologie Catholique,* VII (Paris, 1923).

CHAPTER V

Burghardt, Walter J., *The Image of God in Man according to Cyril of Alexandria.* Washington, Catholic University of America, 1957.

Cherniss, H., *The Platonism of Gregory of Nyssa.* Berkeley, University of California Press, 1930.

Daniélou, J., *Platonisme et théologie mystique. Doctrine spirituelle de saint Grégoire de Nysse.* Paris, Aubier, 1944.

Daniélou, J., and Musurillo, H., *From Glory to Glory.* New York, Scribner, 1961.

Diepen, H. P., *Aux origènes de l'anthropologie de saint Cyrille d'Alexandrie.* Bruges, 1957.

Du Manoir, H., *Dogme et spiritualité chez saint Cyrille d'Alexandrie.* Paris, 1944.

Gallay, P., *La vie de saint Grégoire de Nazianze.* Lyons, 1943.

Hummer, *Des hl. Gregor von Nazianz des Theologen Lehre von der Gnade.* Kemten, 1890.

Jaeger, W., *Two Rediscovered Works of Ancient Christian Literature: Gregory of Nyssa and Macarius.* Leiden, E. S. Brill, 1954.

Kerrigan, A., *St. Cyril of Alexandria: Interpreter of the Old Testament.* Rome, 1952.

Lefherz, F., *Studien zu Gregor von Nazianz.* Bonn, 1958.

Leys, R., *L'image de Dieu chez saint Grégoire de Nysse.* Bruxelles, L'Edition Universelle, 1951.

Pegon, J., *Centuries sur la charité de S. Maxime le Confesseur,* in *Sources Chrétiennes,* IX. Paris, Aubier, 1943.

Pinault, H., *Le platonisme de s. Grégoire de Nazianze.* La Roche-sur-Yon, G. Romain, 1925.

Plagnieux, J., *S. Grégoire de Nazianze Théologien.* Paris, Éditions Franciscaines, 1952.

Sherwood, Polycarp, *St. Maximus the Confessor: The Ascetic Life and the Four Centuries on Charity,* in *Ancient Christian Writers,* XXI. Westminster, Md., Newman, 1955.

———, *The Earlier Ambigua of St. Maximus the Confessor.* Rome, Herder, 1955.

Struckmann, A., *Die Eucharistielehre des hl. Cyrill von Alexandrien.* Paderborn, 1910.

Thunberg, Lars, *Microcosm and Mediator: The Theological Anthropology of Maximus the Confessor.* Copenhagen, Lund, 1965.

Ullmann, C., *Gregor von Nazianz, der Theologe.* Gotha, 1867.

Völker, W., *Gregor von Nyssa als Mystiker.* Wiesbaden, F. Steiner, 1955.

von Balthasar, H. Urs, *Présence et Pensée—Essai sur la philosophie religieuse de Grégoire de Nysse.* Paris, Beauchesne, 1942.

von Campenhausen, Hans, *The Fathers of the Greek Church.* New York, Pantheon, 1959.

Weigl, E., *Die Heilslehre des hl. Cyrill von Alexandrien.* Mainz, 1905.

Dalmais, I. H., "La fonction unificatrice du Verb Incarné d'après les oeuvres spirituelles de Saint Maxime le Confesseur." *Sciences Écclesiastiques,* 14 (1962).

Devreese, R., "La vie de S. Maxime le Confesseur et ses recensions." *Analecta Bollandiana,* 46 (1928).

Disdier, M., "Les fondaments dogmatiques de la spiritualité de S. Maxime le Confesseur." *Echoes d'Orient,* 29 (1930).

Du Manoir, H., "Cyrille d'Alexandrie," in *Dictionnaire de Spiritualité,* II (1953).

Dunstone, A. S., "The Meanings of Grace in the Writings of Gregory of Nyssa." *Scottish Journal of Theology,* 15 (Sept., 1962).

Gauthier, R. A., "Saint Maxime le Confesseur et la psychologie de l'acte humain." *Recherches de Théologie Ancienne et Medievale,* 21 (1954).

Godet, P., "Grégoire de Nazianz: III Doctrine," in *Dictionnaire de Théologie Catholique,* VI (Paris, 1923).

"Gregor von Nazianz," *Real-encyclopädie fur Protestantische Theologie und Kirche,* VIII (1899).

Grumel, V., "Maxime le Confesseur," in *Dictionnaire de Théologie Catholique,* X (Paris, 1928).

———, "Cyrille, saint, patriarch d'Alexandrie," in *Dictionnaire de Théologie Catholique,* III (Paris, 1908).

Hausherr, I., "Philautie: De la Tendresse pour Soi à la Charité selon S. Maxime le Confesseur," *Orientalia Christiana Analecta,* 137 (Rome, 1952).

Janssens, J., "Notre filiation divine d'après saint Cyrille d'Alexandrie." *Ephemerides Theologicae Lovanienses,* 15 (1938).

Koch, Hugo, "Das Mystiche Schauen beim hl. Gregor von Nyssa." *Theologische Quartalschrift* (1898).

Lieske, L., "Theologie der Christus-mystik Gregors von Nyssa." *Scholastik* (1939).

Mahé, J., "La sanctification d'après saint Cyrille d'Alexandrie." *Revue d'Histoire Écclesiastique,* 10 (1909).

Sherwood, Polycarp, "Notes on Maximus the Confessor." *American Benedictine Review,* I (1950).

———, "Survey of Recent Work on St. Maximus the Confessor." *Traditio,* 20 (1964).

CHAPTER VI

Braybrooke, Neville, ed., *Teilhard de Chardin: Pilgrim of the Future.* New York, Seabury Press, 1964.

Cognet, Louis, *Le Père Teilhard de Chardin et la pensée contemporaine.* Paris, Flammarion, 1952.

Crespy, Georges, *La pensée théologique de Teilhard de Chardin.* Paris, Éditions Universitaires, 1961.

Cuenot, Claude, *Teilhard de Chardin.* Baltimore, Helicon Press, 1956 (contains a complete bibliography).

de Lubac, Henri, *The Religion of Teilhard de Chardin.* New York, Desclee, 1967.

———, *La Prière de Père Teilhard de Chardin.* Paris, Artheme Fayard, 1964.

Faricy, Robert, *Teilhard de Chardin's Theology of the Christian in the World.* New York, Sheed and Ward, 1967.

Fessard, Gaston, "La vision religieuse et cosmique de Teilhard de Chardin," in *L'Homme devant Dieu,* III. Paris, Aubier, Montaigne, 1964.

Francoeur, Robert, ed., *The World of Teilhard.* Baltimore, Helicon, 1961.

Mooney, Christopher F., *Teilhard de Chardin and the Mystery of Christ.* New York, Harper, 1966.

Murray, Michael H., *The Thought of Teilhard de Chardin.* New York, Seabury Press, 1966.

Rabut, Olivier, *Teilhard de Chardin: A Critical Study.* New York, Sheed and Ward, 1961.

Raven, Charles E., *Teilhard de Chardin, Scientist and Seer.* New York, Harper, 1962.

Rideau, Emile, *La Pensée du Père Teilhard de Chardin.* Paris, Éditions du Seuil, 1965.

Smulders, Pierre, *The Design of Teilhard de Chardin.* Westminster, Md., Newman, 1967.

Trestmontant, Claude, *Pierre Teilhard de Chardin.* Baltimore, Helicon Press, 1959.

Wildiers, N. M., *Teilhard de Chardin.* Paris, Éditions Universitaires, 1960.

Daniélou, Jean, "Signification de Teilhard de Chardin." *Études,* 212 (1962).

Donnelly, William, "The Thought of Teilhard de Chardin." *The Clergy Review,* 45 (1960).

Journet, Charles, "La vision Teilhardienne du monde." *Divinitas,* 3 (1959).

Malevez, Leopold, "La Methode du P. Teilhard de Chardin et la phenomenologie." *Nouvelle Revue Théologique,* 89 (1957).

Mooney, Christopher F., "Blondel and Teilhard de Chardin." *Thought,* 37 (Winter, 1962).

North, Robert, "Teilhard and the Problem of Creation." *Theological Studies,* 24 (1964).

Vass, George, "Teilhard de Chardin and Inward Vision." *The Heythrop Journal,* 2 (1961).

Vollert, Cyril, "Toward Omega: Man in the Vision of Teilhard de Chardin." *The Month,* 23 (1960).

Von Balthasar, H. Urs, "Die Spiritualität Teilhard de Chardin." *Wort und Wahrheit,* 17 (1963).

CHAPTER VII

Abott, W., ed., "Pastoral Constitution on the Church in the Modern World," in *The Documents of Vatican II,* New York, Guild Press, America Press, Association Press, 1966.

Boros, L., *The Mystery of Death.* New York, Herder, 1965.
Bouyer, Louis, *Christian Humanism.* Westminster, Md., Newman, 1959.
Buber, Martin, *I and Thou.* New York, Scribners, 1958.
Cox, Harvey, *The Secular City.* New York, Macmillan, 1966.
Duquoc, C., ed., *Spirituality in the Secular City. Concilium,* Vol. 19, New York, Paulist Press, 1966.
Gogarten, F., *Der Mensch zwischen Gott und Welt.* Stuttgart, Vorwerk Verlag, 1956.
Lehmann, Paul F., *Ethics in a Christian Context.* New York, Harper and Row, 1963.
Marcel, G., *The Mystery of Being.* Chicago, Regnery, 1960.
Maritain, Jacques, *True Humanism.* New York, Scribners, 1938.
Mesthene, Emmanuel, "Religious Values in the Age of Technology," in *Concilium,* Vol. 26, *The Evolving World and Theology.* New York, Paulist Press, 1967.
Munby, D., *The Idea of a Secular Society.* New York, Oxford University Press, 1963.
Niebuhr, H. R., *The Responsible Self.* New York, Harper and Row, 1963.
Schillebeeckx, E., "The Church and Mankind," in *Concilium,* Vol. 1, *The Church and Mankind.* New York, Paulist Press, 1964.
The Christian in the World: Readings in Theology. Compiled at the Canisianum, Innsbruck. New York, Kenedy, 1965.
Thils, Gustav, *Théologie des Réalités.* Bruges, Desclée de Brouwer, 1946.
Van Buren, Paul, *The Secular Meaning of the Gospel.* New York, Macmillan, 1963.
von Balthasar, H. Urs, "Meeting God in Today's World," in *Concilium,* Vol. 6, *The Church and the World.* New York, Paulist Press, 1965.
White, H. C., Jr., ed., *Christians in a Technological Era.* New York, Seabury, 1964.

Wilmore, G. S., *The Secular Relevance of the Church.* Philadelphia, Westminster Press, 1962.

Clarke, T., "The World Is Already Christic." *America* (May 29, 1965, pp. 800–803).

NOTES

Introduction

1. Jack Kerouac, *On the Road* (New York, Viking, 1957), pp. 162–163.
2. Dietrich Bonhoeffer, "Thy Kingdom Come" (an essay written in 1932), in J. D. Godsey, *Preface to Bonhoeffer* (Philadelphia, Fortress, 1965), pp. 28–29.
3. E. Schillebeeckx, ed., *The Church and Mankind,* in *Concilium,* Vol. I (New York, Paulist Press, 1964), pp. 81–82.
4. The Chalcedonian formulation reads in part: ". . . one and the same Christ, Son, Lord, only-begotten, made known in two natures without confusion, without change, without division, without separation, the difference of the natures being by no means removed because of the union, but the property of each nature being preserved and coalescing in one *prosopon* and *hypostasis,* not parted or divided into two *prosopa,* but one and the same Son, only-begotten, divine Word, the Lord Jesus Christ. . . ." *Cf.* J. N. D. Kelly, *Early Christian Doctrines* (New York, Harper, 1960), p. 340.
5. Amos N. Wilder, "Art and Theological Meaning" in Nathan A. Scott, ed., *The New Orpheus: Essays toward a Christian Poetic* (New York, Sheed and Ward, 1964), p. 407.

Chapter I

1. C. K. Barrett, *From First Adam to Last: A Study in Pauline Theology* (New York, Scribner, 1962), p. 87.
2. P. Benoit, "L'horizon paulinien de l'Épître aux Ephesians," *Exégèse et Théologie* (Paris, 1961), p. 88.
3. *Ibid.*, pp. 91–92.
4. *Cf.* also Eph. 4:15–16: "Rather by professing the truth, let us grow up in every respect in love and bring about union with Christ who is the head. The whole body is dependent on him. Harmoniously joined and knit together, it derives its energy in the measure each part needs, only through contact with the source of supply. In this way the body grows and builds itself up through love."
5. H. Schlier, "Anakephaloioomai," *Theologisches Wörterbuch,* III (Stuttgart, W. Kohlhammer, 1938), pp. 681 ff.
6. Joseph Huby, *Les Épîtres de la Captivité* (Paris, Beauchesne, 1935), p. 40, cited by Christopher Mooney, "The Body of Christ in the Writings of Teilhard de Chardin," *Theological Studies,* 25 (December, 1964), pp. 604–605.
7. Karl Rahner, *Theological Investigations,* I (Baltimore, Helicon, 1960), p. 165.

Chapter II

1. *Ecclesiam Suam* (New York, Paulist Press, 1965), p. 30.
2. Pierre Benoit, "Corps, tête, et plérôme dans les Épîtres de la Captivité," *Exégèse et Théologie* (Paris, 1961), p. 147.
3. *Ibid.*

Chapter III

1. Some of the more recent outstanding scholarship done in this area can be found in the following works: C. H. Dodd, *The Interpretation of the Fourth Gospel* (New York, Cambridge University Press, 1953); R. H. Strachan, *The Fourth Gospel,* 3rd ed. (London: S. C. M. Press, 1941); B. F. Westcott, *The Gospel according to St. John* (Grand Rapids, Mich., Eerdmans, 1954); W. F. Howard, *The Fourth Gospel in Recent Criticism,* 4th ed., rev. by

C. K. Barrett (Naperville, Ill., Allenson, 1955); J. H. Bernard, *The Gospel according to St. John,* 2 vols. (Edinburgh, Clark, 1928); F. L. Cross, ed., *Studies in the Fourth Gospel* (London, A. R. Mowbray, 1957); J. N. Sanders, *The Fourth Gospel in the Early Church* (Cambridge, Cambridge University Press, 1943); R. H. Lightfoot, *St. John's Gospel: A Commentary,* ed. by C. F. Evans (New York, Oxford University Press, 1956).

2. It was Theophilus of Antioch (*c.* 180) who first ascribed the Fourth Gospel to a St. John but even he does not clearly affirm that he was the Apostle. From then on, it was generally assumed that he was. The Muratorian Canon (possibly between 170–240 A.D.), the oldest type of canon of New Testament writings, and of unknown authorship, attributes the Fourth Gospel to St. John the Apostle. Thus, from the end of the second century St. John the Apostle is accepted both in the East and the West as the author of the Fourth Gospel.
3. Outstanding work on the Gnostic Nag Hammadi discoveries in Egypt has been done by W. C. van Unnik: *cf.* his "Newly Discovered Gnostic Writings," *Studies in Biblical Theology* 30 (Naperville, Ill., Allenson, 1960). *Cf.* also R. M. Grant, *Gnosticism and Early Christianity* (New York, Columbia University Press, 1959). The literature on the Qumran Dead Sea Scrolls is voluminous. More relevant to the relationship of the scrolls to John's Gospel are K. Stendhal, ed., *The Scrolls and the New Testament* (New York, Harper, 1957) and W. F. Albright, "Recent Discoveries in Palestine and the Gospel of St. John," in W. D. Davies and D. Daube, eds., *The Background of the New Testament and its Eschatology* (New York, Cambridge University Press, 1956).
4. R. Bultmann, *Das Evangelium des Johannes* (Gottingen, Vandenhoeck and Ruprecht, 1956).
5. C. T. Wood, *The Life, Letters and Religion of St. Paul,* (Edinburgh, Clark, 1925), p. 320.
6. "O gladsome radiance of the holy glory of the Father immortal, heavenly, holy, blessed, Jesus Christ! In that we now are come unto the setting of the sun and behold the light of evening, we hymn thee, Father, Son and Holy Spirit, God. For it is just that at all times thou shouldst be magnified by voices propitious, O Son of God, who bestowest life. For this all the world does glorify Thee."

7. *In Joann.* (Pg IX, 47, 1264).
8. *Commentarium in Joannem* (Pg XIV, 1, 28, 73).

Chapter IV

1. For some leading books and articles on Irenaeus, cf. the Bibliography, Chapter IV.
2. For a thorough treatment of Gnosticism, cf. R. M. Grant, *Gnosticism and Early Christianity* (New York, Columbia University Press, 1959); W. C. van Unnik, "Newly Discovered Gnostic Writings," *Studies in Biblical Theology,* 30 (Naperville, Ill., Allenson, 1960).
3. *Adversus Haereses* (hereafter listed as *AH*), IV, 38, 3–4, pp. 521–522. Quotations from Irenaeus are from *The Ante-Nicene Fathers,* I, ed. by A. Roberts and J. Donaldson (Grand Rapids, Mich., Eerdmans, 1962), unless otherwise noted. Quotations used with permission.
4. *Proof of the Apostolic Preaching* (hereafter listed as *Dem.*) trans. by Joseph P. Smith, *Ancient Christian Writers,* 16 (Westminster, Md., Newman, 1952), p. 62.
5. K. Rahner, *Nature and Grace* (New York, Sheed and Ward, 1964), p. 117.
6. G. B. Ladner, *The Idea of Reform* (Cambridge, Mass., Harvard University Press, 1959), p. 84.
7. G. Wingren, *Man and the Incarnation* (Philadelphia, Muhlenberg, 1959), p. 18.
8. *AH,* V, 2, p. 544.
9. The history of the word *anakephalaiosis* is most interesting. According to John Lawson (*The Biblical Theology of Saint Irenaeus,* London, Epworth Press, 1948, pp. 140 ff.), Gustave Molwitz in his Latin work, *De "Anakephalaiosis" in Irenaei Potestate* (Dresden, 1874) is the first scholar to treat of its meaning. He points out that the word does not come from *kephale,* meaning *head,* and hence (contrary to many translators of St. Paul, Eph. 1:10) does not refer to the summing up of things under a head, and therefore it does not refer to the Headship of Christ. But the word comes from *kephalaion,* meaning the chief point or summary, the whole containing the parts. Lawson gathers together all possible interpretations of Irenaeus' complicated term and offers as the chief interpretation the following meanings: to unite under a

single head, to restore to the original, to make a new start, to bring to a climax, to go over the ground a second time.

10. Irenaeus borrows this word from St. Paul and also from Justin: "In his book against Marcion, Justin well says: 'I would not have believed the Lord Himself, if He had announced any other than He who is our framer, maker and nourisher. But because the only begotten Son came to us from the One God who both made this world and formed us and contains and administers all things, summing up His own handiwork in Himself, my faith towards Him is steadfast and my love to the Father immoveable, God bestowing both upon us" (*AH,* IV, 6, 2, p. 468).
11. *AH,* V, 21, 1, pp. 548–549.
12. *Ibid.*, IV, 34, 1, p. 511.
13. *Cf.* Mircea Eliade, *The Sacred and the Profane* (New York, Harper Torchbooks, 1961), pp. 80 ff.
14. *AH,* V, 9, 2, p. 535; *cf. ibid.*, V, 8, 1, p. 533; V, 12, 4, p. 538.
15. *Ibid.*, V, 12, 2, p. 537.
16. *Dem.*, 5, p. 51, *cf. ibid.*, 97, p. 108.
17. *AH,* 36, 1, p. 566; *cf.* I Cor. 7:31.
18. *AH,* 36, 1, pp. 566–567.
19. *Ibid.*, 36, 3, p. 567.
20. *Paedagogos,* II, 119, p. 241. All citations from the works of Clement are from *The Ante-Nicene Fathers,* II, ed. by A. Roberts and J. Donaldson (Grand Rapids, Mich., Eerdmans, 1962). Quotations used with permission.
21. *Stromata* (hereafter listed as *Strom.*), I, 28, p. 340–341.
22. R. B. Tollinton: *Clement of Alexandria, I* (London, Williams and Norgate, 1914), p. 351.
23. *Protrepticos* (hereafter listed as *Protrep.*), 10, p. 199.
24. Clement does show in several places that he holds a clear distinction between image and likeness; but he rarely abides by the distinction in his stress on the unity of man's progressive assimilation to God. "For is it not thus that some of our writers have understood that man straightway on his creation received what is 'according to the image', but that what is according 'to the likeness' he will receive afterwards on his perfection?" (*Strom.*, II, 22, p. 376; *cf.* also *Paedagogos,* I, 12, p. 234).
25. *Protrep.*, 1, p. 174.
26. *Strom.*, VI, 12, p. 504.
27. R. B. Tollinton, *Clement of Alexandria,* II, *op. cit.*, pp. 99–100.

28. For some leading books and articles on Origen, cf. the Bibliography.
29. *Cf.* C. Butterworth, *Origen: On First Principles* (New York, Harper Torchbooks, 1966), pp. xlvi–lii, for a rather complete presentation of Rufinus' translation. Citations from Origen's *De Principiis,* hereafter listed as *OFP,* are taken from this edition. Quotations reprinted with the permission of Harper Torchbooks, Harper & Row, Publishers, Inc., New York.
30. Cited by H. Urs von Balthasar, *Origène: Esprit et Feu,* Paris, Editions du Cerf, 1959, frontispiece.
31. *OFP,* I, 2, 2, p. 24.
32. *Ibid.,* I, 4, 4, p. 42.
33. *Ibid.,* I, 6, 2, p. 53; *cf.* also, II, 1, 3, p. 78.
34. *Cf. OFP,* I, 3, 5, p. 34: "The Son, being less than the Father, is superior to rational creatures alone (for He is second to the Father); the Holy Spirit is still less, and dwells within the saints alone. So that in this way the power of the Father is greater than that of the Son and of the Holy Spirit, and that of the Son is more than that of the Holy Spirit, and in turn the power of the Holy Spirit exceeds that of every other holy being." C. Butterworth, *op. cit.,* pp. liv–lv, claims that this admits of an orthodox interpretation.
35. *OFP,* Preface, I, 5, p. 4.
36. Origen's opinion whether the devils also will be eventually saved has been greatly disputed through the centuries. In his preface to the *De Principiis* he seems to rule out this possibility: ". . . the apostolic teaching is that the soul . . . shall, after its departure from the world, be rewarded according to its deserts, being destined to obtain either an inheritance of eternal life and blessedness, if its action shall have procured this for it, or to be delivered up to eternal fire and punishments, if the guilt of its crimes shall have brought it down to this" (*OFP,* p. 4). It is probably fair to say that Origen takes no absolutely fixed position in this matter. In many passages, in his desire to highlight the goodness and omnipotence of God, Origen seems to include also the devils in the final recapitulation whereby all creatures will reach their proposed end.
37. *In Ioann.* I, 16 (PG XIV, 49D); cited from *Patrologiae Cursus completus, Series Graeca* (abbrev.: PG), ed. J. P. Migne, Paris, 1857 ff.

38. For some leading books and articles on Athanasius, cf. the Bibliography, Chapter IV.
39. Archibald Robertson in his Introduction, *St. Athanasius: Select Works and Letters,* Vol. IV of *A Select Library of Nicene and Post-Nicene Fathers of the Christian Church* (Grand Rapids, Mich., Eerdmans, 1957), p. lxxii. All citations from Origen will be taken from this translation, pagination corresponding to Vol. IV, unless otherwise indicated. Quotations used with permission.
40. Dr. T. E. Pollard maintains that St. Athanasius inherited from Origen the problem of Arianism that haunted his whole life. Origen encountered difficulties with his Logos doctrine, maintaining a subordinationism to the Father, contrary to the traditional teaching of the Church on the equality of the Son of God with the Father. Origen failed to complement his Logos doctrine with an adequate teaching on Christ's Sonship. The Arian heresy arose as an attempt to solve Origen's problem by distinguishing between the uncreated Logos and the created Son. The Son, according to this teaching, was only man while the Logos was only God. *Cf.* T. E. Pollard, *Logos and Son in Origen, Arius and Athanasius, Studia Patristica,* II (Berlin, 1957), p. 287.
41. *Contra Arianos,* II, 64, p. 383.
42. John Henry Newman, *Select Treatises of St. Athanasius, II* (London, Longmans and Green, 1895), p. 465.
43. *Contra Arianos,* III, 33, p. 412.
44. *Contra Arianos,* I, 51, p. 336.
45. *De Incarnatione,* 7, p. 38.
46. *Contra Arianos,* II, 70, p. 386.
47. *Die Erlosungslehre des Hl. Athanasius* (Fribourg-en-Brisgau, 1894), p. 140.
48. *Vita S. Antonii,* 7, p. 197; 14, p. 200; 19, p. 201; 55, p. 211.
49. *Ad Serapionem* IV, 19 (PG XXVI, 668A).
50. *De Incarnatione,* 30, p. 52.

Chapter V

1. For some leading books and articles on St. Gregory Nazianzus, cf. the Bibliography, Chapter V. His principal works can be found in the following editions: *S. Gregorii Nazianzen Opera Omnia* (PG XXXV–XXXVIII); *Anthologia Graecorum Carminum Christianorum,* ed. by W. Christ and M. Paranikas (Leipzig,

1871); *St. Gregory Nazianzen, Nicene and Post-Nicene Fathers,* 2nd Series, VII (Grand Rapids, Mich., Eerdmans, 1955). All citations of Gregory's writings, unless otherwise noted, are from this edition. Quotations used with permission.

2. *Ibid., Oratio* 21, 33, p. 279.
3. *Oratio* 38, 13; p. 349.
4. *Cf. Oratio* 41, 12, p. 383.
5. *Epistola ad Cledonium* (PG XXXVIII, 181).
6. *Oratio* 7, 23; p. 237.
7. *Oratio* 38, 18; p. 351.
8. *Ibid.*
9. For some leading books and articles on St. Gregory of Nyssa, cf. the Bibliography, Chapter V.
10. *A Select Library of Nicene and Post-Nicene Fathers of the Christian Church,* 2nd Series, V (Grand Rapids, Mich., Eerdmans, 1953), p. 1. All citations of St. Gregory of Nyssa's works will be from this edition unless otherwise indicated. Quotations used with permission.
11. *Life of Moses,* trans. from the French edition by J. Daniélou. *Grégoire de Nysse, La Vie de Moise,* in *Sources Chrétiennes,* VI (Paris, Editions du Cerf, 1941), pp. 110–111.
12. Leys, *L'Image de Dieu chez Saint Grégoire de Nysse,* Brussels, L'Edition Universelle, 1951, p. 98.
13. Daniélou, *Platonisme et Théologie Mystique: Doctrine Spirituelle de Saint Grégoire de Nysse* (Paris, Aubier-Montaigne, 1954), p. 54.
14. *De Oratione Catech. Magna,* 25, p. 495.
15. *Ibid.,* 26, p. 489.
16. *Ibid.,* 37, pp. 504–505.
17. *In Cant. Cant.* (PG XLIV, 1037).
18. *De Anima et Resurrectione,* p. 450.
19. For some leading books and articles on St. Cyril, cf. the Bibliography, Chapter V.
20. Cited by Campenhausen, *The Fathers of the Greek Church* (New York, Pantheon, 1959), p. 155.
21. *Contra Julianum* VII (PG LXXVI, 877).
22. *Epistola ad Calosyrium,* cited by Burghardt, *The Image of God in Man according to Cyril of Alexandria* (Washington, Catholic University Press, 1957), p. 53, fn. 9.
23. *Homilia in Lucam* (PG LXXII, 71, 688).

24. *In Ioann.*, 20:17 (PG LXXIV, 700B).
25. *Thesaurus,* 34 (PG LXXV, 597A–C). *Cf. De Trinitate* (PG LXXV, 1088B ff.).
26. *In Ioann.*,I, cited from 9th ed., P. E. Pusey, *Sancti Patris Nostri Cyrilli Arch. Alexandrini in D. Joannis Evangelium,* I., 9th ed. (Oxford, 1872), p. 111.
27. Of the Greek Fathers, Maximus the Confessor has been the last one to come under thorough study by theologians and patristic scholars, probably because of his difficult thought. For some of the leading authors who have written recently on Maximus, cf. the Bibliography, Chapter V.
28. Monothelitism was a Christological heresy that arose within the Byzantine Empire in the 7th century. It originated as a compromise theory in an attempt to reunite the Monophysites to Chalcedonian orthodoxy. Monothelitism maintained that in Christ there was only one will (*thelema*) from which there flowed only one source of activity or operation; however, it accepted the Chalcedonian doctrine of the two distinct natures in Christ. After it was condemned by Pope Martin I in the Lateran Synod of 649, it was condemned in the Sixth Ecumenical Council, held at Constantinople in 681.
29. Polycarp Sherwood, *St. Maximus the Confessor: The Ascetic Life and The Four Centuries on Charity,* "Ancient Christian Writers" series, XXI (Westminster, Md., Newman, 1955), p. 5. Citations (below) from *The Four Centuries on Charity* are abbreviated *CC;* the series as *ACW*.
30. Cf. R. J. Deferrari, *The Sources of Catholic Doctrine*. This is a translation of Denziger's *Enchiridon Symbolorum,* 30th ed. (St. Louis, Herder, 1955), pp. 60–61.
31. Thunberg, *Microcosm and Mediator: The Theological Anthropology of Maximus the Confessor* (Copenhagen, Lund, 1965), pp. 77–78. Cf. G. Maloney, "Eastern Christian Asceticism," *John XXIII Lectures,* I (New York, Fordham University, John XXIII Center, 1966), pp. 48 ff.
32. *Ambigua* (PG XCI, 1081C).
33. *CC,* I, 95; in *ACW,* p. 151.
34. *CC,* II, 17; in *ACW,* p. 155.
35. *CC,* III, 3; in *ACW,* p. 173.
36. Hesychasm derives from the Greek word *hesychia* and refers to that type of asceticism that strives through solitude and vigilance

to control the passionate elements in oneself so as to arrive at a state of *apatheia* or tranquility. This was effected by fasting, long vigils and prayers, strict control over thoughts and a constant repetition of the prayer: "Lord, Jesus Christ, Son of God, have mercy on me, a sinner." *Cf.* I, Hausherr, "L'Hesychasme, Étude de spiritualité," *Orientalia Christiana Periodica,* 22 (Rome, 1956), pp. 5–40, 247–285.

37. Vladimir Lossky, *The Mystical Theology of the Eastern Church* (Naperville, Ill., Allenson, 1957), p. 111.

Chapter VI

1. Pierre Teilhard de Chardin, *The Divine Milieu,* trans. by B. Wall, *et al.* Copyright 1957 by Editions de Seuil, Paris; English translation Copyright © 1960 by Wm. Collins Sons & Co., London, and Harper & Row, Publishers, Inc. Reprinted by permission of Harper & Row, Publishers, and Wm. Collins Sons & Co., p. 14.
2. *Cf. ibid.,* pp. 94, 110.
3. Teilhard de Chardin, *Letters from a Traveller,* trans. by B. Wall, R. Hague, V. Hammersley, N. Lindsay, *et al.* (New York, Harper, 1962), p. 264.
4. *Ibid.,* pp. 133–134.
5. Teilhard de Chardin, *The Phenomenon of Man,* trans. by Bernard Wall (New York, Harper Torchbooks, 1959), pp. 226, 228.
6. *The Divine Milieu, op. cit.,* p. 118.
7. *Ibid.,* p. 21.
8. Adam worked before the Fall, but after the Fall his work was associated with hardship and exertion—"sweat."
9. *The Divine Milieu, op. cit.,* p. 35.
10. *Ibid.,* p. 23.
11. *Ibid.,* p. 89.
12. *Ibid.,* p. 101.
13. *Super-Humanité, Super-Christ, Super-Charité, Oeuvres de Pierre de Chardin,* 9 (Paris, Seuil, 1965), p. 213.
14. *The Future of Man,* trans. by N. Denny (New York, Harper, 1964), p. 309. The three verses are taken from I Cor. 15:26, 27, 28: "The last enemy that shall be destroyed is death. For he hath put all things under his feet. But when he saith, all things are put under him, it is manifest that he is excepted, which did put all things under him. And when all things shall be subdued unto him,

then shall the Son also himself be subject unto him that put all things under him, that God may be all in all."

15. *The Phenomenon of Man, op. cit.*, p. 244.
16. *The Future of Man, op. cit.*, pp. 82–89.
17. *Super-Humanité, op. cit.*, p. 209.
18. A reference to St. Paul's Greek expression "*en pasi pana theos*" in I Cor. 15:28.
19. *The Phenomenon of Man, op. cit.*, p. 294.
20. *The Divine Milieu, op. cit.*, p. 95.
21. *Mon Univers* (1924), *Oeuvres, 9, op. cit.*, pp. 85–94.
22. *Cf.* Letter of Dec. 12, 1919, *Archives de Philosophie,* 24 (1961), pp. 139–140.
23. *Cf. Le Christique,* (1955).
24. *Comment je vois* (1948), unedited.
25. *La Vie Cosmique* (1916), *Écrits du Temps de la Guerre, 1916–1919* (Paris, Grasset, 1965), pp. 39–40, 47.
26. *Super-Humanité, op. cit.*, p. 211.

26a. Olivier Rabut, *Teilhard de Chardin: A Critical Study* (New York, Sheed and Ward, 1961), p. 167.

27. *Super-Humanité, op. cit.*, p. 211.
28. Christopher Mooney, "The Body of Christ in the Writings of Teilhard de Chardin," *Theological Studies* (Dec. 1964), p. 586.
29. *The Divine Milieu, op. cit.*, p. 101.

29a. Teilhard de Chardin, *Le Milieu Mystique,* 1917, p. 23, as cited by Christopher Mooney, "Anxiety in Teilhard de Chardin," *Thought,* Winter 1964, p. 520.

30. *The Divine Milieu, op. cit.*, p. 104.
31. *A.A.S.*, 50 (1958), p. 212. Pope John XXIII in his encyclical *Pacem in Terris* (New York, Paulist Press, 1963) expressed a similar thought: "They [Catholics] should endeavor, therefore, in the light of their Christian faith, and led by love, to insure that the various institutions—whether economic, social, cultural or political in purpose—should be such as not to obstruct, but rather to facilitate or render less arduous man's self-betterment both in the natural order and the supernatural" (#146).
32. Cited by H. de Lubac, *The Religion of Teilhard de Chardin* (New York, Desclée, 1967), p. 123.
33. Letter of December 1, 1919, cited by H. de Lubac, *ibid.*, p. 123.
34. *The Divine Milieu, op. cit.*, p. 101.
35. *The Phenomenon of Man, op. cit.*, p. 298.

36. *Ibid.*, p. 265.
37. *Comment je vois.*
38. Letter of October 9, 1950, cited by Christopher Mooney, *Teilhard de Chardin and the Mystery of Christ* (New York, Harper, 1966), p. 159.
39. Letter to M. Teilhard-Chambon, Sept. 6, 1953; in *Letters from a Traveller, op. cit.*, p. 344.
40. Cited by de Lubac, *op. cit.*, p. 192.
41. *Ibid.*
42. Letters of November 9, 1948 and October 4, 1950, cited by de Lubac, *op. cit.*, p. 192. Teilhard also describes the Church as conforming, through its dogma of papal infallibility, "to the great law of 'cephalization' which dominates all the biological evolution." *Cf. The Future of Man, op. cit.*, pp. 223–224.
43. *Letters from a Traveller, op. cit.*, p. 299. "I always feel that the Church is phylectically essential to the fulfillment of the Human," he wrote in a letter of August 16, 1951, cited by Claude Cuenot, *Teilhard de Chardin* (Baltimore, Helicon Press, 1965), p. 367.
44. *Super-Humanité, op. cit.*, pp. 212–216.
45. *Ibid.*, p. 213.
46. *Ibid.*, p. 215.
47. *Comment je vois.*
48. *The Future of Man, op. cit.*, p. 267.
49. *The Divine Milieu, op. cit.*, p. 136.
50. *Ibid.*, p. 137.
51. Jean Daniélou, "Signification de Teilhard de Chardin," *Études* (February, 1962), p. 161.

Chapter VII

1. *Cf.* Karl Rahner, *Mission et Grace,* I, "XXe siècle, siècle de grace," in *Collection Siècle et catholicisme* (Brussels, Mame, 1962), pp. 213–214.
2. Karl Rahner, *L'Appartenance à l'Eglise d'apres la Doctrine de l'Encyclique "Mystici Corporis Christi," Écrits Théologiques* II (Bruges, Desclée, 1959), pp. 97–112.
3. *Ibid.*, pp. 102–105.
4. Edward Schillebeeckx, ed., *The Church and Mankind,* in *Concilium,* I (New York, Paulist Press, 1965), pp. 84–85.

5. Cited by Harvey Cox, *The Secular City* (New York, Macmillan, 1965), p. 2. Copyright © Harvey Cox, 1965–1966.
6. Cox, *op. cit.,* p. 2.
7. Teilhard de Chardin, *The Divine Milieu,* trans. by Bernard Wall (New York, Harper, 1960), pp. 35–36.
8. *De Ecclesia* (Washington, National Catholic Welfare Conference, 1964), p. 3.
9. *Ibid.,* pp. 14–16.
10. Edward Schillebeeckx, *Christ the Sacrament of the Encounter with God* (New York, Sheed and Ward, 1963), pp. 215–216. We have seen how Teilhard de Chardin conceives the Church as a "phylum of salvation" that spreads its inner life and superpersonalism, informed by the life of the physical Body-Person of Christ in a movement of greater consciousness, until the completion of the whole human race in the Body of Christ in the Parousia. *Cf. The Phenomenon of Man,* trans. by Bernard Wall (New York, Harper Torchbook, 1959), p. 298.
11. Karl Rahner, *Mission et Grace,* I, *op. cit.,* p. 213.
12. Henri Bergson, *Les deux sources de la morale et de la religion* (Paris, Alcan, 1930), p. 343.
13. Irenaeus, *Adversus Haereses,* III, 19, 1, 448.
14. Louis Bouyer, *Christian Humanism* (Westminster, Md., Newman, 1959), p. 101.
15. Irenaeus, *Adversus Haereses,* IV, 18, 5, 486.
16. *Cf.* Roger Troisfontaines, *I Do Not Die* (New York, Desclée, 1963); Ladislaus Boros, *The Mystery of Death* (New York, Herder and Herder, 1965); R. W. Gleason, *The World to Come* (New York, Sheed and Ward, 1958); Karl Rahner, *On the Theology of Death* (New York, Herder and Herder, 1960); M. F. Sciacca, *Morte e Immortalitá* (Milan, 1959); A. Winklhofer, *The Coming of His Kingdom* (New York, Herder and Herder, 1963).

Appendix

1. *Adversus Haereses* (abbrev.: AH), IV, 38, 3–4, pp. 521–522. Excerpts from the writings of Irenaeus are from *The Ante-Nicene Fathers,* I, ed. by A. Roberts and J. Donaldson (Grand Rapids, Mich., Eerdmans, 1962). Quotations used with permission.
2. *Stromata* (*Strom.*), VII, 10, p. 538. Excerpts from the writings of Clement of Alexandria, including the *Protrepticos* (*Protrep.*) are

from the above cited work, Vol. II. Quotations used with permission.

3. *On First Principles* (*OFP*), I, 22, p. 160. Excerpts from this work of Origen (based on Rufinus' Latin version *De Principiis*) are from the translation by C. Butterworth, *Origen: On First Principles* (New York, Harper Torchbooks, 1966). Reprinted with the permission of Harper Torchbooks, Harper and Row, Publishers, Inc., New York.
4. *Contra Gentes,* 41, p. 26. Excerpts from the writings of Athanasius are quoted with permission from Archibald Robertson, *St. Athanasius: Select Works and Letters, Vol. IV, A Select Library of Nicene and Post-Nicene Fathers of the Christian Church* (Grand Rapids, Mich., Eerdmans, 1957), except those cited from *Patrologiae Cursus completus, Series Graeca* (abbrev.: PG), ed. J. P. Migne, Paris 1857ff.
5. *Oratio,* 29, 2, p. 301, *St. Gregory Nazianzen, Nicene and Post-Nicene Fathers,* 2nd Series, VII (Grand Rapids, Mich., Eerdmans, 1955). All excerpts from the works of St. Gregory Nazianzen are from this edition. Quotations used with permission.
6. *De Opif. Hom.,* 16, 16, p. 406. All excerpts from the writings of St. Gregory of Nyssa are quoted with permission from *A Select Library of Nicene and Post-Nicene Fathers of the Christian Church,* 2nd Series, V (Grand Rapids, Mich., Eerdmans, 1953) or from PG (as noted).
7. *In. Ioann.,* PG LXXIV, 11, 560. All excerpts from St. Cyril of Alexandria are from PG (as noted).
8. *Capita Theologica et Oeconomica,* PG XC, 1108 A–B. All excerpts from St. Maximus the Confessor are from PG, except No. 66 (as noted).
9. *The Earlier Ambigua,* trans. by Polycarp Sherwood (Rome, Herder, 1955), pp. 170–171.

INDEX